W9-BIU-128

Developing and Managing Requests for Proposals in the Public Sector

First Edition

Khi V. Thai, Ph.D.
Florida Atlantic University

Prepared for the National Institute of Governmental Purchasing under the LEAP Program. All rights are conveyed to the NIGP upon completion of this book.

Developing and Managing Requests for Proposals in the Public Sector

Copyright ©2004 by NIGP, Inc. All Rights reserved. Printed in the United States of America. Except as permitted under the United States Copyright Act of 1976, no part of this publication may be reproduced or distributed in any form or by any means, or stored in a database or retrieval system, without the prior written permission of the publisher.

ISBN number 1-932315-04-7

This book was set in Berkeley Oldstyle
Design and layout by Vizual, Inc.
Printing by HBP.

LEAP
Learning and Education
to Advance Procurement

The National Institute of Governmental Purchasing gratefully acknowledges financial contributions from the following organizations.

Patron Sponsors

Office Depot

IAPSO

U.S. Communities

Gold Level Friends

Florida Association of Public Purchasing Officers, Inc.

LES Professional Development Foundation

Virginia Association of Governmental Purchasing Chapter of NIGP, Inc.

Silver Level Friends

CDW Corporation

Georgia Chapter of NIGP

Louisiana Chapter of NIGP

Southeast Florida Chapter of NIGP

Bronze Level Friends

Columbia Chapter of NIGP

Mr. Steven H. Corwin, CPPO, C.P.M.

Governmental Purchasing Association of Georgia Chapter of NIGP

Gulf Coast Association of Governmental Purchasing Officers, Inc. Chapter of NIGP

Kentucky Public Procurement Association Chapter of NIGP

New York State Association of Municipal Purchasing Officials Chapter of NIGP

Ontario Public Buyers Association, Inc. Chapter of NIGP

San Antonio Public Purchasing Association Chapter of NIGP

Southeast Louisiana Chapter of NIGP

Southeast Texas Association of Public Purchasing Chapter of NIGP

Tampa Bay Area Chapter of NIGP

Wisconsin Association of Public Purchasers Chapter of NIGP

The contributions listed above were received and recorded as of **June 23, 2004.**

Patron Level - $50,000 • Gold Level Friends - $10,000 - 19,999
Silver Level Friends - $5,000 - $9,999 • Bronze Level Friends - $1,000 - 4,999

CONTENTS

PREFACE

Governmental entities employ a variety of solicitation methods that are dictated by the goods or services to be purchased. This book focuses on the Request for Proposal (RFP) method and process and is based on the National Institute of Governmental Purchasing, Inc.'s (NIGP) guidelines and suggested procedures. As procurement practices vary among governmental entities, this text provides basic knowledge and skills that are useful for those who select competitive sealed procurements and negotiations. While most agencies find that complex procurements are better facilitated through the RFP process, some entities are unable to incorporate the suggested practices and knowledge found within this book. As each governmental entity has its own procurement law, regulations and process, the reader may need to modify the information provided in order to comply with the agency's legal requirements.

As mentioned above, this book was based on the NIGP training curriculum developed for the LEAP (Learning and Education to Advance Procurement) program. However, it has intentionally covered more than may be covered in a typical training course, thus allowing trainers the opportunity to pick and choose subjects they may explore in their training program. It must be noted that the book has not covered in depth many activities or areas of public procurement, best and final offers (BAFOs), among other things. The reader can easily find information on the solicitation of BAFOs in private sector purchasing and supply management books.

Finally, I would like to thank NIGP for the use of its training manuals, including *General Public Procurement* (2000), *Intermediate Public Procurement* (1999), and *Advanced Public Procurement* (1999). I would like to acknowledge particularly the assistance and leadership of the LEAP Project members, including Donna Beach, Rick Grimm, and Carol Hodes. I also wish to thank the NIGP instructors, particularly Nancy Davis, Tony R. Ellis, Horace L. Ford, Elene Fromanger, Ralph Gilbert, Aaron D. Howell, James E. Park, Jeannie E. Ready, Stefan Rollwage, Jim Totty, and Larry Wellman, who reviewed the first draft of the book and made valuable comments and suggestions. Finally, acknowledgment must be made of Michael Asner and Steve H. Corwin for their drafting of parts of several chapters of this book.

CHAPTER 1

Request for Proposal: An Overview

Introduction

A clear and concise Request for Proposal (RFP) document serves to promote
fair and just competition while allowing the procuring entity the flexibility in evaluation through weighted criterion, in contrast to competitive bids
that are awarded on price alone. Through the RFP process, public agencies
acquire innovative solutions as well as the associated prices, as recommended
by the supplier community. The term "value engineering" is often associated
with the use of RFPs as governments recognize that the best propositions for
problem resolution come from field experts who deal with such conflicts on a
daily basis. As this text will illustrate, an RFP allows for give-and-take on the
parts of both sides of the contracting process.

According to the earliest records, the RFP was introduced in the Armed
Services Procurement Act of 1962 and by the Competition in Contracting Act
of 1984 as the "competitive proposal" technique (Nash, Cibinic, & O'Brien,
1999, p. 1). As both RFP and competitive bidding procedures share common
traits, an RFP provides flexibility for both public agencies and their vendors
to establish a relationship through shared information, rules and decrees, time
lines, and requirements.

Goods and services must be procured in a timely fashion to meet the public
entity's needs, recognizing that governmental resources are limited. It is

imperative that public procurements be conducted efficiently through the minimization of administrative operating costs and through effective acquisition of goods and services at a reasonable price. Most important, public procurements should be conducted with integrity, fairness, and openness. In order to achieve the multiple goals of their public procurement needs, government entities have issued strict procurement laws and regulations and established sound procurement systems with which procurement officials must comply. These processes vary by jurisdiction as well as by the types of goods or services to be purchased.

Submittals received in response to RFPs reflect the interpretation of the agency's contracting desires. As such, creativity is encouraged through insightful thinking. If there is one thing that procurement officials will agree on, it is that to know a lot about a variety of items is to know nothing at all. Vendors that know everything about one thing are in a far better position to propose cost-saving innovations to governments. The following are situational (but not all-inclusive) examples in which the RFP process would best be applied:

- Specifications cannot be established in order to provide a clear picture of the item, process, or output desired by the buyer.[1]

- In order to accomplish a particular task, there exists a need for the concurrent interactive exchange of information and materials among several contractors that cannot be segregated.

- Negotiation of pricing is desired.

- The best price or value is determined not by the initial cost of a good or service but by the combination of a series of factors assessed over the life of the product or service.

- Technology is changing at such a rate that the most cost effective solutions to public problems may need to be created as analyses of the problems are made.

During the initial preparation of an RFP, through an acquisition team, a budget is created based on supplier research, program/project requirements, and the buyer's awareness of possible solutions. Vital to the success of any project is the ability of the team to clearly assess the requirements of the project so that a clear financial picture can be provided. A strongly defined set of requirements and outcome expectations aid in establishing budgetary figures that are achievable.

[1]The term "buyer" is intended to be interchangeable with government, agency, entity, jurisdiction, etc., and is used to indicate the party to a contract that is seeking to purchase a commodity or service. Similarly, the use of the word "vendor" is interchangeable with supplier, offeror, proponent, contractor, etc.

In order to accomplish a realistic budget, needs must be translated into requirements, and all parties to a project must share in a singular vision, devoid of tangential objectives. Consensus must be built so that all members move in a direction conducive to meeting the goals and mission of the entity (Figure 1).

Needs Identified and Determination of Program Requirements→

　　Market Research on Available Products/Services and Associated Costs→

　　　　ROI / Cost-Benefit Analysis→

　　　　　　Budget Formation and Adoption.

Figure 1 - *The Appropriations Process.*

RFPs generated in response to the above process must also take into account contributing factors, such as contract administration, project management, and financial and labor (union) implications. All possible scenarios must weigh in as part of the panoramic picture of project acquisition. A summary of the appropriations process can be better presented as follows:

- An agency need is identified and targeted for possible resolution through the acquisition of commodities or services.
- A plan for the purchase is created to aid in communicating the need to possible suppliers.
- Identify suppliers that are able to provide the good or service or appropriate solutions to the problem.
- Through the budgetary process, seek recognition of need and budgetary approval for the acquisition.
- Establish an acquisition team and project schedule appropriate to ensure program success and to clearly convey measurable outcomes and/or deliverables.
- Formulate monitoring and evaluation criteria to ensure continued success.

As mentioned above, the procurement function in operations is the main focus of public procurement, which consists of a procurement organization and personnel, procurement methods or techniques, asset and inventory management and, particularly, the procurement process (popularly known as the "acquisition process" in the Federal Government). The National Association of State

Purchasing Officials (NASPO) in its *State and Local Government Purchasing Principles and Practices* (1997, p. 3) makes a distinction between the terms "procurement" and "purchasing": procurement represents "the entire spectrum of the acquisition process, more frequently than 'purchasing,' which tends to be limited to a segment of that process." This distinction is found in the Federal Acquisition Regulation (FAR), which defines acquisition as "the acquiring by contract with appropriated funds of supplies or services (including construction) by and for the use of the Federal Government through purchase or lease" [emphasis added] (FAR, 2002, Part 2.101). Actually, "acquiring by contract" or contracting does not begin until funds are appropriated.

Public procurement is a very complicated process, which is normally described in the government entity's procurement manual. The procurement process consists of different steps or phases, depending on the types of goods and services to be purchased. According to Harink (1999), while authors describe it differently, the most common procurement process model consists of six phases: specifying, selecting, contracting, ordering, monitoring, and/or servicing (after sales). Harink then groups these six phases into two simple phases: pre-award phase (consisting specifying, selecting, and contracting) and post-award phase (ordering, monitoring, and/or servicing). The pre-award phase is called "tactical procurement"; the post-award phase is called "operational procurement." In reality, the procurement process varies, depending on a number of factors, such as (a) the nature of goods, services, capital assets, and information technology to be acquired and (b) the relationship with the suppliers concerned. Harink's model is more applicable to procurements of office equipment and supplies/materials than of other types, such as construction and major systems procurements. Moreover, although it describes the most common phases in a procurement process, Harink's model does not recognize the importance of strategic planning, funding, and contract planning.

In reality, the procurement or acquisition process encompasses many activities or steps: assessing needs and determining requirements; requesting and appropriating funds; planning acquisition; preparing and processing a requisition; determining the contractor source selection method and drafting and issuing a solicitation; evaluating bids or proposals and awarding a contract; administering the contract; receiving and accepting the goods or services; and managing delivery, payment, and contract closeout. These activities or steps can be grouped into three phases: requirement determination and procurement funding or appropriations, contract formation, and contract administration and closeout, as shown in Figure 2. The contract formation and contract administration phases are commonly called the *contracting process*.

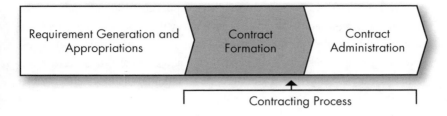

Figure 2 - *The Public Procurement Process.*

Requirements Generation and Appropriations Phase

There cannot be a sound procurement budget without a strategic plan, and there cannot be procurement without a contract authority that leads to budget appropriations. Strategic planning is a process of determining the long-range direction of an organization and establishing the means by which this direction will be maintained. The process includes the defining of missions and objectives, which are statements of how the organization sees its purpose and the implementation of it. Fundamentally, strategic planning is basically the road map intended to help an organization respond to new challenges and develop its future opportunities. Thorough planning is critical as agencies are always facing budget constraints that cannot satisfy government entities' goods and services needs.

An effective strategic plan should anticipate changes in the agency's requirement for technological capabilities and should identify goods, services, and capital assets that are critical to implement the plan. Goods and services that government entities need consist of the following:

- Low-dollar-value, commercial items, such as paper, paperclips, laptop or desktop computers, office equipment (routine) maintenance, and travel: as these types of goods and services become basic needs for the government's daily operations, there is no need for strategic planning, and budget requests and decisions regarding these goods and services are simple: planning and budgeting are basically on an incremental basis. In other words, needs and funding are based on the previous year's level.

- Major capital projects requiring large-dollar-value funding, such as information technology, major defense weapons, and infrastructure construction: major capital projects need to be well planned and are greatly scrutinized. Thus, the process becomes more complicated, as explained in the following sections.

Annually, agencies (users) have to establish a capital acquisition plan by assessing their existing capital assets in order to identify the capital asset gap between planned and actual performance and defining the gap or capital asset needs, commonly called "wish list." All needed capital assets have to be assessed in terms of functionality; full life-cycle costs, including all direct and indirect costs for planning, procurement, operations, and maintenance (operational analysis are used to evaluate condition and any negative trends on cost projections for assets in use), and disposal; the affordability of full life-cycle costs relative to expected funding levels; associated risks; and agency capacity to manage the assets.

Finally, agencies establish capital acquisition objectives in terms of requirements to be achieved and prepare an original portfolio of capital acquisitions. Identifying more detailed capital acquisition requirements than those established in the annual performance plan can help identify the proper size and scope of potential options. Detailed functional requirements for capital acquisition options also need be defined. These functional requirements should be defined in terms of the mission, purpose, capability, agency components involved, schedule and cost objectives, and management capacity, not in terms of equipment or software terms. Figure 3 shows the relationship between needs and requirements.

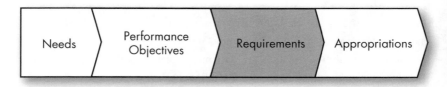

Figure 3 - *Strategic Planning: Requirements Generation.*

Requirements generated through the strategic planning phase produce information for decision-makers on the agencies' projected mission needs. Capital acquisition plans require careful selection. A plan selected without adequate analysis may face overrunning both cost and schedule, while falling short of expected performance.

In order to meet all procurement goals, the contracting process becomes a very complicated, lengthy process, consisting of many activities beginning with procurement planning and ending with contract closeouts. These activities are grouped into two major phases: pre-award and post-award or contract formation and contract administration.

Contract Formation or Pre-Award Phase—RFP Planning

Regardless of the size of the project, a RFP should be well planned and thought out. The RFP is but one small component of a much larger project or program, as the eventual award of the RFP will mark the initiation of the "real" project. The planning stages of the RFP take the initial work of the appropriations phase and fold it into a set of requirements and specifications that can be easily understood by potential suppliers.

> **Contract Planning**. Contract planning is the process by which the efforts of all personnel responsible for an acquisition are coordinated and integrated through a comprehensive plan for fulfilling the agency need in a timely manner and at a reasonable cost. It includes developing the overall strategy for managing the acquisition" (Federal Acquisition Institute, 1999, p. 6-6).

Simply stated, after the goods or services requirements are determined and funds for goods or services are appropriated, a plan is drawn up to obtain them. The plan identifies the people involved and what they must do in an established time frame. Contract planning is different from the government entity's strategic planning: While strategic planning is involved in assessing a government's procurement needs, specifying requirements that meet the needs and proposing programs, according to priorities, for legislative appropriations, contract planning is an administrative action to effectively implement all funded procurement programs/items. According to NIGP (1999a, p. 137), contract planning "must be done by the procurement department itself." Actually, there are two types of plans: central procurement office/division's procurement plan and contract plan for a procurement project (good, service or capital asset).

The following are tasks most often associated with the RFP Development Process:

- Project organization and team formulation;
- RFP task identification and schedule determination;
- Research of commercially available products and services;
- Technical requirements determined and reviewed with end-users;
- Sourcing document generated using standardized and legally approved formats;
- RFP issuance and pre-proposal questions/conferences;
- Supplier evaluation and selection; and
- Post-award RFP tasks—debriefings and retention of documents.

Following procurement planning is a series of activities to be performed until a contract is awarded. This series of activities is called contract formulation (Cibinic & Nash, 1998), pre-award phase, or tactical procurement (Harink, 1999). Contract formulation is a process consisting of major activities, depending on the type of procurement methods being used—be it invitation for bids, request for proposal, request for quotation, emergency procurement, or small purchase. For the "request-for-proposal" method, the process consists of five major activities: solicitation document preparation, solicitation of offers, evaluation, negotiation, and contract award, as shown in Figure 4. Each of these major activities, in turn, becomes a process, such as solicitation document process, bid/proposal evaluation process, or negotiation process. As these activities are the focus of this book, they are not explained here.

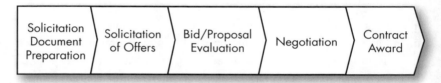

Figure 4 - *Contract Formulation.*

Procurement Phase: Contract Administration

Contract administration can be simple or a very complicated process, depending on the type of contract and the nature of good or service to be purchased. For commercial items, contract administration consists of ordering, monitoring ordered items' quantity and quality, paying invoices, and keeping a good accounting record; and there is no need for contract closeouts. For construction, the contract administration is very well structured and more complicated, consisting of major phases, including initiating work (and/or modification) or ordering, contract monitoring, payment/accounting, and contract closeout/termination, as shown in Figure 5.

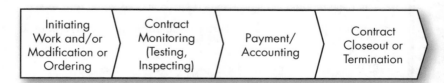

Figure 5 - *The Contract Administration Process.*

After a contract is awarded, a designated contract administrator issues a notice to proceed that sets the contract administration in motion. Although most government entities do not require a formal contract administration plan, procurement officials are responsible for ensuring that the parties have complied with all terms and conditions of the contract. The decision to conduct a post-award conference depends on the following variables:

- Size and complexity of the project;
- Contract type;
- Urgency of the project; and
- Contractor's performance history.

While contractors perform their contracts, the procurement official or their designated contract administration team need to carefully monitor their contract performance. There are many areas to be monitored, including quality, schedules, acceptance, conflicts, contractor's performance, changes, and budget and payment.

Although finance departments are in charge of payment and accounting, procurement officials are involved in the payment process. There are three types of payment: advance payments or prepayments (an extension of credit to the supplier by the organization), interim payments (frequently utilized in contracts for construction, capital equipment, certain professional services, and other labor intensive and/or capital intensive contracts), and final payment (work or product already delivered, tested, inspected, and installed). As procurement officials are the ones who know when the contract needs to be paid, all payments have to be authorized by them.

The final payment is authorized only when the contract is closed out. As shown in Figure 5, a contract can be terminated or closed out. If contractors fail to perform according to contractual provisions, legally, they have breached the contract and are in default. Breach of contract usually results in order cancellation or contract termination. Mostly, contractors honor their contracts; and, when the contract is honored, the contract has to be closed out.

Contract closure involves several activities. Unlike a purchase order where receipt of the items ordered and subsequent payment constitute closure, a contract, before being closed out, has to meet the following requirements:

- All contractual issues have been met.
- All changes, if any, have been incorporated into the final document.
- All deliverable items (hardware, data, and reports) have been received.

- All bailed (borrowed) equipment and all classified documents have been returned.
- Final payment has been made.

Once all these items are complete, the procurement official or contract administrator writes a formal closure document. This closure document contains a narrative identifying and discussing the contractor's strengths and weaknesses in the performance of the contract. This document is invaluable if disputes subsequently arise. This file is also useful later when new jobs develop and potential contractors are being considered.

It should be noted that not all phases receive equal attention. In practice, some phases are occasionally omitted. This will depend on a number of factors, such as the nature of the good or service to be purchased, and the contract arrangement, such as open-ended contracts. For example, for capital assets procurement, the contract award and ordering phases often coincide: once the contract has been signed, the goods have, in effect, been ordered. Another case is an existing blanket order for office supplies: new orders can be placed (the ordering phase) at the same time that invoices for previous orders are being paid (the monitoring phase).

Factors Determining Procurement Method Selection

According to many government entities' procurement regulations, the Competitive Sealed Bid (Federal Acquisition Regulation, 2002) or the Invitation or Request for Bids (American Bar Association (ABA), 2000) is required, as will be discussed later in this section. However, there are circumstances where this procurement method may not be the most appropriate; and selecting an appropriate procurement method becomes a very important, but difficult, decision. The procurement or sourcing method selection is determined by two major factors: the type and size of good or service to be purchased and the market uncertainty and risk for that type of good or service.

Types of Goods and Services to Be Purchased

Government entities purchase a wide range of goods and services. The Federal Government's Federal Acquisition Regulation lists six major types of goods and services:

- Commercially available items,
- Major systems,
- Research and development,
- Construction and Architect-Engineer (professional services),
- MRO Services, and
- Utilities services.

In general, these types of goods and services can be classified into three types, in terms of market availability:

- Items of a type customarily available in the marketplace, called commercial items, such as office supplies and equipment;
- Items of a type customarily available in the commercial marketplace with modifications, such as spare parts for jetfighters and warships; or
- Items used exclusively for governmental purposes, such as many weapons systems and information technology.

Depending on supplies or services to be purchased, requirements should be stated in terms of:

- Functions to be performed;
- Performance required;
- Essential physical characteristics; or
- A combination of the above.

Commercial Items. Commercial items or non-developmental items consist of all items that are sold competitively in the market. For these types of goods and services, government entities should specify their needs using market research in a manner designed to:

- promote full and open competition; and
- only include restrictive provisions or conditions, when necessary, to satisfy their specific needs.

Moreover, requirements should be defined in terms that:

- enable and encourage vendors to supply commercial items, or, to the extent that commercial items suitable to meet the end-user's needs are not available, non-developmental items, in response to their solicitations; and

- provide vendors of commercial items and non-developmental items an opportunity to compete in any acquisition to fill such requirements.

In the preparation of specifications, standardized commercial items should be used. The use of standardized items enables an entity to obtain lower prices, reduce its handling costs, carry smaller inventories, and have fewer quality problems. Inappropriate or too stringent standards will not guarantee the integrity of goods or services and may contribute to a higher cost. A jurisdiction's requirements should not be written so as to require a particular brand name, product, or feature of a product peculiar to one manufacturer, thereby precluding consideration of a product manufactured by another company, unless:

- the particular brand name, product, or feature is essential to the government's requirements, and market research indicates other companies' similar products, or products lacking the particular feature, do not meet, or cannot be modified to meet, the agency's needs;
- the authority to contract without providing for full and open competition is supported by the required laws justifications and approvals; and
- the basis for not providing for maximum practicable competition is documented in the file when the acquisition is awarded using simplified acquisition procedures.

Major Systems. Systems acquisitions normally designated as major are those programs that, as determined by the agency head (1) are directed at and critical to fulfilling an end-user mission need, (2) entail allocating relatively large resources for the particular end-user and (3) warrant special management attention, including specific agency-head decisions" (FAR 34.003).

Major systems include mainly new weapon developments and IT systems. This type of good and service is used exclusively for governmental purposes and requires a lot of procurement attention. Such major system procurement includes the functions of concept exploration, design engineering, prototyping or demonstration, full-scale development, and full production. For this type of purchase, the procurement process is very complicated; negotiated contracting is probably appropriate, if allowed by law.

Research and Development. Research and development is funded mostly by the Federal Government but also by state governments and universities. Research consists of two types: applied and basic. Basic research is to increase knowledge in science and develop a fuller knowledge or understanding of the subject under study rather than any practical application of that knowledge. Applied research, which normally follows basic research but may not be detachable from the related basic research, attempts (1) to determine and exploit the potential of scientific discoveries or improvements in technology, materials, processes, methods, devices, or techniques and (2) to advance the state of the art (FAR 35.001).

Development means the systematic use of scientific and technical knowledge in the design, development, testing, or evaluation of a potential new product or service (or of an improvement in an existing product or service) to meet specific performance requirements or objectives. It includes the functions of design engineering, prototyping, and engineering testing. It excludes subcontracted technical effort that is for the sole purpose of developing an additional source for an existing product (FAR 35.001).

Research and development projects, which must be awarded on a competitive procedure (either IFB or RFP), usually consists of the following:

- *Awards Based on a Broad Announcement.* The announcement, general in nature, identifies areas of research interest, including criteria for selecting proposals, and solicits the participation of all offerors capable of satisfying the government's needs. The award is based on a peer or scientific review (FAR 6.102).

- *Unsolicited Research Proposal.* Government entities may decide to award a contract without competitive solicitation, such as an unsolicited research proposal. In the opinion and to the knowledge of the government evaluator, the proposal, a product of original thinking submitted in confidence by one source, is meritorious; contains new novel or changed concepts, approaches, or methods; was not submitted previously by another; and is not otherwise available within the entity. In this context, the term does not mean that the source has the sole capability of performing the research (FAR 6.003).

Construction and Architect-Engineer. Performed or approved by a person licensed, registered, or certified, professional services of an architectural or engineering nature include studies, investigations, surveying and mapping, tests, evaluations, consultations, comprehensive planning, program management, conceptual designs, plans and specifications, value engineering, construction phase services, soils engineering, drawing reviews, preparation of operating and maintenance manuals, and other related services (FAR 36.102). In state and local governments, the construction procurement may consist of design, construction, operation, operation, and maintenance. According to FAR 36.103, sealed bid procedures should be used for actual construction procurements alone, and negotiated contracting procedures should be used for architect-engineer services. The American Bar Association (2000, Article 3-203.1.c) recommends the use of competitive sealed proposals for contracts for the design-build, design-build-operate-maintenance, or design-build-finance-operate-maintenance project delivery methods that include all aspects of the project, such as A/E services and the actual construction.

Services. Some of the areas that are normally contracted out include:

- Maintenance, overhaul, repair, servicing, rehabilitation, salvage, modernization, or modification of supplies, systems, or equipment;
- Routine recurring maintenance of real property; housekeeping and base services;
- Advisory and assistance services (professional services);
- Operation of government-owned equipment, facilities, and systems;
- Communications services;
- Architectural-Engineering; and
- Transportation and related services.

Depending on the types of services, competitive sealed proposals or the negotiated contracting method may be used.

Market Uncertainty and Risk

Government vendors face a level of uncertainty and risk caused by the following factors:

- *Type and Complexity of the Desired Goods or Services (Requirements)*. Complex requirements, particularly those unique to the government, usually result in greater risk assumption by the government. This is especially true for complex research and development contracts, information technology, and communications contracts when performance uncertainties or the likelihood of changes make it difficult to estimate performance costs in advance. As a requirement recurs or as quantity production begins, the cost risk should shift to the contractor, and a fixed-price contract should be considered.
- *Urgency of the Requirement*. If urgency is a primary factor, the government may choose to assume a greater proportion of risk, or it may offer incentives to ensure timely contract performance.

- *Period of Performance or Length of Production Run.* In times of economic uncertainty, contracts extending over a relatively long period should provide for economic price adjustment terms.
- *Size of Purchases.* The dollar value of purchases also adds to the level of market uncertainty and risk.

Abi-Karam (2001) suggests that every project should be evaluated for six types of risk:

- Proposal risk, depending on how well the vendor understands what the proposal requires;
- Price risk, depending on how accurately the price reflects what the procurement will cost;
- Schedule risk, depending on whether the required item(s) will be delivered on time;
- Performance risk, depending on whether the vendor delivers the item(s) with the expected quality;
- Contractual risk, depending on how well the contract documents cover unforeseen issues and protect the public organization in case of problems; and
- Surety/liability risk, depending on the potential liabilities that the government organization or vendor may encounter.

In general, the more specific the type, the higher dollar value; the higher the complexity of the desired goods and services, the more urgent the procurement; and the longer the period of performance or production, the higher the risk becomes and the higher the cost government entities may have to pay. According to Pettijohn and Qiao (2000), vendors add an average of approximately 20% to most fixed-price contracts because of uncertainty and risk caused by unclear specifications.

Contracting Methods

The American Bar Association (2000, p. 22) lists seven procurement methods, including competitive sealed bidding, competitive sealed proposals, small purchases (or "micro" purchases, as used by the Federal Government), sole source procurement, emergency procurements, and architectural and engineering services. In addition to these methods, FAR 13 also allows the use of simplified acquisition procedures. For the purpose of this text, the focus will be on competitive sealed proposals, also known as RFPs, and related sub-structural components such as requests for information and qualifications.

In understanding the nature of public procurement, one must consider the mechanics of how the procurement process works. Everything must be considered individually and a plan devised to satisfy each need and/or requirement. Government was established to meet and serve the needs of its customers (constituents). Procurement is the mechanism whereby government translates its needs and/or requirements into products and services for its customers. The methodology employed by government to obtain needed products and services usually determines the efficiency and effectiveness of that operation.

For a government unit to acquire a repetitive low cost maintenance or repair item, it should do so at minimal cost. Conversely, a high dollar acquisition involving multi-year contracts requires cost and time of a governmental entity. Thus, supplying and meeting the governmental entity's needs is key to efficiency and effectiveness for overall operations. The role of procurement is to create efficiency and effectiveness for the entity to provide products and services that taxpayers can afford.

Request for Information (RFI)

How the procurement unit performs its obligations becomes a key factor in the governmental entity's operation. The key is to create methodologies that are cost efficient, workable, and also satisfy needs. A little used strategy in procurement is that of issuing a Request for Information (RFI). The RFI is used in complex procurements such as RFPs. In using a RFI, the procurement officials can obtain valuable information from potential suppliers of goods, relatively simple services, and complex services by simply asking for the information from known and qualified firms. The RFI process can be helpful in assisting the jurisdiction in obtaining several solutions for its needs.

Usually, potential suppliers will provide enough information to enable the entity to look at several possible solutions to their need and eventually develop a short-list of firms capable of providing the goods and services or meaningful solutions that are considered by all to be fair and competitive. Although RFIs take time to set up and obtain information, their value should never be underestimated. The use of a RFI is discussed later in the text as one methodology in the overall RFP process. The usefulness of a RFI comes from the fact that potential suppliers will provide method-valuable information, alternative solutions, and enable the entity to evaluate their approach to the procurement of the good or service.

If an organization has no intention of procuring goods and services, it should not issue a RFP. If an entity is interested in learning about products and services available in the marketplace, a simpler procedure exists. The more formal, less expensive approach is to use a Request for Letters of Interest, as is done in Broward County, Florida. The organization identifies the types of problems or types of services in which it is interested and invites suppliers to provide information to determine what vendors, if any, are interested in this type of work.

Another approach to acquiring previously undefined items is to make contact with two or three vendors and invite them to present information about their products, services, or solutions. Most procurement officials know that vendors will gladly provide information about their products and services and will welcome the opportunity to learn more about an organization, including its problems and requirements. There is no conflict nor is there any impropriety in inviting vendors to present their credentials. Inviting one supplier to present its credentials may raise some concerns about favoritism. Inviting several competing suppliers to brief an organization on their capabilities is not favoritism, but good business—simply keeping up to date with a changing marketplace. This process is commonly referred to as a pre-solicitation conference. For example,

> Suppose a jurisdiction wanted to retain a firm to review its expansion plans for their local area network and required $5,000 worth of help. They wanted to hire an expert to review their existing equipment and software and identify various scenarios. In some jurisdictions, the procurement officials or the information technology manager would phone a company, confirm the assignment, and send them a purchase order/contract. Typically, as the value of the estimated contract increases, the process becomes more formal. In each procurement, it is vital to ensure that the procurement effort is consistent with the complexity and dollar value of the resulting contract.

For $25,000 worth of design assistance, three companies may be called and asked to submit letter-proposals. The level of internal approval and formality increases until it reaches a pre-defined threshold, often $50,000. A formal RFP process with a project plan, public advertisement, evaluation teams and all the other formality is required. For some organizations, only suppliers on their pre-qualified vendors bid list are contacted for these more formal procurements. Purchasing must always ensure that all vendors have equal access and opportunity to compete for the government's business.

Limited Competition Procurement

This is a process used in some jurisdictions to reduce the cost of the process. For some products and services, there may be hundreds of responsible suppliers. Suppose a jurisdiction needs a firm to provide project management services. There may be hundreds of suppliers in that state or city. In some jurisdictions, the procurement officials argue that it is contrary to the public good to invite 200 suppliers to submit proposals for project management services. They argue that each supplier would spend $10,000 on its proposal for a $50,000 contract. In total, they argue, that if 100 suppliers responded and each spent $10,000 on its proposal, then the industry would have spent more than $1,000,000 to obtain one $50,000 contract. To avoid this situation, some jurisdictions permit the procurement officials to restrict the competition to a limited number, say 20, suppliers. They do this by selecting names from their suppliers list on a random basis or some rotational system or by only issuing 20 RFPs on a first-come-first-served basis. In some cases, the anticipated price differential between offers is so small, why get 100 bids when 5 to 10 will provide excellent competition. Whatever method is used, the procurement officials must use an equitable and transparent process.

Request for Proposals (RFP)

The most intensive type of "full and open" procurement employs a RFP, which is more formally known as "Competitive Sealed Proposals" (ABA, 2000; FAR, 2002). This procurement technique is used when the requirements are not clearly known, are qualitative rather than quantitative, or when the procurement official is looking for a solution to a problem, and/or the selection of a supplier is being made not only on price but on a combination of non-price-factors, as will be discussed later in this text.

Differences Between the RFB and the RFP

In procurement organizations, a competitive sealed bid or Request for Bids (RFB) and a competitive sealed proposal or Request for Proposal (RFP) are the two accepted methodologies for formalized procurements normally set at a predetermined high dollar figure. The objective is the same, but the methodology of acquisition varies. As entities specify needs, procurement officials determine the procurement methodology to meet these needs. The common approach used in procurement is that competitive sealed bids are used when the dollar value reaches a certain value and the entity has the ability to adequately describe its need for potential bidders to adequately respond in a competitive nature (i.e., there are enough bidders who can respond to the bid, thereby ensuring fair and open competition). Bids are opened at an announced time, and each bidder is identified along with the bid amount. Award is made to the lowest responsive and responsible bidder. This is an objective bid.

Conversely, a RFP is used by a entity to meet a complex need that is difficult to specify; however, the agency's need may be expressed through a Statement or Scope of Work to be done along with criteria to evaluate responses from potential offerors. Once publicly advertised, proposals are received at a stated date and time and subject to jurisdiction regulations, and no additional information is revealed. In some cases, the names of the offerors are not made public until an award is made. Following receipt, an Evaluation Committee will review the proposals and may discuss the proposals with respective offerors individually. Often, the offerors of proposals determined to be the most advantageous to the entity are requested to submit best and final offers. Based upon professional analysis by each team member, the committee will recommend an award of the contract. Table 1 highlights the differences between an RFB and an RFP.

In Florida for instance, Government in the Sunshine requires full disclosure of all information related to the RFP process at any given point in the process. For other states, no information is released until an award recommendation has been made.

Table 1

Comparison of Competitive Sealed Bids and Competitive Sealed Proposal

Activity Description	Competitive Sealed Bids	Competitive Sealed Proposal
When to Use	When specification or statement of work is well-defined	When government looks for proposer to develop and provide ideas or solutions
Type of Specifications	Any type	Preferably performance
Opening	Public—price announced; and all data available to other bidders and the public	Public—only names of proposers are read; no pricing or other data made available (subject to local laws)
Evaluation	Based strictly on Technical Specifications—NO material changes allowed	Based on quality with multi-member Criteria Evaluation Committee assigning weighted values to various parts of each proposal
Discussion	None	Discussions may ensue with each proposer to determine understanding of proposal requirements
Negotiations	None	Each qualified supplier is requested to submit a Best and Final Offer as a result of the in-depth review
Award	Lowest Responsive and Responsible Bidder	Best Value Proposal-not necessarily the lowest price

Source: National Institute of Governmental Purchasing, Inc. (NIGP) (2000). *General public procurement*. Herndon, VA: NIGP; Corwin, S. (1999). *How to handle competitive negotiations*. A paper presented at the Annual Forum of the National Institute of Governmental Purchasing, Inc., Halifax, Canada.

Conclusion

The RFB is employed at a pre-determined dollar amount requiring a formalized process to be followed. Taking into account the potential contract value, jurisdictions must ensure that the resultant contract is governed by a set of general and specific terms and conditions in the solicitation document. While the RFB is strictly an objective award, the RFP is a semi-subjective award based upon the highest score given by an evaluation team for rating on established criteria. While members of the Evaluation Committee may see things slightly different from one another, each member must be consistent in their evaluation of all proposals. In addition, the RFP is primarily used when there are high start-up costs in the contract and the term of contract is multi-year. Very technical and complex procurements tend to utilize the RFP, as offerors have much more leeway in solutions to the entity's need. The RFP tends to take much more time and involve more cost to the entity. A good rule of thumb in both the RFB and the RFP is the 70/30 rule; that is, spend 70% of the time on planning and preparation and 30% of the remaining time on execution. The end result will always yield better results, and less time will be spent in protests and resoliciting the need. It is noted that procurement officials can never spend too much time on preparation.

The RFB is used when all of the requirements are mandatory. The RFP is used when the evaluation is based on more than price. Often, the evaluation is based on the offeror's experience on similar projects, its project plan, the effectiveness of the proposed solution, and an assessment of the risks. More specifically, the RFP is used when the organization wants to:

- use a contract other than a fixed-price type;
- conduct written and/or oral discussions with offerors concerning technical and price aspects of their proposals;
- afford offerors the opportunity to revise their proposals once short-listed;
- compare the different price, quality, and contractual factors of the proposals submitted; and
- award a contract in which price is not the determining factor.

The RFB is generally the standard or traditional method in public contracting. It is simpler, cheaper, faster, and seemingly more objective than the RFP. The RFB process does not permit negotiations or discussions, and all the requirements are mandatory. Consequently, very few supplier protests are received. The ABA's *2000 Model Procurement Code* contains a good commentary on the use of each technique:

- For the RFB, judgmental factors are used only to determine if the bid meets the requirements stated in the RFB. For compliant bids, "award is made on a purely objective basis to the lowest on the basis of price" (p. 26). For the RFP, judgmental factors are used to evaluate the relative merits of competing proposals. (Proposal A obtained 8 points for the quality of the project management plan; proposal B obtained 12 points.) For compliant proposals, the award is made on the basis of which proposal is most advantageous as (usually) reflected in the highest total score (p. 26).

- For the RFB, no changes are allowed once the bids are opened. For the RFP, discussions and revised offers are permitted (pp. 26-27) and even encouraged.

Procurement Method Selection: A Multi-Dimensional Approach

*T*here are many factors that procurement officials need to consider before selecting a procurement method. Moreover, they need to be aware of the goals of procurement, which are often complicated.

Goals of Public Procurement

How does one judge a jurisdiction's success in acquiring needed supplies, capital assets, and services? This question is often viewed as relevant only to the contracting (purchasing) office. Yet, the contracting office is only one of the many jurisdictional units that play a role in the acquisition process. Hence, the goals of the acquisition system should be conceived broadly and encompass the contribution of all shareholders (concerned parties) to the process, including requiring activities, audit activities, budget activities, and the like.

The goal of public procurement is to satisfy the internal customer by obtaining the optimum market response to end-user needs at a fair and reasonable price with exactly what is needed (i.e., quality) and when it is needed (i.e., timeliness) while serving the government's long term interests by minimizing business and technical risks, accomplishing socioeconomic objectives, maximizing competition, and maintaining integrity.

There are many suggested procurement method selection models. Using two sets of variables—relative expenditure and difficulty of securing supply—The Government of Queensland, Australia (2002), suggests another quadrant model showing circumstances under which procurement methods should be used. For the same purpose, Pettijohn and Babich (2004) suggest a quadrant model, using two sets of variables—cost/complexity and risk/uncertainty. As there are many factors influencing a procurement method, many similar quadrant models can be suggested; however, these models simplify each of the variables, as each variable has only two levels—low and high. In reality, each variable may have more than two scales or levels. As shown in Table 2, the purchase size variable (or "relative expenditure" in the Queensland model, and "cost" in the Pettijohn and Babich model) has four levels—small-value or micro purchase (up to $2,500, or as determined by each governmental entity), simplified purchase threshold (between $2,500 and $25,000, or more or less depending on each government entity), large purchase (over a set threshold, say $25,000, or more or less depending on each government entity), and major systems (large and risky procurement projects). Similarly, the "market availability" variable has three types or levels—items of a type customarily available in the commercial marketplace; items of a type customarily available in the commercial marketplace with modifications; and items used exclusively for governmental purposes.

Table 2

Factors Determining the Types of Contracting Methods: Market Availability and Purchase Sizes

Market Availability	Small-Value or Micro Threshold*	Simplified Purchase Threshold*	Large Purchase	Major Systems
1. Items of a type customarily available in the commercial marketplace	Purchase order, Purchase card	Simplified Process	Mostly RFB	
2. Items of a type customarily available in the commercial marketplace with modifications		Simplified Process, Negotiated Contracting	RFB, RFP	
3. Items used exclusively for governmental purposes			Mostly RFP or Sole Sourcing	Mostly RFP or Sole Sourcing

* The thresholds for small purchases vary significantly among government entities. For the U.S. Federal Government, it is up to $2,500. The thresholds for the simplified procurement process also vary widely. For the U.S. Federal Government, it is up to $100,000.

Cost

The cost of supplies and services is more than just the price (i.e., dollar amount) of the contract. There are other associated costs, including any costs for acquiring the supplies or services not covered in the contract price, such as the cost of delivery when the contract provides for F.O.B. Origin, under which the buyer pays the cost of shipping and risk of loss during transportation.

Quality means the extent to which the end-users' specified requirements are exactly met.

For capital assets, their life-cycle costs (LCC) should be considered. A comprehensive cost analysis should not be based only on the initial acquisition price offered by bidders or offerors, but on the estimated operational costs over the life of the product. For example, two bidders/offerors (A and B) offer products that meet both per-formance and quality requirements. The product of A requires more electricity than the product of B; however, A's purchase price is less. Whether A's offer represents the best value is not only a matter of the purchase price but also of the net pre-sent value of the cost of electricity over the useful life of the product. LCC actually accounts for all costs that will be incurred over the useful life of the product, less its asset value at the time of disposal.

Quality

Quality means the extent to which the end-users' specified requirements are exactly met. Quality should be addressed in every source selection. According to the U.S. Federal Acquisition Regulation, this is done in part by:

- Defining the need in functional terms;
- Describing the performance and/or design characteristics that are necessary to satisfy the need (e.g., height, weight, energy usage, reliability, maintainability, useful life, etc.);
- Prescribing standards for determining whether a deliverable is acceptable (i.e., meets the need as defined in the contract); and
- When appropriate, establishing inspection and testing procedures for measuring the deliverable against those standards.

As a factor in evaluating competing contractors, quality may be expressed in terms of past performance, technical excellence, management capability, personnel qualifications, prior experience, and schedule compliance.

Timeliness

With respect to supplies, timeliness means delivering the requisitioned supplies to the end-user at the time necessary for the end-user's purposes. With respect to services, timeliness means performance at the time necessary for the end-user's purposes. With respect to construction and other capital asset projects such as information technology and possible new weapons systems, timeliness means that various phases of these projects are completed as scheduled so that the whole project can be completed on time to meet the government entity's mission. When planning to meet an agency's needs at the predetermined time, the procurement officials should consider the time it will take to:

- prepare specifications and purchase descriptions;
- obtain funding and administrative approvals for purchase requests;
- solicit offers, make source decisions, and award contracts; and
- complete, inspect, and accept the work.

When the requirement is for supplies, the procurement office must also factor in time for:

- shipping and distributing supplies to the designated location;
- receiving and inventorying the supplies; and
- physically distributing supplies to the end-users.

In addition, forecasts of time required for an acquisition should be cast in terms of the probable risk of delay that is inherent in any acquisition.

Minimizing Risks

In a contractual relationship, both the jurisdiction and the contractor want to achieve their desired objectives. While the jurisdiction wants to achieve its mission within its budget, the contractor wants to maximize his/her profits. Both parties recognize certain contract risks and try to minimize them. When the risks associated with those objectives are perceived as being too high or unfairly apportioned, either or both parties will probably be unwilling to enter into the contract.

There are three types of risks—business, financial, and technical. Unfortunately, no contractor can forecast with absolute certainty the cost of doing work under a contract. Unpredictable perils, such as strikes, equipment malfunctions, turnover of key personnel, financial setbacks, defective parts, bottlenecks in the availability of raw or semi-finished goods, general inflation, and unexpectedly long learning curves, may happen at any time. In an effort to minimize the types of risks, bidders/offerors may inflate proposed prices to cover the anticipated worst-case scenarios. For the jurisdiction, the main financial risk is payment of an inflated price (that intends to protect worst-case scenarios that never materialized). Thus, procurement officials need to consider specific protection against such an inflated price on one hand; but, on the other hand, they need to consider specific options to avoid the risk of an unfulfilled contract, caused by unpredicted perils and understand the suppliers' problems.

For standard commercial (off-the-shelf) supplies and services, the risks, both business and technical, to both parties tend to be minimal. However, for more complex and uncertain items, such as developing a new computer program, building to a structural specification, or conducting research and development, particularly in the age of rapid technology advances, risks may become a significant factor in establishing and negotiating the terms and conditions of the contract. For the contractor, technical risks are strongly related to financial risks. Any possible problem in meeting technical requirements might require more effort (labor and material costs) than was contemplated at the time the price was agreed to. The contractor may even discover that the work is literally impossible at any price. For the government entity, technical risks lead to unpredicted higher budget allocation and, particularly, possible failure of the intended project. From the government's standpoint, business and technical risk goes beyond financial impact; the jurisdiction's very mission may be at risk (FAI, 1999).

Without a reasonable allocation of risk, one or both of the parties may be unwilling to enter into a contract. Thus, many governmental entities have developed alternatives to negate specific types of risk.

Accomplishing Social and Economic Objectives

Government entities in the United States (including Federal, state and local) spent over $700 billion in 2001 (the Public Purchaser, Nov./Dec. 2001). This magnitude of government procurement outlays has created opportunities for implementing selected national policies. Indeed, government entities can require, for example, that contractors maintain fair employment practices, provide safe and healthful working conditions, pay fair wages, refrain from polluting the air and water, give preference to American local contractors and to small or women/minority-owned businesses, and promote the rehabilitation of prisoners and the severely handicapped.

Maximizing Competition

Competition is defined as "the effort of two or more vendors to secure business of a third party by the offer of the most favorable terms as to price, quality, promptness of delivery, and/or service" (NIGP, 1996). A sound procurement system needs to promote and provide full and open competition in soliciting offers and awarding government contracts, except:

- contracts awarded using the simplified or emergency procurement procedures (sole source procurement);
- contracts awarded using contracting procedures that are expressly authorized by statute;
- contract modifications, including the exercise of priced options that were evaluated as part of the initial competition, and that are within the scope and under the terms of an existing contract; and
- orders placed under definite-quantity contracts.

Full and open competition, when used in respect to a contract action, means that all responsible sources are permitted to compete. Competition provides major incentives to industry and government entities to reduce cost and increase quality. Moreover, in the area of high technology, competition is critical for providing innovation. Procurement officials need to comply with statutory requirements for competition when they acquire goods, capital assets, and supplies. At the same time, they need to take all necessary actions to promote a competitive environment, including:

- ensuring that prime contractors foster effective competition for major and critical products and technologies; and
- ensuring that qualified international sources are permitted to compete.

Occasionally, in order to promote full and open competition, government entities may exclude a particular source from a contract action in order to establish or maintain an alternative source or sources for the supplies or services being acquired. This action is allowed if the government entity determines that to do so would:

- increase or maintain competition and likely result in reduced overall costs for the acquisition or for any anticipated acquisition;
- ensure the continuous availability of a reliable source of supplies or services;
- satisfy projected needs based on a history of high demand; or
- satisfy a critical need for medical, safety, or emergency supplies.

In addition, the U.S. Department of Defense has frequently used this source-exclusion practice in order to have a facility (or a producer, manufacturer, or other supplier) available to furnish the supplies or services in case of a national emergency or industrial mobilization; or to establish or maintain an essential engineering, research, or development capability to be provided by an educational or other nonprofit institution or a Federally-funded research and development center. In order to avoid possible intentional or unintentional abuse of this practice, any source exclusion must to be authorized (signed) by an appropriate administrator. State and local jurisdictions have made extensive use of this type of procurement as part of their emergency response or disaster plans. Some geographic areas are subject to hurricanes, tornadoes, flooding, and other types of natural disasters (force majeure). It is imperative that each purchasing department have an Emergency Procurement Plan in order to effectively respond in these type of situations.

Maintaining Integrity and Transparency

As will be discussed in detail later in this text, at any given point of the procurement process, protests frequently occur. Hence, in order to avoid protests, the procurement process needs to be integral and transparent. There are many ways to maintain integrity and transparency. FAI (1999) suggests that procurement officials:

- deal fairly and in good faith;
- maintain impartiality and avoid preferential treatment; and
- avoid any appearance of conflict of interest or in any way compromise public trust in the procurement system.

Procurement method selection requires a thorough analysis of all elements, as previously discussed. Procurement statutes and/or regulations of each jurisdiction is a factor that has not been discussed. Normally, procurement thresholds and procurement methods are clearly stated in the entity's regulations and statutes. Legal requirements take precedent and cannot be ignored. Within the legal boundary, procurement officials should select a procurement method that will meet procurement goals by carefully examining the variables discussed above. The best selection approach is to involve a procurement team in the selection process.

In the Federal Government, as stated in FAR, the RFP method is used only when the RFB method is not appropriate. This requirement is independently applied at the state and local government levels. In many entities, the first decision related to procurement method selection deals with ways of avoiding a competitive solicitation process.

- Is there a statewide contract?

- Can another department provide the required goods or services?

- Is there another department that has a similar contract and that permits purchases by additional departments?

- Can this procurement be handled as one of the designated exceptions, e.g., emergency, collective purchasing, exempt from competition, single source, etc.?

- Can the procurement be handled as an RFB, where all specifications, terms and conditions are mandatory?

In selecting a procurement strategy, the treatment of cost is always an important consideration.

Determination That Competitive Sealed Bidding is Neither Practicable Nor Advantageous

If it is determined that the RFP method is the best approach, the next step is to justify that competitive sealed bidding is neither practicable nor advantageous. The procurement official must make this determination in writing, and it should incorporate the required conditions for the use of the method. A practical approach for making the determination involves two steps. First, the end-user prepares a justification and requests a determination from procurement that competitive sealed bidding is neither practicable nor advantageous. Second, the chief procurement official develops a written determination based on the justification, assigns staff to the procurement project, and appoints an evaluation committee for the solicitation. Then, the RFP process begins. As mentioned above, the RFP process consists of many phases that vary, depending on the types of procurement. In this book, a standard RFP process is proposed, as shown in Figure 6, and this standard RFP process will be explored in detail.

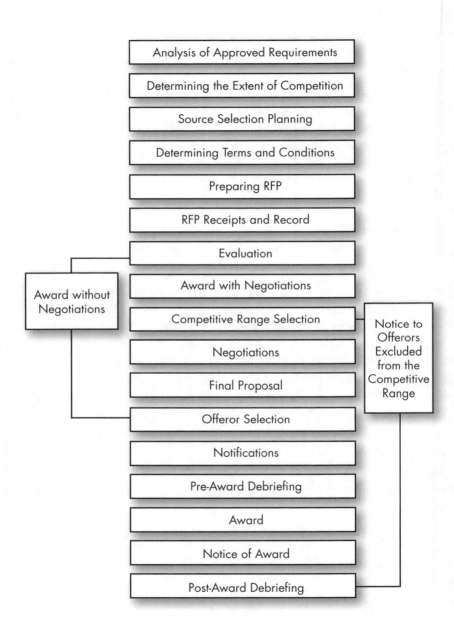

Figure 6 - *The Standard RFP Process.*

Conclusion

When the RFP method was first introduced as a procurement method is still unknown. In the academic world, it is known for the Federal Government's research and development programs. The RFP method is used when the flexibility of evaluation criteria found in the RFB is not appropriate. Chapter 2 will focus on the procurement plan and explore the key steps and activities in the RFP process. Considered as a source selection method, the RFP process ends when an award is granted, unsuccessful vendors are debriefed, and the contract administration process begins.

References

Abi-Karam, T. (2001). Managing risks in design/build, technical programs and proceedings. Pittsburgh, PA: The Association for the Advancement of Cost Engineering (AACE) Internatinal, 45th Annual International Conference. Pittsburg, PA.

American Bar Association (2000). *The 2000 model procurement code for state and local governments*. Chicago, IL: American Bar Association.

Associated Press (2001). *New Hanoi Airport terminal opens*. Available from www.aol.com.

Cibinic, J., Jr., & Nash, R. C., Jr. (1998). *Formulation of government contracts* (3rd ed.). Washington, DC: George Washington University, National Law Center.

Corwin, S. (1999). *How to handle competitive negotiations*. A paper presented at the Annual Forum of the National Institute of Governmental Purchasing, Inc., Halifax, Canada.

Federal Acquisition Institute (1999). *The federal acquisition process*. Washington, DC: Federal Acquisition Institute.

Federal Acquisition Regulation Web site, *http://www.arnet.gov/far/loadmainre.html*.

Geroski, P. (1990, July). Innovation, technological opportunity and market structure. *Oxford Economics Papers*, 42.

Harink, J. H. A. (1999). *Excelling with e-procurement*. Alphen aan den Rijin, The Netherlands: Samson.

McCrudden, C. (Ed.). (1999). *Regulation and deregulation*. Oxford, England: Clarendon Press.

Nash, R. C., Jr., Cibinic, J., Jr., & O'Brien, K. R. (1999). *Competitive negotiation: The source of selection process* (2nd ed.). Washington, DC: The George Washington University, Government Contract Program.

National Association of State Purchasing Officials (NASPO) (1997). *State and local government purchasing principles and practices*. Lexington, KY: NASPO.

National Institute of Governmental Purchasing, Inc. (NIGP) (1996). *Dictionary of purchasing terms*. Herndon, VA: NIGP.

National Institute of Governmental Purchasing, Inc. (NIGP) (1999a). *Advanced public procurement*. Herndon, VA: NIGP.

National Institute of Governmental Purchasing, Inc. (NIGP) (1999b). *Intermediate public procurement*. Herndon, VA: NIGP.

National Institute of Governmental Purchasing, Inc. (NIGP) (2001). *General public procurement.* Herndon, VA: NIGP.

Office of Federal Procurement Policy (1982). *Proposal for a uniform federal procurement system.* Washington, DC: Office of Federal Procurement.

Office of Management and Budget (1997, July). *Circular A-11, supplement to part 7, capital programming guide.* Available from www.whitehouse.gov/omb/circulars/index/htlm.

Pettijohn, C., & Babich, K.S. (2004). Sourcing in the public sector. Herndon, VA: NIGP

Pettijohn, C., & Qiao, Y. (2000). Procuring technology: Issues faced by public organizations. *Journal of Public Budgeting, Accounting, and Financial Management, 12,* 441-461.

Thomas, A. G. (1919). *Principles of government purchasing.* New York: D. Appleton and Company.

CHAPTER 2

The Request for Proposal Process

Introduction

*P*ublic procurement is one of the most, if not *the* most challenging functions of government due to the size of procurement expenditures, its various and conflicting goals, and particularly its fair and open competition process. Government procurement agencies and individual procurement officials are accountable not only to the end-users and suppliers but also to their whole jurisdiction, elected officials and the public for the efficient, cost-effective and fair conduct of their procurement. The Request for Proposals (RFP) method is different from other procurement methods, particularly the Invitation to Bid, in that the contract award decision is not based purely on pricing offered by prospective proposers, but also on other weighted criteria. These non-price factors cannot be objectively measured and depend heavily on professional judgments that may be challenged by disgruntled offerors.

Thus, procurement officials should establish and make publicly known the RFP procedures and should follow the stated process without infraction throughout the entire procurement. In order to ensure transparency of the procurement process, avenues for filing and reviewing questions should be available. Jurisdictions purchase a wide range of goods and services, and each entity enjoys its independence and autonomy. Thus, the RFP procedures, as will be discussed later in this chapter, vary with each type of good and service and among agencies; however, commonality exists for most procedures. Relying on this assumption, this chapter will describe basic activities or steps in the RFP process, noting that the RFP is one of several source selection methods and ends when a contract agreement is reached. For further discussion on the public contracting process, refer to *Introduction to Public Procurement*, published by the National Institute of Governmental Purchasing, Inc. (NIGP) in 2004.

Following the illustration of a typical RFP process, this chapter will briefly cover a very complicated RFP process for major systems most commonly illustrated by an information technology system acquisition. Where applicable, the U.S. Federal, state and local government practices have been added as examples. Although the procurement process is an ongoing, step-by-step process and each step leads to the next (Federal Acquisition Institute [FAI], 1999), it will be shown that many steps can be taken simultaneously to reduce the procurement cycle. Moreover, not all steps receive equal attention; and some may be omitted altogether.

...the RFP process should "begin as soon as the agency need is identified..."

According to the General Accounting Office (GAO) appropriation law (1999), Federal Government agencies cannot encumber and expend funds until the budget is appropriated by legislation and apportioned by the Central Budget Office. However, because it is so time-consuming, the RFP process should "begin as soon as the agency need is identified, preferably well in advance of the fiscal year in which contract award is necessary" (Federal Acquisition Regulation [FAR] 7.104a). Thus, due to time constraints, procurement officials need to have a very well prepared action plan. The purpose of the action plan is to ensure that procurement meets the agency's needs in the most effective, economical, and timely manner. Furthermore, knowledge gained from prior acquisitions should be used to further requirements and procurement strategies.

Initial Steps

Preparing a Procurement Action Plan for Large Acquisitions

The process begins by:

- forming a team consisting of all those who will be responsible for significant aspects of the procurement, such as contracting, fiscal, legal, and technical personnel;

- coordinating with and securing the concurrence of end-users in all planning; and

- consulting requirements and logistics personnel who determine type, quality, quantity, and delivery requirements.

In order to comply with procurement policies and goals as established by a jurisdiction, the plan should comply with all established procedures to:

- encourage offerors to supply commercial items;
- solicit offers in such a manner to promote and provide for full and open competition;
- conform to established criteria and thresholds at which greater detail and formality are required, such as dollar value, size, complexity, scope, nature, and circumstances of the procurement;
- provide for the review and approval of acquisition plans and revisions to such plans;
- establish criteria and thresholds at which design-to-cost and life-cycle-cost techniques will be used; and
- structure contract requirements to facilitate competition by and among small business concerns. While like-type commodity and service bundling may provide substantial benefits to jurisdictions, unnecessary and unjustified bundling that precludes small business participation as contractors should be avoided.

In addition to a well-written procurement plan (Table 3), procurement should establish a feasible procurement schedule.

Table 3

Elements of a Typical Federal Acquisition Plan

1. Acquisition Background and Objectives

- Statement of need
- Applicable conditions
- Cost
- Capability or performance characteristics
- Delivery or performance-period requirements
- Trade-offs (among cost, schedule, etc.)
- Risks
- Acquisition streamlining

2. Plan of Action

- Sources
- Competition
- Source selection procedures
- Contracting considerations
- Budgeting and funding
- Product descriptions
- Priorities, allocations, and allotments
- Contractor v. Government performance (OMB Circular A-76)
- Management information requirements
- Make or buy
- Test and evaluation
- Logistics considerations
- Government-furnished property
- Government-furnished information
- Environmental and energy conservation considerations
- Security considerations
- Milestones for the acquisition cycle
- Identification of participants in acquisition plan preparation
- Other considerations, such as standardization concepts and foreign sales implications

Source: Federal Acquisition Regulation, Part 7.105.

Preparing and Processing a Procurement Request

Although sound procurement planning starts well in advance of the fiscal year in which contract award is budgeted, the actual procurement function takes place once the end-user prepares and forwards an approved purchase requisition to the purchasing department.

Preparing a Purchase Requisition (PR)

The purpose of a PR is to provide the purchasing agent (or contract officer in the Federal Government) with the information and approvals necessary for initiating procurement. When preparing a PR, end-users should consult with purchasing to ensure a clear and concise understanding of the goods needed or services desired. The more the end-user consults with procurement, the more precise the document will be. Procurement that starts with a poorly prepared PR is likely to be troublesome at some point in the process. For example, if a single-source acquisition is initiated without justification and approval, the action may later be protested and the entire process disrupted and delayed. Other consequences of a poorly prepared requisition might include:

- need to cancel a solicitation because of improper approval or lack of funds;
- failure to order the most cost-effective quantity, considering acquisition and storage; or
- failure to include price-related evaluation factors in the solicitation.

There is no standard form for PRs. As a result, PRs often vary in format from one jurisdiction to the next. Despite differences in form, PRs generally tend to have certain elements in common, as shown in Table 4.

Table 4
Typical Elements of a PR

Description of the requirement

Quantity of the item(s) to be procured

Delivery or performance requirements

Any recommended special packaging and marking requirements

Inspection and acceptance requirements

Recommended sources

Any recommended special contract administration requirements

Any recommended special provisions or clauses (e.g., options, government-furnished property)

Any recommended price-related factors for award

Any recommended non-price evaluation factors for award (if factors in addition to price are applicable)

Justifications and approvals for other than full and open competition, if needed

Acquisition plan, if required

Certification of funds available for the procurement

Management reviews and approvals as required by agency policies

Source: Federal Acquisition Institute (1999). *The federal acquisition process.* Washington, DC: Federal Acquisition Institute.

Processing of Purchase Requisitions

After receiving a PR, the purchasing agent reviews and approves the procurement and begins the contracting process. Should major deficiencies or omissions be identified, the PR is returned to the end-user to obtain any missing information or to make the necessary corrections. After accepting a PR, the purchasing agent often:

- establishes a contract file;

- counsels end-users on protecting source selection information from unauthorized disclosure;

- enters the PR in the "tracking" system; or

- starts the clock on the "Procurement Administrative Lead Time" (PALT). PALT represents the time between (1) acceptance of the PR and (2) award of the contract (FAI, 1999).

Funding

For budget control purposes, the RFP process cannot start without appropriate administrative approval, as a completed RFP process results in a contract award that commits appropriated funds to honor the contract established. In other words, a contract award is a fund obligation.

It is improper to issue a RFP unless there is a reasonable expectation that a contract will be awarded. As contracts cannot be awarded without adequate funds, the availability of funds must be certified on the PR prior to procurement action. Similarly, funds must be available when processing a contract modification that will increase the contract price.

The following aspects of funding are of particular importance to procurement officials:

- Funds are appropriated for either a specific use or for a category of uses. For example, some funds are only used for research and development programs, while others are used for operations and maintenance. The contracting officer (CO) must ensure that the correct funds are cited.

- Funds have a life in terms of a date by which they must be obligated. In some cases, funds may be used only for work completed within a given fiscal year. Funds are normally "good" for one year or for a specific number of years. The procurement officials must ensure that the procurement is completed (from solicitation of offers to contract award) before the funds "expire."

- Funds must be adequate for the procurement. If the procurement officials believe the funds are inadequate, they might request that the end-users either make additional funds available or reduce the quantity of supplies or level of service to be procured.

In principle, appropriations laws require agencies to comply with the appropriated amount of funds, the time, and purpose (GAO, 1999). Thus, the procurement official needs to ensure that the amount of funds is available for the authorized procurement project for the specified fiscal year(s). Failure to do so could result in delay or cancellation of the procurement. Even worse, from a personal standpoint, if a procurement official awards a contract and there are insufficient funds, as an individual, they may be personally responsible for payment under the provisions of the Anti-Deficiency Act.

On occasion, agencies process procurements without appropriated funds by:

- making the solicitation "subject to the availability of funds";
- including options for increased quantities or extension of the contract period;
- using "Indefinite Quantity or Requirements" terms and conditions; or
- incorporating clauses that provide for year-by-year funding of multi-year requirements. (non-appropriation clauses).

Market Research

*M*arket research is defined as "collecting and analyzing information about capabilities within the market to satisfy agency needs" (FAR 2.101). The results of market research are used

"to arrive at the most suitable approach to acquiring, distributing, and supporting supplies and services" (FAR 10.000). For more information on market research, see McVay's (1996) *Getting Started in Contracting.*

Normally, the procurement researches markets even before developing new specifications for an acquisition by end-users, before soliciting offers for acquisitions with an estimated value in excess of the sealed bid threshold, and before soliciting offers for acquisitions with an estimated value less than the sealed bid threshold, when adequate information is not available and the circumstances justify its cost. The extent of market research and analysis will vary depending on the urgency, value, and complexity of the proposed acquisition. Data collected may include:

- the availability of a commercial item suitable as is, or with minor modifications, for meeting the need;
- common practices of firms engaged in producing, distributing, and supporting the products or services, such as terms for warranties, buyer financing, maintenance and packaging, and marking;
- requirements of any laws and regulations unique to the supplies or services being acquired;
- number and time frame for sales to occur to provide reasonable assurance that a particular product is reliable;
- the availability of items that contain recycled materials and items that are energy efficient;
- distribution and support capabilities of potential suppliers, including alternative arrangements and cost estimates;
- size and status of potential sources;
- customary practices regarding customizing, modifying or tailoring of items to meet customer needs and associated costs; or
- extent to which commercial items or non-developmental items could be incorporated at the component level.

Market data normally come from a variety of sources including:

- technical personnel, commodity specialists, price analysts, and other in-house experts for a commodity or service and its market;
- acquisition histories available for the jurisdiction;
- catalogs and periodicals, including those published online;
- references from other purchasing professionals in and around the agency;
- buyers for the same or similar supplies or services;
- sources sought for synopses and surveys of potential suppliers;
- trade and professional associations;
- nonprofit standards and testing labs; or
- government and non-government databases (FAI, 1999).

Market data is very important and applicable to virtually all pre-award duties and tasks. Market information is needed for cost and price analyses in (1) determining whether the requirement can be met by a commercial item and, therefore, is to be procured and (2) reviewing proposed requirements documents to ensure that they encompass all acceptable products (if any) in the market. They are equally important for:

- determining when to buy, establishing delivery schedules that are realistic in terms of market conditions and practices;
- identifying potential sources for the solicitation mailing list;
- reviewing sole source justifications;
- determining whether to set the procurement aside for small business concerns;
- determining whether to buy or lease;
- identifying price-related and non-price evaluation factors;
- identifying terms and conditions for the solicitation (e.g., those that are customary in markets for commercial items);
- establishing quantity breaks; and
- estimating the proper price level or value of the supplies or services.

Normally, market research is a continuing effort by all procurement professionals. Equipped with a comprehensive and broad network of peers that provides information for all types of goods and services that their jurisdictions may need, today's buyer has ready access to current data on market activity. However, as the market is constantly changing, procurement officials still need to do their homework to include what has been done before for similar requirements. Market research is the identification of existing offerors that are likely able to satisfy the requirements, types of solutions, customary practices, and other agencies' approaches to solving similar requirements. It is often done jointly by end-users and the procurement officials and prior to the development of Specifications or the Statement/Scope of Work (SOW) when agencies identify their needs and develop requirements to meet their needs (Thai, 2004). Then, market research is done again, concurrently with the development of the SOW. The information obtained influences the development of the specifications or Statement/Scope of Work, as well as the selection process.

Market data is very important and applicable to virtually all pre-award duties and tasks.

A host of information is available from practitioners willing to share advice and experiences. In addition, NIGP maintains a valuable technical library for a multitude of products and services that have been procured from a cross section of public procurement practitioners.

Another market research tool is the supplier community, and information is often acquired through the Request for Information (RFI) method. A RFI is a non-binding method whereby a jurisdiction publishes via newspaper, Internet or direct mail its need for input from interested parties for an upcoming solicitation. An agency prepares a general statement of what product or service is contemplated, requesting interested parties to respond with any input that may be considered for planning such a purchase. Typically, potential suppliers willingly offer information and advice to aid jurisdictions in gathering sufficient details prior to the creation and issuance of an RFP. The give and take of information benefits both parties and aids in the determination of whether the RFP process is the best strategy to use. A RFI emphasizes the jurisdiction's desire for fair and open competition once the process begins. In some cases, an agency may choose to invite one or more potential offerors to a meeting to discuss the acquisition process. This meeting is called a Pre-Solicitation conference. From a legal standpoint, this type of meeting is not a public meeting or offer to purchase; and as such, it is not legally necessary to invite all potential offerors as in the case of a formal Pre-Bid or Pre-Proposal conference. Some jurisdictions feel that inviting all known suppliers prevents any future criticism of their procedures. Procurement officials either alone or with the procurement planning team can meet separately with each of the interested parties. However, it is necessary to remember the requirement of impartiality and transparency in all public procurements. It is a good practice for the procurement officials to meet with any of the parties who request a meeting in advance of the solicitation and ensure that the same topics are covered with all potential offerors.

When conducting conferences, procurement officials should be careful not to give the appearance of favoring one potential offeror over another and ensure that comparable access to government officials is granted to all potential offerors. Do not disclose information from prospective offerors, if doing so would reveal that offeror's confidential business strategy. When specific information about a proposed acquisition that would be necessary for the preparation of proposals is disclosed to one or more potential offerors, make that information available to the public as soon as practicable, but no later than the next general release of information.

Additional resources include hiring consultants with knowledge of both the RFP process and technical expertise in the specific area of the jurisdiction's need. While consultants can be retained to provide technical and administrative advice, an agency should consider the overall cost of such assistance. A good consultant is expensive, and dependence on the consultant's advice may lock the jurisdiction into a path with few options, especially for future expansion.

There are many different ways to perform market research, depending on the complexity of the problem, the value of the contract, the industry involved, and the time and staff available. Input can be sought directly from industry through:

- discussions and briefings prior to constructing a procurement document;
- issuance of a draft SOW, specification, or draft solicitation document; or
- issuance of a Request for Information.

Input can also be obtained from non-industry sources by:

- contacting knowledgeable individuals in government about market capabilities to meet requirements;
- reviewing the results of recent market research undertaken to meet similar or identical requirements;
- querying government databases that provide information relevant to agency acquisitions; and
- obtaining source lists of similar items from other contracting activities or agencies, trade associations, or other sources.

Getting input from industry is a valuable exercise and well worth the time and effort. Some of the benefits include:

- input from industry may permit requirements to be refined and made less restrictive, removing barriers acquiring commercial items;
- development of more effective acquisition strategies and procurements; and
- preparation of better specifications, Statements/Scopes of Work, or evaluation processes.

Developing an RFP Document

As the RFP procurement method is used for sophisticated procurement items, the development of a RFP document is vitally more important. In preparing the requirements documents, agencies may select from existing

RFP documents, modify or combine the other entity's requirements documents, or create new requirements documents to meet agency needs. In order to demonstrate that an item has achieved commercial market acceptance, the criteria in the solicitation should reflect, at a minimum, the need of the end-user; the item's performance and intended use, and include consideration of items satisfactorily supplied under recent or current contracts for the same or similar items.

Many months and even years prior to the start of the RFP process, agencies identify their mission needs and analyze requirements for procurement authorization. Moreover, the requirements result in budget appropriations (Thai, 2004). Requirements prepared for procurement authorization and appropriations may become out of date, particularly in the age of rapid technological changes. Thus, in preparing the requirements documents, agencies may select from existing requirements documents, modify or combine existing requirements documents, or create new requirements documents to meet end-user needs.

Requirements documents include Specifications or Statements/Scopes of Work and related elements of the purchase requisition. The procurement officials may accept requirements documents proposed by the end-user as is or recommend improvements to the documents. In making this determination, procurement officials review the proposed documents to ensure that the documents meet certain criteria.

- The documents should be phrased in terms that that market can satisfy.
- The documents should describe functions to be performed, the performance required, or essential physical characteristics rather than design characteristics.
- The documents should establish a valid and reliable benchmark for determining whether offered supplies or services meet the functional need.
- The documents should enable and encourage offerors to supply commercial items or (to the extent that commercial items suitable to meet the agency's needs are not available) other non-developmental items.
- The documents should allow evaluators to consider "technically acceptable" commercial or other non-developmental items that can meet the functional need.
- The documents should exclude all products or services (commercially available or not) from consideration that cannot meet the actual functional need.

- The documents should include restrictive provisions or conditions only to the extent necessary to satisfy the needs of the agency or as authorized by law.

- The documents should promote full and open competition (or maximum practicable competition when using simplified acquisition procedures) with due regard to the nature of the supplies or services to be acquired.

Preparing Specifications (Specs) and Statement/ Scope of Work (SOW)

As a very important element of the RFP method, specifications will have a great impact throughout the RFP process. Specs and SOW's have a great impact on the offered price (Harink, Telgen, & Streefkerk, 1999; Harink, 1999). Moreover, they are a major source of protests and complaints. According to NIGP (2000), a good specification or SOW contains the following elements:

- It identifies a minimum requirement.

- It allows for maximum competition.

- It identifies the test methods to be used to verify compliance with the requirement.

- It contributes to obtaining best value at the lowest possible cost using a fair, equitable, and transparent (easy to understand) contract award process.

There is a quick method of determining whether a specification or SOW contains these four elements and is adequate to achieve proper results. If the answer to the following questions is an unequivocal "yes," chances are it is appropriate.

- Is the text legible and the wording precise? (Ambiguity is a source of potential problems.)

- Is the overall message clear and understandable both to procurement and the potential suppliers? (Misunderstandings can be expensive.)

- Does the use of the specification simplify the process?

- Are the tolerances and performance expectations reasonable? (Unnecessary precision is expensive and may discourage some potential suppliers from submitting proposals.)

- Is it relatively easy to perform the verification, which will govern acceptance or rejection? (A specification that cannot be checked is useless.)

- Is the specification exact and the SOW clear and well defined? (There should not be any loopholes that could be used by offerors to evade any of the provisions.)

- Does the specification identify one or more brands already on the market?

- Is it fair to all potential suppliers? (Specifications written around specific products may reduce or eliminate fair competition.)

- Is there some built-in flexibility? (Depending on the age of the specification, progress made by the industry may have contributed to a better product.)

Due to its importance, the scribing of specifications and SOWs will be addressed in the next chapter. Prior to soliciting offers, purchasing agents should obtain feedback from the market on the proposed requirements documents. Such feedback can be obtained through early exchanges with prospective offerors through such means as:

- pre-solicitation notices;

- pre-solicitation conferences;

- request for Information, request for qualifications, and draft request for proposal;

- one-on-one meetings.

When preparing or reviewing requirements documents, end-users and purchasing representatives should consider the impact of these documents on soliciting competition. Requirements documents should exclude only those products or services that cannot satisfy the government's actual needs. For example, a deliverable compatible with the equipment of XYZ Corporation may be required if such compatibility is really needed. Otherwise, that requirement may improperly rule out products of other corporations that can meet the need.

Revealing Budgetary Figures

One of the current points of debate about offeror selection surrounds the issue of whether the procurement is enhanced by publishing a budget as part of the solicitation. Proponents of publishing a budget suggest that there are significant benefits to creating a level playing field and comparing offerors' proposals solely on their technical merits. If all the potential offerors are charging the same amount of, the Evaluation Committee has only to select the firm that offers the greatest technical approach along with having the most desirable credentials. Cost is no longer an issue.

Opponents of publishing a budget maintain that it is not possible to measure the level of effort or cost of many requirements. Further, many suggest that it is not wise to restrict the effect that competition can have on the prices offered by offerors. There is obviously no need to publish a budget when choosing an offeror based on the lowest price and the lowest cost-per-point selection methods, because competition considers price along with other issues. For the other vendor selection methods, each procurement representative will need to decide on their own whether to publish a budget. Home rule dictates an agency's ability to safeguard information from public review with regard to the RFP process. Individuals involved in public procurement are encouraged to familiarize themselves with the local rules and legislation of their given entity.

Solicitation

Approval Levels

In undertaking a competitive procurement, purchasing should verify the applicable approval levels. Typically, the approval levels required of competitive procurements, like the signing levels, are higher than for a sole-source procurement. Most often, the approval levels for the amendments to a competitive procurement match those of non-competitive procurements. The basic premise for this is that the market itself will act as a control on what is appropriate; and, therefore, the jurisdiction does not need to be as concerned with establishing extra controls or checks on vendor fees for the amended/additional services.

Further, the procurement office is responsible for verification of which competitive approval levels apply. In most jurisdictions, different approval levels have been set for commodities and services, professional services, and construction services to reflect the unique aspects of each commodity. Typically, the approval levels for commodities are the least restrictive, those for construction services the most.

In many jurisdictions, the authority to purchase certain goods and services up to a particular dollar value has also been delegated to the internal clients themselves. In these cases, procurement's role may be one of advisor to the client. When this occurs, purchasing should prepare guidelines and basic instructions to help the end-user with the procurement. In addition, purchasing must remember that delegation does not absolve them of overall procurement oversight responsibility.

Due to the checks and balances built into the procurement process when planning the schedule for the procurement, buyers need to take the time required to obtain approval and award the contract. As will be discussed in later chapters, purchasing's main role is to clearly document all relevant information related to the solicitation and evaluation in order to expedite the award phase.

The approval levels set for the requirement will also determine what steps will be required in advance of the solicitation and after the evaluation of the proposals. In some jurisdictions, prior approval must be sought from a higher authority in order to proceed with the solicitation. In other cases, special approval is required only when there is something unique about the solicitation, the terms and conditions, or the proposal evaluation and offeror selection methods. In other jurisdictions, the procurement plan itself may require approval.

Depending upon the approval level for the requirement, purchasing ensures that the process followed possesses all of the supporting pricing documentation required and meets the exact definition of competition. For example, in some jurisdictions, when only one proposal is found to be compliant, the approval level set for a sole source requirement is required; and a need to provide additional justification for the proposal price in order to obtain approval to proceed with the contract award may be necessary.

Public Notice

For Federal procurement officials, public notice must be made in advance of a solicitation. The U.S. Federal Government publicizes proposed contract actions at least 15 days prior to solicitations. In cases such as requirements purchased under the North American Free Trade Agreement (NAFTA) rules, the notice period is set at 40 days. Typically, these notices are posted or published for a pre-scribed period of time in newspapers, trade journals, electronic bulletin boards, or official Web sites and serve as a mechanism to solicit proposals instead of using source lists to identify interested parties. In other cases, the notices merely advertise in advance that the jurisdiction will be seeking to procure a requirement. The notices are also used in cases where the jurisdiction is intending to sole-source a requirement to ensure that there are no alternative sources.

Electronic Solicitation Web Sites

Electronic solicitation is becoming more and more common in public procurement as a form of public notice. In some cases, electronic bulletin boards are used only to post or publicize the upcoming requirements. In other cases, vendors can view the electronic boards and order solicitation documents that interest them. For most state and local agencies, potential offerors can only receive documents by downloading them from the Web. An example of electronic solicitation (in Canada) using the Internet can be found at http://www.merx.

cebra.com (MERX). Notices of Proposed Purchases (NPPs) are posted on the MERX site to satisfy the NAFTA and possibly other international requirements for public notice. Vendors who use the service can review Notices of Proposed Procurements, Advance Contract Award Notices, Expressions of Interest, Standard Acquisition Contract Clauses, and information on international procurements. The service covers the Federal, most of the Provincial, and the Territorial Government market. Vendors identify their areas of interest and are notified of specific opportunities matching their jurisdiction's profile. Vendors pay a fee only when they want to download the solicitation documents.

Another similar example is FedBizOpps, the Federal Business Opportunities Web site produced by the General Services Administration (GSA) that announces products and services wanted or offered by the U.S. Government. Procurement information is available either electronically for:

- all proposed procurements of $25,000 or more by civil and military agencies;
- all contract awards of $25,000 or more;
- non-U.S. Federal Government procurement opportunities;
- surplus U.S. Government property sales;
- non-U.S. standards that may affect U.S. exports; or
- special notices and the occasional announcement of business-related events, such as procurement conferences.

Although the use of electronic solicitation tools is growing very quickly, security issues surrounding the receipt of proposal packages from offerors are still a concern in many jurisdictions and, therefore, prevent their use.

Other Methods of Publicizing

Solicitation notices can be publicized in a variety of ways.

- Posting solicitation notices in public places (required when the award price is expected to range between $10,000 and $25,000 or, in the case of Defense agencies, between $5,000 and $25,000), or as dictated by the rules and regulations of the individual entity;
- Electronic dissemination available to the public at the procurement/ contracting office;
- Periodic handouts listing proposed contracts;
- Announcements to local trade associations;

- Announcements to newspapers and other media for publication without cost (paid advertising requires special authority and is seldom used);
- Electronic bulletin boards;
- Mailing of flyers to potential suppliers listed on the Vendors Mailing List.

Distributing the Solicitation

The RFP solicitation documents are made available to interested parties by:

- issuing the solicitation to firms on the mailing list;
- mailing to other interested sources upon request (advising the requestor of any limits on competition);
- providing a courtesy copy to publishers, trade associations, and other such interested parties;
- retaining a copy for review and duplication upon the request of an interested party; and
- distributing the solicitation electronically (may limit availability of the solicitation to the applicable electronic medium when employing electronic commerce).

Although it is not legally required to notify all vendors registered on the Vendors (bidders) List, should a jurisdiction choose not to distribute the solicitation document to all the vendors on the list, the vendors must be so advised at the time they register with the jurisdiction. Keep in mind that some interested vendors may not receive solicitations; and, as a result, those vendors who did not receive a solicitation may file protests.

Dealing with Pre-Award Inquiries

Pre-award inquiries are questions and comments from prospective offerors about specifications, terms, and/or conditions in the solicitation. In order to avoid situations that might be viewed as improper disclosure, all inquiries should be referred to the procurement representative responsible for the project. It must be made very clear that the only contact point for potential offers is the designated procurement representative. To ensure fairness to all potential offerors, there must be only a single point of contact. Technical or other information may be transmitted only by those individuals possessing contractual authority.

Improper release of information may result in a protest that could delay or void the entire procurement. Thus, only general information not prejudicial to other offerors (i.e., not giving one offeror an unfair advantage over any other offeror) may be furnished upon request, e.g., explanation of the meaning of a clause, directions for locating a facility, etc.

Pre-Proposal Conference

The procurement official may conduct a pre-proposal conference for any or all of the following reasons:

- providing for inspection of work site or government-furnished property;
- explaining complicated specifications and requirements;
- explaining revisions to requirements; and/or
- addressing numerous offeror inquiries.

Increasingly, procurement is faced with the prospect of seeking competitive proposals of a highly technical or complex nature. Consultant or professional service contracts often fall into this category. This type of solicitation typically has a greater chance of unforeseen problems that may require a special understanding by the potential offerors in preparing their proposals. In such circumstances, procurement agents are relying on the use of pre-proposal/bid conferences as a mechanism to meet with the prospective offerors and discuss the upcoming procurement.

Chaired by the purchasing representative, the Pre-Proposal Conference provides an opportunity to discuss with the prospective offerors the specifications in detail, explaining the scope, objectives, and techniques expected as part of the proposed purchase. The Request for Proposal stipulates the time, date, and location of the Pre-Proposal Conference. It is highly recommended that that questions be submitted in writing. The timing of the conference should be sufficiently early in the solicitation to allow prospective offerors to adjust their submittals according to the information received at the conference.

At the actual conference, it is important to note in writing all of the questions as well as the answers provided for any prospective offerors unable to attend the conference. Just as with questions raised by prospective offerors in the normal bid solicitation process, clarification may be provided to all. A cutoff date for questions should be established in order for the schedule to be maintained. If not, it may become necessary to extend the proposal closing date in order to issue additional addenda and allow sufficient time for proposal response preparation.

Pre-Proposal Conferences are most useful when the client's requirement is unique or has special qualities not typically seen by the specific vendor community; however, this usefulness is often tempered by fear from the vendor community of revealing proprietary information through their questions. As a consequence, the procurement official and the end-user often present information they expect may be contentious but may receive little in the way of real questions at the conference.

Pre-Proposal Conferences are most useful when the client's require- ment is unique...

Pre-Proposal Conferences contribute to the climate of competition. They provide an excellent source of information for the agency, often operating as a type of focus group with potential suppliers. Additionally, they allow potential offerors to obtain a better understanding of the needs of the jurisdiction, thereby increasing the quality of responses to the solicitation. On occasion, conferences may be necessary to insure competition (National Association of State Purchasing Officials [NASPO], 1997, p. 53).

Amendments/Addenda to Solicitations

Frequently, after the RFP is solicited but prior to proposal deadline, changes need to be made in such items as specs, SOW, delivery schedules, quantities, etc., or ambiguous provisions need to be clarified, or errors and oversights need correction and clarification. These changes may or may not have been brought to the attention of procurement by the potential supplier at events such as the proposal conference. Verbal changes may not be made and interpretations of a material consequence must not verbally be made to potential offerors who inquire. All offerors who have been asked to submit proposals and have received a solicitation package must be informed in writing by an addendum of any such changes that are made. This action is necessary to ensure that all offerors are proposing on the same knowledge base and have the same understanding of the requirements.

Prior to issuing an addendum, purchasing and the end-user must consider the period of time remaining before proposal submission deadline. If additional preparation time is likely to be required by the offeror, the amendment should extend the deadline for a reasonable period of time. When only a short period of time remains before the deadline, the potential offerors may be notified by telephone, telegram, or fax with confirmation provided later by a written amendment. This process is difficult in those jurisdictions using electronic means, such as bulletin boards, to solicit proposals, as they can only notify those who have requested RFP documents. Notices may need to be posted on these bulletin boards to advise any future requestors.

When insufficient time remains for the offerors to adjust their proposals, purchasing must issue an addendum to extend the submission deadline or cancel the solicitation and start it anew with the corrected information. In all circumstances, procurement has the responsibility of informing all offerors that inquiries relating to the interpretation and technical details of the RFP must be referred to the procurement official and not to the end-user.

Additional Solicitation Provisions

Socio-economic Considerations and Conditions

Increasingly, many purchasing agencies face the challenge of incorporating new solicitation rules into the already complicated procurement process. These changes are meant to satisfy new laws that use the public procurement process as a means to strengthen small and disadvantaged businesses in the competitive marketplace. The thrust of many of these laws is to restrict competition for public contracts in a variety of ways, ranging from proposal preferences to set-asides, whereby only targeted groups can participate in the RFP solicitation. In many cases, procurement is also required to work with various business development advocacy agencies to develop mechanisms to assist these disadvantaged suppliers.

Other laws establish new contracting goals or provide for outreach programs intended to assist targeted groups in obtaining public contracts through the identification, training, and removal of systemic impediments that work against small or disadvantaged businesses. The exact definition of who is disadvantaged depends upon the jurisdiction. Typically, businesses owned and controlled by minority individuals, who have historically been disadvantaged through discriminatory practices, are considered socially or economically disadvantaged businesses. Socioeconomic procurement laws typically use various methods of directing public contracts to disadvantaged businesses.

Set-Asides/Preferences/Goals

The setting aside of certain contracts for competitive participation by only targeted businesses has been practiced by both the American and Canadian federal governments for many years as well as random state and local entities. One example of such a program can be found under the Small Business Act in the United States, whereby government agencies place contracts for a portion of their requirements with the Small Business Administration that, in turn, subcontracts to only small businesses.

In several jurisdictions, procurement laws mandate that certain factors (location of business, recycled material content, etc.) be considered in the comparison of proposal prices for targeted groups versus other vendors. These may take the form of a straightforward percentage discount factor or the use of graduated percentages, depending on the value of the contract. This form of assistance is referred to as "preferences."

Another form of assistance is the establishment of goals for general contractors to achieve. A given percentage of the contract amount or a specific dollar amount is targeted for the general contractor to award to disadvantaged groups. Jurisdictions have used subcontract requirements to provide opportunities for historically underutilized, small/disadvantaged, women-owned, and other small business concerns. In some procurements, the apparently successful offeror is required to submit a subcontracting plan. The plan describes how the offeror will provide subcontract opportunities to historically underutilized, small/disadvantaged, women-owned and other small business concerns. If awarded through the procedures of FAR Part 15, this plan is subject to negotiation if the procurement official concludes that the plan, as submitted, is not adequate.

The emergence of socio-economic laws and equal opportunity programs has added tremendously to the complexity of the public procurement process. Those who are not affected now may be affected sometime in the future. One proactive response for public procurement jurisdictions is to shift to other areas of support, such as training sessions, in order to foster opportunities for disadvantaged businesses without compromising the integrity of the public procurement process. A focus can be placed on the identification of small, minority, or disadvantaged business for inclusion on source lists. One recent example of this can be found in the Canadian Federal Government's effort to identify and list businesses owned by members of the First Nations in a central registry.

Once potential sources have been found, emphasis can turn to ensuring they are aware of the jurisdiction's solicitation practices. Where proposals are advertised, extra effort can be taken to also advertise in publications that target minority readerships. The increasing use of electronic bulletin boards has helped somewhat to "level the playing field" by removing some of the barriers to access to solicitation notices, while it also must be acknowledged that a "digital divide" exists for small and disadvantaged businesses.

Consideration can also be given to the use of presentations by the agency's procurement representative at events, such as reverse trade shows, to identify the opportunities available to these businesses and to elicit a discussion about possible barriers to competition. Rather than focusing on the narrowing of the public market to accommodate these disadvantaged groups, procurement can help these suppliers become more competitive and, in turn, widen their marketplace.

Extent of Competition

One of the goals of the procurement process is to obtain competition from sources that provide supplies and services; however, other mitigating factors may result in limiting competition. The extent to which procurement officials foster competition depends on factors such as:

- requirements in law or regulation to use specific suppliers;
- requirements for "maximum practicable" and "full and open" competition;
- the validity and suitability of an unsolicited proposal;
- requirements to set aside procurements for small business; and
- availability of suppliers under the Federal 8(a) small business program.

Sources

Once purchasing clearly understands the requirements of the end-user, the focus turns to the sources for supplying the required goods or services. It is at this stage where procurement usually decides if there are sufficient sources available to "compete" the requirement. In choosing to solicit for the requirement, the buyer will want to ensure that enough vendors are asked to submit proposals to allow a comparison or competition among the responsive proposals. Many purchasing departments will assemble a list or use a preexisting list of qualified vendors (source list) who will be asked to prepare proposals for the required good or service in addition to advertising the requirement (NIGP, 2001, pp. 132-137).

Creating a Qualified Source/Bidders List

The Qualified Source List is a classification of suppliers of pre-qualified goods and services who are possible sources from whom proposals may be solicited. In assembling the register, the procurement official needs to consider a number of additional factors to those discussed above, such as the experience of the firms qualified to provide the requirement, the quantity required; the likelihood of availability. and how the good or service is traditionally distributed.

Many entities maintain source lists of qualified vendors, classified according to the type of goods or services they provide. "These lists need not include every firm in the relevant industry, but there should not be any artificial or unreasonable limitation, such as size or location of firm, used in determining what vendors may be suitable" (NASPO, 1997, p. 17). These are also referred to as Pre-qualified Vendor or Pre-qualified Products lists.

Where a list does not exist, the procurement official needs to create a list of vendors from which a proposal can be solicited. The list needs to be sufficiently broad and as inclusive as possible, because the more competition, the greater the assurance that the best possible product(s) and prices will be obtained. However, for a simple commodity or service, the procurement official may choose to limit the number of firms solicited.

Generally, the procurement official uses various factors to pre-qualify vendors for inclusion on the list. In other cases, the procurement official uses several techniques after the proposals are submitted to post-qualify the vendors as capable of satisfying the requirement. Regardless of whether the procurement official uses the pre-qualification or post-qualification method, the following points when determining who might be a responsive offeror or who should be included on the vendors list and, therefore, receive the RFP documents will need to be considered.

- Size of firm;
- Past experience with the firm;
- Financial status of the firm;
- Management staff and their capabilities;
- Labor relations;
- Internal procedures of the firm;
- Capacity of the firm, amount of work in progress, amount of back-orders awaiting production;
- Bonding capacity;
- Reference checks of previous clients;
- Service-after-sale experience with the firm;
- Facilities and reserve facilities of the firm;
- Location of the firm; and
- Professional credentials of the people to be assigned to the project.

Published Sources

Given the uniqueness of many requirements, it is not always easy to know where to look for sources of supply for new or novel requirements. In the market, there are a variety of published source references that the procurement official can use to find suitable vendors. Table 5 provides a list of relatively common source references.

Table 5

List of Relatively Common Source References

General Industrial Registers or Directories
- Thomas's Register of American Manufacturers
- Conover-Mast Purchasing Directory
- MacRae's Blue Book
- Sweet's Catalogue
- Metropolitan and regional directories provided by Chambers of Commerce and industrial development agencies

Industry Sources
- Industry associations
- Trade associations
- Trade papers and journals
- Professional associations
- National and regional association publications
- Specialized industry buyer's guides

Classified Telephone Directories
Professional Source Services
- Microfilm libraries
- Computer-based data retrieval services
- Inquiry services

Manufacturers' Catalogues and Sales Literature
Random Sources
- Interviews with salespeople (expect some bias)
- Discussions with other buyers
- Trade and product shows
- Interviews with personnel from other functions (such as the client)

Foreign Sources
- U.S. Department of Commerce, DFAIT/Industry Canada
- Commercial attaches of foreign missions
- Chambers of Commerce in foreign cities
- Trade Directories of the World, Croner Publications, Inc.
- Made in Europe (lists sources of foreign-made goods)

Other Sources
- Internet searches
- Computer-based information retrieval systems

Use of Source Lists

As indicated above, many jurisdictions maintain pre-existing lists of vendors, categorized by the type of goods or services they provide. In order to be listed on these "Source Lists," vendors usually register with the procurement jurisdiction responsible for the maintenance of the lists. Typically, vendors identify the type of good or service they wish to supply and are then listed by that grouping or commodity code. NIGP developed the Commodity/Service Code system for use in categorizing vendors onto source lists and for coding purchases on procurement cards. The NIGP Code system has found wide acceptance throughout the United States. The use of the NIGP system affords an agency compatibility with many other jurisdictions and suppliers. One of the most commonly used groupings in Canada is based on the Goods and Service Index Numbering system, developed initially for categorizing goods in the U.S. military. No matter what system the jurisdiction uses, the potential supplier should be given a list of the codes at the time it registers as a potential offeror.

In order to be registered on the source lists, vendors are often required to provide additional information, such as ownership, financial stability, number of employees, licensing arrangements, geographic location, etc. In cases where a set-aside or preferential program exists, the vendors may also be asked to abide by stricter requirements or provide some form of certification in order to be listed on the appropriate source list.

Some jurisdictions require vendors to pay for their registration or to pay a one-time fee or a fee every time they receive solicitation documents. However, in many of these agencies, revenue generated from the listing and sale of documents may not equate to the actual cost of maintaining the list or the administrative burden of the registration process itself.

Much like Vendors Lists, the Source Lists help procurement officials identify the appropriate commodity for a specific requirement. Purchasing may send out copies of the solicitation advertisement or notices describing the upcoming requirement to all of the vendors listed on the source list. Interested vendors are then invited to either submit a proposal or, in the case of the notice, ask for copies of the solicitation documents.

Restrictions on the Use of Source Lists

Certain restrictions may be imposed on the use of a Source List. A number of restrictions relate to the requirement itself. The dollar value of the requirement may be too small to cover the additional time and costs associated with preparing and mailing solicitations in a competitive environment. The requirement may be for a proprietary good or service that only one vendor can provide, or the requirement may be urgent and there is not enough time to warrant the time required of a competitive requirement. In such cases, procurement officials may want to consider single sourcing the item to only one vendor.

In other cases, restrictions may be a result of the size of the actual list or the ability to create new lists when established source lists are maintained by the jurisdiction. The objective of the list is to obtain sufficient numbers of responsive proposals to assure that the best possible product(s) and prices have been obtained; however, for many kinds of goods or services there are literally thousands of sources available. As a consequence, procurement might want to consider restricting the firms listed to a reasonable number that can be evaluated in a short period of time. In many jurisdictions, it is standard practice to require a sufficient number of vendors on the list to ensure that at least three responsive vendors can be identified. To be fair, all potential suppliers need to know that they might not receive a solicitation for every procurement.

...the Source Lists help procurement officials identify the appropriate commodity for a specific requirement.

In order to ensure fairness to all vendors, procurement should also consider rotating the vendors registered on the source list to allow each vendor the opportunity to submit proposals. In other cases, procurement officials have used some factor, such as geographic location or size of firm, to reduce the number of vendors on the lists in order to minimize the amount of time required for proposal evaluations and contractor selection. Unfortunately, such practices usually leave jurisdictions vulnerable to claims of preferential treatment and do not always result in the best price or product.

An additional issue associated with the use of source or vendors lists is the need to update and maintain the lists. The creation of new lists each time a requisition is received adds to the overall time necessary to obtain the good or service required by the client, particularly where pre-qualification of the vendors occurs at the time of assembling the Vendors List; however, updating and maintaining pre-existing lists of qualified vendors is equally time-consuming.

Clearly defining the categories of commodities and services within the commodity code alleviates some maintenance problems, but the addition of new categories [or new requirements for qualifying on the lists] presents challenges, such as notifying those already registered. Additionally, there are some areas of procurement, such as computer services and management consulting, under which literally hundreds of vendors have been known to register (NASPO, 1997, p. 53).

Many jurisdictions have programs that remove vendors from the list if they have not responded to a specific number of requests or over a stated period of time.

One final complication in the use of Source and Vendor lists relates to the issue of non-performance. In general, the lists are predicated on the belief that all of the vendors on the list are capable of satisfying the requirement. Occasionally, the vendor fails to provide the good or service in the manner promised in the proposal. The procurement official then needs to look at what it will and can do to ensure that the incident does not happen again. Often, consideration is given to "de-listing" the vendor. Unfortunately, this practice sounds easier that it often is in reality. Very few procurement officials have the necessary resources required to review and judge vendor performance. Further, few have succeeded in developing fair and just policies with regard to how long a vendor can be removed from the list, the mechanisms to review the decision, and the process by which a vendor can appeal the decision.

Alternatives to Source Lists

Increasingly, governmental jurisdictions are using public advertising as a way of identifying their requirements, inviting interested parties to respond by submitting a proposal. Originally, newspapers and special publications, such as the *Commerce Business Daily*, were used as supplementary or alternative vehicles to advertise the requirements. Over time, this way of finding the preferred vendor became the only method for many jurisdictions to source certain types of requirements. Laws and regulations were created to determine the appropriate format, notice period, and process for these advertisements. In more recent years, both the American and Canadian Federal and Provincial governments have moved to using electronic bulletin boards and Internet Web pages to identify the requirements and to solicit responses to proposals.

In both cases, rules have been established to set the required amount of time for posting on these boards or pages and the required processes to be followed by all parties. One of the advantages of using these alternatives to the Vendor List is the removal of the need to maintain current source lists for all types of goods and services. One of the disadvantages relates to the issue of qualification of the vendors with these electronic vendor systems, as the vendor qualification forms part of the proposal evaluation process. The cost of mailing for the jurisdiction or the cost of downloading the documents for the potential offeror has made jurisdictions using electronic solicitation methods reconsider the quantity of proposal documents that need to be sent to the vendors for solicitation purposes. In some cases, attempts have been made to limit the requirement description to one page, with just enough information to allow a vendor to determine whether it wants to request the full RFP document. In other cases, jurisdictions have made available, in advance and often for a fee, descriptions of the standard clauses. When solicitation documents are sent to the vendors, number or code can then reference clauses, thus limiting the space required for standard "tombstone" information.

Circumstances Permitting Other than Full and Open Competition (FAOC)

There are circumstances where the procurement cannot be conducted in full and open competition. Each jurisdiction may have a host of such circumstances. Table 6 provides an example.

Table 6

Circumstances Permitting Other than
Full and Open Competition

1. Only one responsible source and no other supplies or services will satisfy agency requirements, such as when:
   - No other source is available.
   - The contract is a "follow-on" for the continued development or pro- duction of a major system or highly specialized equipment or for the provision of highly specialized services, if switching contractors would result in unacceptable delays or a substantially higher cost.
   - The contract is in response to an unsolicited research proposal.

2. Unusual and compelling urgency, for example, delay in award would result in serious financial or other injury.

3. Industrial mobilization; or engineering, developmental, or research capability, when there is a need for:
   - Maintaining a facility, producer, manufacturer, or supplier in case of a national emergency or wartime industrial mobilization, or
   - An essential engineering or research and development capability to be provided by educational or nonprofit institutions or federally funded research and development centers.

4. International agreements, when the terms of an international agreement or treaty preclude open and full competition.

5. Authorized or required by statute, as is the case when procuring from:
   - UNICOR (Federal Prison Industries).
   - Qualified Nonprofit Agencies for the Blind or other Severely Handicapped.
   - GPO or GPO contracts for printing and binding.
   - Other required sources.

6. National Security, when it would be compromised by broad disclosure of needs.

7. Public Interest, when the agency head determines that FAOC would be contrary to it.

Source: Federal Acquisition Institute (1999). *The federal acquisition process* (p. 6.33). Washington, DC: Federal Acquisition Institute.

Evaluation

*A*n important step in the RFP process is planning for evaluation. While the evaluation process will be explored at length in Chapter 5, this sec- tion summarizes the basic elements required for a comprehensive evaluation process. As mentioned in Chapter 1, by using the RFP method, jurisdictions intend to select the best-value contractor. Best value is a result of the best price and the best quality (determined by non-price factors) combined. Thus, vendors tend to think that there may be a lack of award objectivity in the evaluation process. This perception results in protests or complaints.

Guiding Principles

The guiding principles in developing evaluation criteria and teams include the following:

- *Integrity*. Evaluation of the responses/vendor selection processes must be open, fair and honest.
- *Client Service*. Client needs should be fully understood; and the evaluation criteria should contribute to the ultimate achievement of performance, time, and cost factors as set by the client.
- *Socioeconomic Objectives*. Where they apply, the evaluations must take into consideration socio-economic policies specific to the particular jurisdiction.
- *Competition*. The process must ensure fair competition and be appropriate for each requirement.
- *Equal Treatment*. The process must ensure that all vendors are subject to the same conditions and considerations.
- *Accountability*. Procurement officials are responsible and accountable for the integrity of the process (NIGP, 2001).

Establishing Evaluation Criteria

The development of evaluation criteria should take into consideration many factors, including the nature of the specific requirement, the ability of the end-user to define the requirement in a clear and concise manner, relevant evaluation criteria, and the jurisdictional culture or environment.

While the end-user ultimately is responsible for the evaluation criteria and the vendor selection, the procurement official must ensure that the integrity of the process is maintained. Typically, the end-user develops the criteria with some assistance and guidance from procurement officials; however, in some cases, procurement officials may be requested by the client to play a more proactive role and actually develop the evaluation criteria. This is an excellent approach. The procurement officials outline the criteria, with the end-user providing the relative importance or weight of each item and their relative values. The end-user and the procurement officials must recognize that every case is likely to be different, and the evaluation procedure must be tailored to the particular requirement.

Offeror Selection Methods

In considering which vendor selection method to use, a procurement official must again consider the actual requirement and, with the client, determine which method will achieve the best value. Generally, best value is determined by the client's view of the relative importance of the technical component of the proposal in comparison to the proposal price that the client is prepared to pay. Different from the request for bids procurement method, which focuses on the lowest responsible bidder, the RFP procurement method does not focus primarily on cost. The selection method is much more complicated. Due to this complicated process, how to select offerors will be discussed at length in a forthcoming chapter.

Dealing with Mistakes in Offers

Unfortunately, offerors often err in estimating costs and calculating proposed prices. Different from the bidding process (McVay, 1996), in the RFP process, mistakes in proposals that surface before award tend to have little impact because:

- discussions are permitted (and especially desirable if a serious mistake is suspected in the proposal otherwise in line for award), and
- the offeror can correct mistakes or withdraw the proposal at any time before award.

However, mistakes in proposals alleged after award are a great concern. On the one hand, the government must avoid giving the offeror "two bites at the apple," to the detriment of the rights of other offerors and the integrity of the Federal acquisition process. On the other hand, ignoring genuine mistakes might:

- force the awardee to work at a significant risk of losing money (with a correspondingly high risk of default or unacceptable performance), while
- denying award to offerors who prepared (often at great expense) legitimate offers—which, in the long run, would tend to discourage them from pursuing government contracts.

For these reasons, the FAR establishes procedures for (1) reviewing proposals for mistakes and (2) resolving mistakes alleged by contractors.

Identifying Potential Mistakes Prior to Award

There are two types of mistakes that procurement officials (POs) should look for when they review proposals.

- Apparent clerical mistakes, such as a missing decimal point; and

- Potential non-clerical mistakes, such as a price that is so much lower than other offers or the purchasing agency's estimate, based on market research, as to indicate the possibility of error.

If mistakes are discovered, POs need to ask the offeror to verify the proposal (FAI, 1999).

Resolving Mistakes

Mistakes can be resolved differently depending on the type of solicitation methods, such as RFBs or RFPs. Based either on a call from the procurement official to verify a proposal or upon the offeror's own independent review of the proposal, an offeror may allege a mistake. If an offeror alleges a mistake prior to award in a negotiated acquisition, the mistake would become a matter for discussion and presumably would be rectified in the offeror's final offer.

Regardless of the method of procurement, if a contractor alleges a mistake in its offer after award, the contractor must request either that the contract be rescinded (i.e., terminated) or reformed (i.e., modified). The procurement official, in turn, may reject the request and hold the contractor to the awarded contract. The procurement official may do otherwise only when:

- the mistake is alleged in writing,

- evidence of the mistake is clear and convincing, and

- the mistake was so apparent as to have charged the procurement official with notice of the probability of a mistake.

Other than for pre-award mistakes in negotiated acquisitions, the procurement official's options are constrained by such considerations as whether the offeror's intended price can be calculated from available evidence, or the intended price would have been lower than the next lowest offer in line for award. Moreover, the procurement official may need to obtain approval for any proposed resolution of the mistake from a higher level (e.g., from the jurisdiction's head or designee, if the decision is to permit withdrawal of a proposal after the submission deadline).

Conclusion

The steps that have to be undertaken in the RFP process are not very different from the steps that are taken in any other competitive solicitation.

The initial steps are developing a procurement action or acquisition plan, preparing a purchase request, obtaining funding, and conducting market research. Developing the solicitation document, issuing and advertising the solicitation, and soliciting qualified potential offerors follows the initial steps. A Pre-Submittal Conference may be held and addenda issued.

The next step is the receipt of the proposals, their evaluation, selection of a successful offeror, award of a contract, and handling any protests. When care is taken by the jurisdiction in the execution of these steps, the solicitation will afford the jurisdiction many benefits.

References

American Bar Association (2000). *The 2000 model procurement code for state and local governments.* Chicago: American Bar Association.

Federal Acquisition Institute (1999). *The federal acquisition process.* Washington, DC: Federal Acquisition Institute.

Federal Acquisition Regulation Web site, http://www.arnet.gov/far/loadmainre.html.

General Accounting Office Web site, http://www.gpoaccess.gov/gaoreports/index.html.

Harink, J. H. A. (1999). *Excelling with e-procurement.* Alphen aan den Rijin, The Netherlands: Samson.

Harink, J. H. A., Telgen, J., & Streefkerk, P. M. (1999). *Purchasing management in municipalities . . . towards professionalism.* Alphen aan den Rijin, The Netherlands: Samson.

McVay, B. L. (1996). *Getting started in federal contracting* (pp. 28-31). Woodbridge, VA: Panoptic Enterprises.

Nash, R. C., Jr., Cibinic, J., Jr., & O'Brien, K. R. (1999). *Competitive negotiation: The source of selection process* (2nd ed.). Washington, DC: The George Washington University, Government Contract Program.

National Association of State Purchasing Officials (NASPO) (1997). *State and local government purchasing principles and practices.* Lexington, KY: NASPO.

National Institute of Governmental Purchasing, Inc. (NIGP) (2000). *Intermediate public procurement.* Herndon, VA: NIGP.

National Institute of Governmental Purchasing, Inc. (NIGP) (2001). *General public procurement.* Herndon, VA: NIGP.

National Institute of Governmental Purchasing, Inc. (NIGP) (2004). *Introduction to public procurement.* Herndon, VA: NIGP.

Thai, K.V. (2004). *Introduction to public procurement.* Herndon, VA: National Institute of Governmental Purchasing, Inc.

CHAPTER 3

Developing the RFP Document

Introduction

*T*he quality of responses received from the Request for Proposal (RFP) is directly related to the quality and completeness of the RFP document, particularly the Scope/Statement of Work (SOW). The RFP must provide potential offerors with a clear understanding of the jurisdiction's needs; it also must provide instructions on how to submit the proposal. Potential offerors are more likely to respond to an RFP that is well written and provides for fair and open competition. An RFP document varies with the type and complexity of goods and services to be procured and the urgency of procurement. This chapter will first describe the typical structure of an RFP document that agencies may use as a starting point. Current technology has presented them with a wealth of RFP samples posted by all levels of government through various Web sites as well as through the Procurement Information Exchange Section on the National Institute of Governmental Procurement, Inc.'s (NIGP) Web site.

Preparing an RFP Document

*A*comprehensive RFP document should include at least the basic elements and suggestions that are explained briefly in this section (adapted from NIGP, 2000).

Cover Page. This page identifies the RFP-issuing jurisdiction, the RFP number assigned by the jurisdiction and the commodity of goods or services for which proposals are being requested.

Table of Contents. This section lists all major sections and attachments included in the RFP and identifies the first page number of each section.

Purpose. This section should state that it is accepting proposals from qualified individuals, firms, partnerships, and corporations having specific experience in the area(s) identified in the RFP.

Objective. This section clearly states the objective to be met through the award of the RFP, e.g., "The objective is to enter into a five-year contract with the selected offeror to furnish and maintain electronic document imaging solutions for various departments of the government."

Existing Environment. The potential offerors should be provided with information as it relates to what conditions are currently in place to meet the needs of the goods or services requested.

Inquiries. This section states that questions related to the RFP must be directed to the designated individual responsible for the procurement (including telephone number, e-mail and mailing addresses). It should indicate that questions shall be submitted in writing and that the jurisdiction will document additional questions raised at any Pre-Proposal Conference. It should note that the jurisdiction will prepare and distribute an RFP amendment/addendum to all potential suppliers who received a copy of the RFP. It explains that the amendment should include a listing of each of the questions received and the jurisdiction's response. It also emphasizes that offerors must clearly understand that the only individual authorized to represent the jurisdiction is the one stated in the RFP.

Method of Source Selection. This section cites the statute, ordinance, or administrative approval that provides authority for issuance of the RFP.

Pre-Proposal Conference. All prospective offerors should be notified of the time, date and location of the Pre-Proposal Conference, all prospective offerors should be urged to attend. It should also state that, if required, tours of the jurisdiction's facility will be conducted at that time with all prospective offerors in attendance.

Determination of Responsibility. This section describes the minimum criteria the jurisdiction will use to determine responsibility of prospective offerors. These criteria can include, for example,

- the minimum amount of experience required in previous projects similar in scope;
- financial strength and capacity; and
- minimum qualifications required.

Projected Timetable. A timetable or schedule of events should be carefully and realistically planned that identifies the projected milestones in the procurement process for completion of the solicitation, contract negotiations and project start-up.

Issue Request for Proposal	January 1, 200x
Questions in Writing Cutoff	January 14,200x
Pre-Proposal Conference and Site Visit	January 15, 200x
Amendment/Addendum to RFP	January 18, 200x
Proposals Due	January 28, 200x
Evaluation of Proposals	February 14, 200x
Contract Negotiations	March 1, 200x
Contract Execution	March 15, 200x
Notice to Proceed	April 1, 200x

Services, Goods, Systems or Other Solutions To Be Provided (Purchase Description, Specification, or Scope/Scope/Statement of Work). This section is essential in the preparation of a quality RFP document and should be prepared by persons with expertise in the area associated with the procurement. The objective is to provide prospective offerors with a clear description of what the entity desires to purchase. There are three terms used to indicate description of what is to be purchased: purchase description, specification, and Scope/Statement of Work. Generally, this section should be written primarily in terms of performance requirements that provide prospective offerors a clear understanding of what outcomes (as opposed to inputs or outputs) are required and afford the prospective offerors an opportunity to offer their best technical and economic solutions. There may be times in complex procurements when a jurisdiction may use the services of a consultant to help prepare this section.

The objective is to provide prospective offerors with a clear description of what the entity desires to purchase.

Constraints on the Successful Offeror. This section identifies any conditions that could impact the offeror's performance of the contract resulting from the RFP. Constraints could include, for example, security requirements, safety requirements, and work-site conditions.

Successful Offeror's Personnel Requirements. This section clearly states any successful offeror's personnel requirements, such as minimum experience and qualifications of personnel assigned to the finalized agreement, as well as any specific license requirements.

Responsibilities of the Jurisdiction. This section identifies items that the jurisdiction will provide to the offeror, such as office space, telephone, utilities, and support services. In addition, it identifies the jurisdiction's role in the performance of the agreement, such as assistance provided or tasks to be performed by the jurisdiction.

Contractor's Reporting Requirements. This section defines any required reporting requirements of the successful offeror, such as evidence of small and disadvantaged business participation or copies of sub-agreements and certified payrolls.

Instructions for Proposal Submittal

*I*t is important to state that proposal responses must be sealed when delivered and consist of one original and as many copies as required. This section also instructs offerors to mark the RFP number, proposal closing date and time on the outside of the proposal envelope or container. The number of copies requested should be sufficient to provide a copy to each of the Evaluation Committee members.

Compliance with the Request for Proposal. The offerors should be instructed that proposal submittals must be in strict compliance with the RFP and that failure to comply with all provisions of the RFP may result in disqualification. If prices are requested, be sure that the solicitation indicates whether the price is to be included as an integral part of the proposal or in a separate sealed envelope.

Proposal Deadline. The time and date for receipt of proposals should be clearly stated. This section should make it clear that any proposal received after the time stipulated will not be considered and will be rejected or returned to the offeror. The RFP document provides offerors with the complete mailing address to which proposals are to be submitted. It also instructs offerors that proposals will be opened publicly in a manner to avoid public disclosure of contents—only the names of the offerors will be read aloud. Some jurisdictions may have Public Disclosure Laws that do not allow this procedure.

Ambiguity, Conflict, or Other Errors in RFP. Offerors should be instructed that any ambiguity, conflict, discrepancy, omissions or other error discovered in the RFP must be reported immediately in writing to the jurisdiction and a request made for modifications or clarification. Modifications should be submitted in writing (addendum), and all parties who have received the RFP will receive the revisions. Offerors are responsible for clarifying any ambiguity, conflict, discrepancy, omission or other error in the RFP prior to award, or it shall be deemed forfeited.

Implied Requirements. Offerors should be instructed that any products and services that are not specifically addressed in the RFP, but are necessary to provide functional capabilities proposed by the offeror, must be included in the proposal.

Proposals and Presentation Costs. This section states that the jurisdiction will not be liable in any way for any costs incurred by the offerors in the preparation of their proposals in response to the RFP nor for the presentation of their proposals or participation in any discussions or negotiations.

Rejection of Proposals. This section states that the jurisdiction reserves the right to accept or reject, in part or in whole, any or all proposals submitted. It also states that the jurisdiction shall reject the proposal of any offeror determined to be unreliable in accordance with any statute, regulation, and/or ordinance. Unreasonable failure of an offeror to promptly supply the jurisdiction with information with respect to responsibility may be grounds for a determination of unreliability.

Exceptions to Format. The RFP document describes the requirements and response format in sufficient detail to secure comparable proposals, recognizing that various proponent approaches may vary widely. It also indicates that proposals that differ from the described format may be rejected.

Requests for Clarification. This section stipulates that requests by the jurisdiction for clarification of proposals should be in writing and that such requests should not alter the offeror's pricing information contained in its cost proposal.

Validity of Proposals. This section specifies how long, in days (either calendar or working), submitted proposals must remain valid from the proposal submission date. The jurisdiction should allow reasonable time for evaluation and contract negotiations. The process for RFP evaluation is longer than for Request for Bids (RFB) evaluation.

Proposal Submittal Format. Offerors should be instructed to use a specific proposal format, if such a requirement exists, for fairness in proposal evaluation. For example, offerors must include the following information in their proposal and should use the following format (Table 7) when compiling their responses.

Table 7

Sample Proposal Format Guidelines

Cover Letter
The response should contain a cover letter signed by a person who is authorized to commit the offeror to perform the work included in the proposal and should identify all materials and enclosures being forwarded in response to the RFP.

Table of Contents
The Table of Contents provides a listing of all major topics, their associated section number, and starting page number.

Executive Summary
The Executive Summary of the proposal shall be limited to three single-spaced typewritten pages. The purpose of the Executive Summary is to provide a high-level description of the offeror's ability to meet the requirements of the RFP.

Description of Relevant Experience, Qualifications, and Capacity
The description details qualifications of the offeror's operations and staff regarding requested goods and services.

Technical Proposal
Offeror's business plan to meet the technical requirements of the Request for Proposal must be included in this section.

Proposed Costs
All costs associated with delivering the requested goods and services must be detailed in the format requested in the Request for Proposal.

Attachments
Additional information, which the offeror feels will assist in the evaluation, should be included. Other attachments may include:
  • Proof of Insurance,
  • Proposal Bond, and
  • Equal Opportunity Employer Affidavit and other required information.

Note: Sections should be tabbed and labeled, and pages should be sequentially numbered at the bottom of the page.

Oral Presentations. In most solicitations, there will be a requirement for oral presentations from the top ranked offerors. Normally, the oral presentations will include only the top three to five offerors. This is commonly called the short list. It is a good idea not to specify the exact number in the solicitation document but allow the Evaluation Committee the option of deciding which offerors have a chance at obtaining the contract. The oral presentations are conducted to allow the offerors to bring to the attention of the Committee any aspects of their offer that may contribute to the selection of their response. It is an opportunity for the offerors to sell the merits of their submission, often using slide shows and illustrative presentations.

> *The ability to download information from the Web has provided government wide exposure and enhanced competition...*

Receipt and Confirmation Form. Manual distribution of solicitation packages allowed for a greater level of awareness on behalf of the procuring agency with regard to prospective proposers. The ability to download information from the Web has provided government wide exposure and enhanced competition, but the ability to have an accurate list of interested parties to the solicitation was virtually impossible. As a result of the increased use of the Internet and Web-based technology to post proposal invitations, as well as receive offers electronically, a jurisdiction must include provisions in their solicitation documents for confirmation that offerors have obtained or received a solicitation document and will be submitting a response. This is crucial to the jurisdiction in that if there are changes to any aspect of the solicitation, all offerors should have the same information provided to them. As noted in an earlier section of this chapter, failure to provide all offerors with exactly the same information at the same time may lead to a dispute or challenge of any subsequent award.

Withdrawal Conditions. Most governments make provision for the withdrawal of offers under certain circumstances, such as events occurring within the offerors' jurisdiction that impair their ability to perform the contract, if awarded. However, this ability to withdraw an offer is almost always limited to "prior to closing date and time." Withdrawal of an offer after the closing date and time, particularly if the submission is low compliant, would suggest that the offeror made an error and does not wish to honor the offer. Most jurisdictions do not allow for the withdrawal of responses after the closing date and time. This section of the solicitation document should clearly state the conditions under which offers can be withdrawn.

Examination of Documents. Agencies use this section of the solicitation document to inform the offerors that when they submit a response to the solicitation, they have acknowledged and agree to all of the requirements and information contained within the solicitation document, thereby removing any ability of offerors to make any subsequent claims for additional payment.

Offerors Checklist. To assist offerors in identifying the crucial information and documents they must provide with their offers, the jurisdiction should provide a checklist. Use of the list by the offerors is not mandatory and does not have to be returned with their response. Table 8 is an example of a checklist.

Table 8

Bidder Checklist for Submitting a Bid or Proposal

1. Everyone involved in putting together the response has read and understood the requirements.	☐
2. The response meets all the mandatory requirements.	☐
3. The response addresses everything asked for, particularly those things in the Project Requirements section.	☐
4. The cover letter has been signed and attached.	☐
5. The response clearly identifies the bidder or proponent and the project.	☐
6. The bidder or proponent's name appears on the response envelope.	☐
7. The appropriate number of copies of the response has been submitted.	☐
8. The response is submitted at the closing location and before the closing time.	☐
9. The response is being delivered by hand, courier or mail, but not by fax or e-mail..	☐
10. All required appendixes have been returned, as stipulated in the solicitation document.	☐

Source: Pettijohn, C., & Babich, K.S. (2004). *Sourcing in the Public Sector*. Herndon, VA:NIGP.

Evaluation Teams. Evaluation Teams are primarily established when a jurisdiction issues an RFP, Request for Statements of Qualifications (RFSQ), Request for Letters of Interest (RLI), and Request for Information (RFI). Evaluation

Teams should be established prior to the release of the solicitation document to the market; and all team members should review, understand, and agree to the criteria, methodology, weighting of factors, and understand their respective roles and responsibilities. Team members should be informed that they will be required to participate in all aspects of the evaluation, independently rank responses and sign off on their respective and joint recommendations. Team members should also be cautioned that any and all information is confidential and cannot be disclosed to anyone outside of the Team.

Evaluation Process and Methodology. Solicitation documents should clearly describe the evaluation process, methodology, criteria, weighting of factors, and points allocated to each category or factor. Offerors may use this information in structuring their responses and place emphasis on those criteria or factors having the greatest impact on their proposal evaluation.

General Terms and Conditions. This section provides the details of the General Terms and Conditions, most of which, if not all, will be replicated in the final agreement or Purchase Order. It is, therefore, important to make these terms and conditions known to offerors and indicate that they will be required to execute an agreement containing provisions for these Terms and Conditions.

Some jurisdictions, rather than repeating every term and condition within the formal 2-party agreement, will provide one clause referencing the solicitation document Terms and Conditions, e.g., solicitation document Number (____) dated (_____) with a closing date of (_____) and as per the offerors' offer dated (_____).

As there is no universally accepted standard set of proposal Terms and Conditions that can be consistently applied to all solicitations, most jurisdictions develop a modified version of another jurisdiction's Terms and Conditions to accommodate their own specific and unique requirements. Generally, these terms and conditions may be applied in most of a jurisdiction's solicitation requirements. Terms and Conditions may vary by category of acquisition (products, services, or construction).

Agreement Terms and Conditions. A copy of the jurisdiction's standard agreement terms and conditions should be attached and made a part of the RFP. In some cases, the actual final contract, if available, should be included. In addition, it generally will be necessary to add Terms and Conditions needed for a particular requirement or category of requirements. This section advises offerors to document any exceptions to the language of the standard agreement Terms and Conditions. Identifying exceptions to terms and conditions at time of proposal submittal will aid in evaluation and contract negotiations.

Insurance Requirements of Successful Offeror. It is important to state the insurance requirements with which the successful offeror must comply during the term of the final agreement.

Bonding Requirements of Successful Offeror. This section states clearly any bonds that will be required from the successful offeror, such as performance and payment bonds. The following are some of the commonly referred to "General Terms" and "Conditions" (Pettijohn & Babich, 2004).

General Terms. The "General Terms" section indicates that the offerors acknowledge they have read, understands and agree to be bound and fulfill the requirements and terms and conditions of the Solicitation. In addition, the jurisdiction should describe and clarify its rights and obligations relative to the solicitation.

Agreement Termination. All provisions of options and agreement termination, extension, and fulfillment of obligations should be detailed in this section. Notice of termination time consideration, rights, manner in which termination is conveyed, and actions resulting for failure to comply should be provided in this section.

Termination for Convenience. Occasionally, a jurisdiction may be required to discontinue a contract prior to completion. This may be due to its own needs and not the breach or poor performance of the selected contractor. Provisions should include the policy of severance and any possible payments to the contractor.

Ownership and Intellectual Property. If the jurisdiction wishes to retain ownership of intellectual property or assign it away, these provisions should be detailed in this section. If there are specific restrictions on the use of information that comes into the possession of the offerors during the term of an agreement, these should also be indicated here.

Evaluation Disclosure. Some jurisdictions do not disclose evaluation information, unless a request is filed under the Freedom of Information Act, and clarify their obligations in this section. Generally, it is considered good policy to debrief unsuccessful offerors after a contract is awarded.

Invoicing and Payment. Detail all requirements for payments, invoices, receipt of products or services, late payment charges, interest, method of payment (electronic fund transfers or checks) net terms, etc.

Assignments. Should the jurisdiction permit assignment of a contact resulting from a solicitation, this should be clarified here, including administrative provisions and the terms and conditions upon which an assignment can be made, such as with the prior written approval of the jurisdiction's designated representative. Likewise, if assignment of a contract is prohibited, this should be stated here along with the consequence for violation.

Infringement. Use this section of the solicitation document to state the jurisdiction's requirements and position on infringement on patents, copyrights, trademarks, intellectual property rights, and the consequences for violation, including costs of defending a claim and indemnification from an action of claim by a third party.

Hours of Work. If there are restrictions on the hours during which work will be performed, they should be clearly stated, as the offerors may have to adjust their pricing or completion dates. Include weekends and holidays. Also, some work sites are adjacent to hospitals, nursing homes, schools, etc., and there may be some restrictions imposed by municipal or local by-laws. Offerors should be made aware of these in this section.

Security Clearance. When on a jurisdiction's premises, there may be security restrictions placed on the contractor. Should this be the case, the jurisdiction should make these restrictions known to offerors during the solicitation and response phases of the procurement process.

Special Terms and Conditions. Not all acquisitions fit a standard or common solicitation format. In many instances, procurement may have unique characteristics and require specific or special clauses that are not common to all other types of acquisitions. These provisions must be contemplated when preparing the sourcing document and provided for within the appropriate section of the document. With more focus on the global economy and engaging e-Procurement or eCommerce in the supply chain, special provisions and clauses must be incorporated into the sourcing document to reflect the jurisdiction's needs and expectations in these areas.

Independent Contractor. This section should clearly state that the contractor or supplier is an Independent Contractor and is not an employee, servant, or agent of the jurisdiction. The contract cannot obligate or commit the jurisdiction to any external third party for the payment of any money.

Describing What is To Be Procured

Describing what is to be procured at the RFP phase of the public procurement process is completely different from describing what is to be procured when agencies prepare for procurement authorization and budget appropriations. Thus, it is important to clarify some basic procurement terms used in this section.

Basic Procurement Terms

In public procurement as well as private sector purchasing, there is no clear distinction among the terms "purchase description," "specifications," and "Scope/Statement of Work." Dobler and Burt (1996, p. 162) wrote: "Purchase descriptions fall into two broad categories: detailed specifications and other purchase descriptions" [emphasis added], as shown in Table 9.

Table 9

Methods Classification

Detailed Specifications	Other Purchase Descriptions
Commercial Standards	Performance Specifications
Design Specifications	Function and Fit Specifications
Engineering Drawings	Brand and Trade Names
Material and Method-of-	Samples
Manufacturing Specifications	Market Grades
	Qualified Products
	Combination of Methods

Source: Dobler, D. W., & Burt, D. N. (1996). *Purchasing and supply management: Text and cases* (6th ed., pp. 161-175). New York: McGraw-Hill Companies, Inc.

Describing or specifying requirements is a long process involving a variety of experts, including procurement officials (Thai, 2004). First, after identifying government entities' needs, authoritative managers (assisted by many experts, including procurement officials) identify alternatives to meeting the needs and select the best alternative. Assuming that a good, service, capital asset, or major system is to be procured to satisfy the jurisdiction's needs, managers have to describe it by specifying basic characteristics, called requirements. A comprehensive requirement description needs market research and input from the industry. The type of procurement requirement has a great impact on the funding level that the end-user seeks. A county sheriff's office may decide to "require" a Mercedes or a Ford for patrol needs. The more comprehensively requirements are specified for the procurement authorization and appropriations phases, the easier the preparation of specifications and SOW will be during the RFP process. The requirements process is summarized in Figure 7.

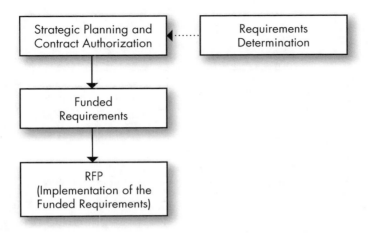

Figure 7 - *Requirements in the Public Procurement Process.*

A few government procurement manuals, including the Federal Acquisition Regulation (FAR), state that procurement officials "prepare requirements" during the RFP process. In fact, one task during the RFP phase is to analyze, and if necessary, modify, the specs or SOW in order to provide a detailed description of these requirements. When procurement officials deal with potential suppliers, the funded requirements must be described as clearly as possible so that potential suppliers understand what the governmental entity desires to procure. This description is called "purchase description," "specifications" or "Scope/Statement of Work." The first step in preparing requirements descriptions is to analyze the approved and funded requirements. Funded requirements or the procurement budget pose three types of constraints that procurement officials have to be aware of, including funding level, procurement object or approved requirements, and time (budget is approved for a certain fiscal year[s]). For RFPs, the requirements description is called specifications. For complicated procurements, requirements may be described in more than one specification. Moreover, in preparing an RFP document, "requirements" consist of two types: requirements for the good or service to be acquired and requirements imposed by general procurement policy and regulations (i.e., fair and open competition and set-aside requirements). Descriptions of these two requirements are called "Scope/Statement of Work," as shown in Figure 8.

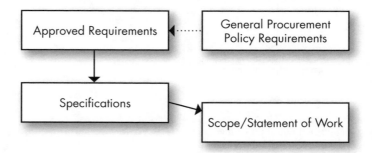

Figure 8 - *Differences Between Requirements, Specifications, and Scope/Statement of Work*

A specification is a "description of the physical or functional characteristics, or of the nature of a supply, service or construction item; the requirements to be satisfied by a product, material, or process, indicating if appropriate, the procedures to determine whether the requirements are satisfied" (NIGP, 1996). Some of the earliest specifications can be found in the Bible for products, such as boats, buildings, and food. Specialization of the Industrial Revolution caused an upswing in specification writing due to the need for consistent and uniform quality. With the coming of the Scientific Revolution, the complexity of modern equipment increased, as did the use of mass-produced components. Thus, in order to ensure compatibility with components manufactured by different companies over time, writing good specifications became very essential. Due to the great diversity of goods and services and rapid changes in goods and services in the market, both back then as well as now, it has always been very difficult to write specifications.

In the private sector, "purchase description is considered as the 'heart of the procurement'" (Dobler & Burt, 1996, p. 160). However, for the public sector, "Scope/Statement of Work" forms the heart of the RFP, because public procurement has become a powerful socio-economic policy tool, not only to procure needed goods and services but also to effect social change. The more clear and precise and the less time procurement needs to spend on responding to prospective offerors' inquiries, the more compliant the proposals will be, the fewer complaints and protests will be, and the easier the contract administration work will be, among other things. Moreover, specifications have a great impact on the price. For example, when writing a specification for office pens, procurement officials may ponder the following requirements:

- Ballpoints, fountain, or felt-tips;
- With or without refills;
- With cap, or retractable point; and
- With an up-market image, just economy type, etc.

In the specification, the choice between a generic ballpoint pen and a gold-tipped fountain pen will have a great impact on the price (Harink, Telgen, & Streefkerk, 1999, p. 15). Moreover, the degree to which specifications are open or restrictive directly affects the extent of competition. Possible impacts of specifications are shown in Table 10.

Table 10

Impact of Specifications on the RFP Process

Effect on:	Poorly Written	Well Written
Number of Offerors	Overly broad or restrictive specifications • Deter potential offerors • Increase costs • Decrease chance of desired results	Complete, clear, concise specifications attract many qualified offerors
Evaluation Process/ Protests	Easily misinterpreted Open to challenge and protest by unsuccessful bidders	Sharp, specific criteria Easier to evaluate Minimizes possibility of protests
Bidder Risk	Unreasonable requirements = higher risk and higher costs	Reasonable requirements Lower assumption of risk by bidder
Type of Contract	Uncertain amount of effort leads to cost reimbursement contract	Well defined effort leads to a firm-fixed-price contract

Legislative and Funding Requirements

Federal legislation concerning employee health and safety and consumer product safety requires increased attention on the part of procurement officials to ensure that products meet government requirements. The legal requirement of the legislation regarding noise level in the workplace is one example that the Occupational Safety and Health Administration (OSHA) has the power to investigate. Furthermore, funding sources often dictate restrictions or reporting requirements associated with the expenditure of funds, such as Davis Bacon Act compliance certification. If it is determined that requirements were not met because of an omission in a contract, it may be that the responsible procurement official will be held responsible. Therefore, it is important for all procurement officials to become familiar with the specifications/SOWs that have been prepared and published to meet government legal and financial requirements.

Design Specifications

This is the most traditional and restrictive type of specification. It has been used in public contracting for buildings, highways, bridges, and other public works. The use of design specifications is essential when a structure or a product is to be constructed or manufactured to meet the client's specific needs. These specifications are so detailed that they even describe how and with which materials the product will be constructed or fabricated.

Generally, design specifications are not well suited for a rapidly changing technological world. They take a long time to develop, and errors and amendments are costly. Moreover, they are totally inappropriate for use in acquiring many commercial products. Quite often, these specifications simply cannot be written for certain items, because the details required make it impossible to generate competition and obtain best value. Even the use of maximums and minimums under this type of specification can present some problems. In an effort to encourage competition, a design specification may be expressed in terms of tolerances or in minimum standards selected from various acceptable products.

Design specifications often have precise requirements that limit competition. These specifications also prevent consideration of the latest technological improvements and discourage innovation. There are also certain risks involved in using design specifications. For instance, a purchaser who details the exact chemical composition when ordering a certain paint automatically assumes responsibility for the paint's performance. What if the color of the paint changes drastically after application or prematurely peels?

The cost of inspection associated with the use of design specifications can be high. This is another reason to use these specifications only for projects and products where the cost of special inspections to ensure compliance with requirements can be justified.

Material and Method of Manufacture Specifications

This type of specification is used primarily by the Armed Forces and by the Department of Energy. Potential suppliers are told precisely what materials to use and how they are to be processed. The buying jurisdiction assumes full responsibility for the performance of the products acquired under this arrangement. Large buyers of paint would use these specifications to request that manufacturers add or delete certain chemicals when producing paint for them. In the industrial sector, for reasons of health or safety, some firms dealing with chemical or pharmaceutical products also use these specifications to describe their requirements.

As in the case of design specifications, many jurisdictions do not use material and method of manufacture specifications because of the high risks assumed by the purchaser, the relatively high costs associated with developing the specifications and inspecting the materials, and the probability of losing out on the latest advancements in technology and in manufacturing. Adequate competition is possible and good pricing normally can be obtained when using the material-and-method-of-manufacture specifications.

Engineering Drawings

Descriptions by blueprints or drawings are recommended when precise shapes, dimensions, close tolerances, and a high degree of manufacturing perfection are needed. Drawings may be used alone; although normally, they accompany other purchase descriptions. Machined parts, forging, castings, construction, and special mechanical parts and components are the types of requirements that would normally justify the use of drawings.

This is an expensive method of describing requirements, both from the point of view of preparing the information and using it in the manufacturing process. The availability of the information in an electronic format and the capability of manufacturing systems to utilize the data should help reduce some of the costs, while increasing the effectiveness of this method of describing and communicating requirements.

Performance Specifications

Performance specifications, also known as functional specifications, are probably the best method of describing requirements and should always be used when the RFP procurement method is used. Instead of describing an item in terms of its design characteristics, a purchaser using a performance specification describes what the item is expected to do. The purchaser is much less concerned about the material composition of the item and the way it is manufactured or assembled, but much more concerned about its performance when put into use. With this approach to procurement, the manufacturer/producer/supplier is not directed to act in a certain way but, rather, is given an opportunity to use ingenuity and to innovate in order to provide (likely at a relatively lower cost) an item which will adequately perform a specific task. Although a high degree of precision and a lengthy text may be used to describe the required performance, suppliers are not told what material to use in fabricating the item or which manufacturing process to use in assembling it.

Depending upon the type of item being purchased, performance may be described as a quantity of units per minute or per hour, power output at a certain speed, time intervals between failures, a designated resistance to abrasion, a pre-determined conductivity capability, operation within a certain range of temperatures, or other measurable outputs. Performance specifications should identify the required operating parameters and the limitations that may necessarily apply under a variety of conditions. For instance, how should traffic cones perform when vehicles zoom by at 50 mph. on a very windy day? Should they be seen from 300 feet at night? What happens when there is fog? If they must be easily moveable when hit, how far should they bounce? Should the cones stack easily for transportation and storage? These are some of the matters to be addressed in terms of performance specifications.

Performance specifications are also used for more complex and expensive equipment.

Performance specifications are also used for more complex and expensive equipment. Indeed, many jurisdictions replacing obsolete but still serviceable machinery use performance specifications when ordering new equipment. The main reason for the use of such specifications is that the ultimate in technological advancements can be obtained, at a competitive price, without the purchaser assuming the risks normally associated with other types of specifications.

The ability to select capable suppliers is a particularly important factor when using performance specifications, because manufacturers and suppliers assume full responsibility for designing and fabricating the items. Potential problems and delays could arise if the manufacturer does not posses the necessary expertise and cannot apply the most advanced technical and manufacturing knowledge. In other words, the supplier must be capable of offering a quality product and stand behind it after installation.

Performance specifications are recommended for use by government purchasing jurisdictions, primarily for services. These specifications allow for maximum competition; they provide some assurance that the required performance will be obtained; and their use facilitates the specification-writing process. Furthermore, the responsibility for a satisfactory product rests with the suppliers, and the opportunity to obtain products containing the latest technological and manufacturing developments is increased. On the negative side, these specifications are not very practical for construction requirements. They make bid comparison somewhat more difficult and their use necessitates the participation of the right kind of suppliers.

Combination

A single type of specification cannot adequately describe many of the more complex products. A combination of two or more types is, therefore, appropriate in such cases. For many requirements, the design-performance combination may be the best approach, with design requirements kept to a minimum while the performance characteristics are very detailed. Combination design-performance specifications are the most common type of specification used in RFP solicitations.

An example of a large combination of specifications relates to the manufacturing of space vehicles. Design specifications would apply to the vehicle configuration; performance specifications would be used to describe numerous overall characteristics; commercial standards or brand names would be appropriate for selected categories of electrical or mechanical hardware; while another design specification would apply to the paint and a sample for its color.

Brand Name "No Substitution" Specifications

Brand name specifications identify, by name, model number or other designations, a specific product manufactured by a specific corporation. One reason for manufacturers to brand a product is to sell that product at a relatively stable price, which is normally higher than that of non-branded products of equal quality. End-users usually have a greater comfort level with a brand name product. It should be pointed out, however, that there is normally a price to pay for this comfort. One example is a battery. Even though they know that the manufacturer of a very popular brand of batteries sells the same item as a generic product at a lower cost, some users will still insist on obtaining the brand name product. The use of brand name specifications in purchasing goods simplifies the responsibilities of a procurement official. Inspection is also easier to perform, since the brand is the quality ordered and expected of the product.

There is little doubt that the use of brand name specifications will reduce competition, because submittals will be restricted to a specific product available only from the distributors of that product. Some will argue that competition is still possible in such circumstances, since there may be multiple distributors of the product; but many will refute this argument on the basis that the perception of restrictive competition is not acceptable in government purchasing. The consequences of a decision to proceed with a purchase, knowing that there may be inequality of opportunity among potential suppliers, less objectivity in the process of awarding a contract and that a higher price was paid, may be unacceptable in a government environment. This may explain why some jurisdictions discourage the use of brand name specifications. In fact, some jurisdictions do not allow the use of brand name products, unless the designated procurement official has made a written determination that only the identified brand name item or items will satisfy the jurisdiction's needs.

In spite of the disadvantages associated with brand name specifications, they have a legitimate, albeit limited, place in public purchasing. For instance, the use of brand name specifications may be allowed, on an exception basis, when the resources and the time required to develop another type of specification are not available or cannot be justified, particularly for low-dollar-value acquisitions. They are also commonly used when buying replacement parts for equipment and for standardization programs such as fleet standardization. Some purchasers are concerned about after-market or generic parts being equal in quality to those provided by the original equipment manufacturer. In the final analysis, the use of such specifications should be permitted only when one specific product will satisfy a particular need and when the decision to proceed can be justified and will withstand scrutiny. Requests from users for brand name products always pose a challenge to a purchaser. Users associate more easily with a brand name and may not immediately agree with the decision of a purchaser to obtain another product that may be even better and acquired at a lower price.

Brand Name or "Approved" Equal Specifications

These specifications go beyond the traditional brand name specifications by demonstrating and emphasizing the idea that any brands or models substantially equivalent to the branded product(s) referred to in the solicitation will be considered for contract award. The procurement official in conjunction with the end-user reserves the right of determining equivalency. Brand name or equal specifications must indicate that the brands designated in the bid documents are for reference purposes only and must not be interpreted as a statement of preference.

Whenever possible, three or more brand references should be used to identify products that contain the characteristics of the item being purchased. In addition, the specifications should list any particular design or functional characteristics that are needed and that are not clearly communicated to potential suppliers by reference to the branded products.

To improve communication in identifying the desired quality level and to encourage competition, procurement officials should attempt to use brand designations that are known throughout the industry. Indeed, all the potential bidders should be provided with sufficient information to determine which of their products are comparable to the designated (referenced) brand names and bid accordingly. It should be noted that suppliers are well aware of the existence of brand name products offered by competitors, and all suppliers know exactly where their respective products stand with regard to public choice and purchasing habits. A solicitation that does not identify the product of a particular manufacturer, even as a reference, may cause that manufacturer to complain, particularly if the omission is observed in several solicitations.

Brand name or approved equal specifications should always be accompanied by wording such as "approved equal" or "similar in design, construction, and performance" to indicate to potential suppliers that any item equal in quality to the identified brand names will be acceptable for competition. The intent can be reinforced in the solicitation documents by inserting a statement such as:

> Any manufacturers' names, trade names, brand names or catalogue numbers used in the specifications are for the purpose of describing and establishing general performance and quality levels. Such references are not intended to be restrictive. Bids are invited on these and comparable brands or products provided the quality of the proposed products meet or exceed the quality of the specifications listed for any item. (NIGP, 2000, p. 107)

Samples

The comparison and testing of samples can effectively substitute for a detailed specification in some instances. Generally, they are used when other methods of specifying a requirement are impractical. For example, it would be quite appropriate to provide samples with the solicitation when specifying that a precise shade of blue is to be used as the color of the needed product. The alternative would be to attempt to describe, in words, the required color.

When specifications call for samples to be provided, the offerors are invited to submit their prices and a sample of their products against a general descriptive specification. The price lists and the samples are segregated, and the samples are then subjected to various comparisons ranging from visual inspection and evaluation to chemical and physical laboratory tests to in-use applications. Data and relative performance results are documented, and determinations are made on a price/performance, cost-effective basis—the best value.

An alternate approach used by some jurisdictions is to obtain the samples after the actual proposal opening. The solicitation documents will then call for samples to be delivered when requested by the procurement official. The procurement official conducts an evaluation of the bids to determine responsibility and other issues of responsiveness of the proposers. The procurement official solicits samples only from those offerors who passed the first cut and appear to offer prices that may result in an award. This significantly reduces the number of samples that a procurement official will have to deal with. The award is then made to the lowest responsive and responsible offeror, which most commonly is the highest ranked proposal whose samples passed the inspection and testing processes.

Another appropriate use of samples is to use them in the conduct of tests after contract award but before production. This method, occasionally referred to as a pilot model or a pilot sample or simply a prototype, may help solve potential problems before all of the units are manufactured and delivered. Unless they are destroyed during testing, all samples obtained and used in evaluations and contract award should be retained for further verification when deliveries are made or for other reasons.

Questionnaires completed by potential suppliers can supplement samples and, in some instances, can substitute for them. These questionnaires, occasionally made a part of the solicitation, call for technical data on the products offered. Valid determinations regarding product acceptability and performance can be made from pertinent technical data as well as from the comparison, examination, and testing of samples. Samples are often utilized when acquiring uniforms, badges, decals, footwear, bulletproof vests, and other items of this nature.

Qualified Products List (QPL)

When acquiring certain products or services, it may be more appropriate to determine in advance of the solicitation whether these products or services meet specifications. Under this arrangement, potential suppliers are pre-qualified through a detailed review and test of the entire process by which compliance with the specifications is ensured. After approval, the products or services of the qualified suppliers are placed on a Qualified Products List (QPL). When applied to goods, Qualified Products Lists are occasionally referred to as Approved Brands List (ABL) or Approved Products Lists (APL). When a solicitation is issued for the products in question, the solicitation is limited to those firms whose products are on the list. Approved products are identified in the QPL by brand name, model number, catalogue number, or other designations that precisely identify a particular product. Vehicles, office furniture, computers, and temporary help services are examples of goods and services for which QPLs are established.

As indicated above, the purpose of this type of specification is to determine in advance which products are acceptable. The evaluation of the bids is simplified, since the price and the qualifications of the bidders become the determining factors in the decision to award a contract. The reduction in the amount of testing required is also a key factor to consider. Once a product is accepted for the list, it does not need to be tested until either the specification or the product changes. Another advantage of the QPL is the elimination of problems resulting from low bidders offering a product whose conformance to specifications is unknown and difficult to ascertain. The QPL process must be fair and equally important; it must be perceived and seen as being fair. Rules must be clear and published prior to soliciting suppliers to submit products for testing. For instance, it is essential to know what will happen when a product does not meet the requirements, when new products are submitted for testing, when existing products are modified, etc. It could be argued that QPLs are living and breathing documents and that rules cannot be changed at will once the process has been initiated. The process should be ongoing and allow for new suppliers and products to be added to the list.

...advantage of the QPL is the elimination of problems resulting from low bidders...

There are some inherent weaknesses in the QPL type of specification. The most obvious is the fact that competition is limited to the products on the list. This problem is not as serious when a new list is prepared; but, over a period of time, those products tend to gravitate to marginal levels of quality and the QPL is not as reliable a tool. Another weakness is that by dealing with products already on the market, QPLs do not encourage nor take advantage of innovation, except perhaps when performance standards are used as the principal criterion for qualification. It is, however, possible to overcome these potential problems to some degree by using the following approach. In designing the qualification procedures, include, where feasible, some qualitative ratings or test scores. Then, evaluate offers by equating these numerical ratings with the quoted prices to arrive at an optimum value. For example, if a truck tire must pass a use test of 25,000 miles to be qualified and six brands of tires passed the test range with averages of 25,000, 26,000, 29,000, 30,000 32,000 and 36,000 miles, it is then possible to determine the lowest average cost per mile by using these figures and the price quoted for each tire.

Samples or documented files should be retained for each item that qualifies. These become contract standards so that contract quality can be enforced if a supplier delivers goods of questionable quality. The need for enforceability results not only from concern over receiving substandard goods but also from another problem associated with QPL specifications. Manufacturers sometimes modify a product without changing its model number or other designations. The product may still be listed as acceptable even though it no longer meets the specifications. Although manufacturers or their representatives agree to inform purchasers when they make such changes, the added assurance of having a documented standard of quality is necessary.

The criteria and the methods for establishing and maintaining a QPL vary for different categories of products. For heavy construction equipment, a written specification might be prepared, while tests in the field of similar models from different manufacturers might be carried out to determine which of them meet the performance requirements. For musical instruments, a committee of musicians acting as advisors might test different brands of a certain instrument according to certain criteria. In the case of truck tires, a number of brands might be tested under controlled conditions and determinations made on their performance. For ready-mixed paints, laboratory tests may be used to accept or reject a brand.

When a QPL program is initiated by a jurisdiction, it is customary to invite a representative group of suppliers to submit products for testing. It should be noted that any potential supplier, even if not originally invited to participate, could offer its products for consideration. QPL test results are considered to be public information and, therefore, available for viewing; however, the information must be prepared in a way that protects the identity of the competitors. One method to accomplish this is to use numerical designations.

The fact that a product has been tested and included in a QPL does not mean that purchasers and inspectors of materials are no longer responsible for ensuring compliance of the products with the requirements of the basic specification of the contract. The responsibility for enforcing the requirements remains.

Market Grades

Market grades are used when procuring commodities that are traded regularly on the commodity exchanges. This type of specification is generally limited to natural products, such as lumber, cotton, tobacco, food products, wheat, hides, fuel, etc. Grading determines the quality of the commodities. It is accomplished by comparing a commodity with standards already agreed upon. Trade associations, commodity exchanges and government agencies are very active in the development and revisions of market grades.

It should be pointed out that this method of describing materials is somewhat subjective, because the grading depends to a great extent on decisions made by inspectors. General market supply is another factor affecting quality and grading. The parameters are, therefore, broader than those found in other types of specifications. Purchasers often have to depend on the suppliers to provide the grade that was ordered. Because price is determined by the grade, it is advisable to deal with reputable firms and to obtain the services of an impartial inspector, if the total value of the order warrants such expenditures.

Writing Specifications

Overview

Specification writers should ask questions of themselves.

- Who will receive the document?
- What do I want people to know or do?
- What should be my tone or approach?
- How detailed and exact should my information be?
- What can I assume about my audience's knowledge of the subject?
- What might their questions be?

A specification should:

- allow for competition at the manufacturing level, although some jurisdictions allow for competition at the distribution level.
- identify those measurable physical, functional and quality characteristics common to at least two manufacturers or distributors.
- be specific in the stipulation of all requirements, either directly or by reference to other specifications, publications, or drawings.

These requirements should include:

- basic design,
- physical dimensions,
- weights,
- percentage and type of ingredients,
- grades of materials, if applicable, and
- function.

There should not be conflict or repetition in matters covered by other specifications and publications to which reference is made. Use only reference specifications, publications, or drawings that are of the same quality and detail as the items or services procurement officials require. Specifications should not be too restrictive for the following reasons:

- A restrictive specification usually limits competition and eliminates items that can satisfactorily meet actual needs.
- Specification writers should be careful not to use in-house jargon and acronyms that may be misunderstood by the offeror.
- Specifications must be well written and communicative.
- A well-written specification is precise in its descriptions and directions. It should be clear, simple and free of vague or ambiguous terms subject to variation in interpretation.
- Abbreviations should be restricted to those in common usage and not subject to possible misinterpretation.

A good specification writer should seek the advice, assistance, and cooperation of all intended users concerning their precise requirements regarding the standard of quality, type, size, etc. for any item(s). Always seek the assistance of individuals who have specialized technical competence in the field for which purchasing is developing the specifications. When an essential requirement is left out of a specification, the purchasing process is relegated to one of competitive assumption or chance. A professional specification writer will deal only with facts; if those facts are not available, it is better to state their absence than to be too creative with content.

No Need for Reinventing the Wheel. Considerable amounts of literature and model documents concerning specification writing are available and are published by:

- The United States Government,
- ASTM,

- Canadian General Standards Board,
- The U.S. Standards Institute, and
- Federal, State, Provincial, Regional, County, and Local Governments.

In addition, NIGP's Specification Library will provide members with sample specifications free of charge. Procurement officials can also subscribe to various magazines that may provide help, such as *Consumer Reports*, *Buyers Laboratory*, and *Dataquests Spec Check*. Material from these sources may not be suitable for use in its entirety, but can be used as a basis for specification development. Sections can be adopted or adapted, and others can show what important points should be emphasized.

Characteristics of a Good Specification.

- A good specification should be simple, consistent and exact, but not so specific that a loophole will allow an offeror to evade any of the provisions and thereby take advantage of its competitors or the buyer. (An example of an improper specification—one having loopholes—is included at the end of this chapter.)
- A good specification should be identified, when possible, with one or more brand specifications already on the market. (Custom goods are expensive.)
- A good specification should be capable of being checked. It should describe the method of checking that will govern acceptance or rejection. A specification that cannot be checked is of little value will only result in confusion.
- A good specification should be reasonable in its tolerance. Unnecessary precision is expensive.
- A good specification should be as fair to the offeror as possible.
- A good specification should be capable of being met by several offerors for the sake of competition.
- A good specification should be clear and up-to-date. Misunderstandings can be expensive.
- A good specification should be flexible. Inflexible specifications impede progress. Invite potential suppliers to suggest cost-saving alternatives or substitutes.

Revisions to Specifications

Changes in specifications should be made as required; however, when revisions are made, all requirements of the specification should be analyzed and brought up to date. Remember, when any change is made in a specification, regardless of how minor, it should be re-dated with the date of the revision and clearly marked "REVISED."

Appropriate Use of Words

The inappropriate use of key words in a specification could have disastrous results, if the supplier is not sure what procurement officials require and what they would like to have. In order to be competitive, suppliers almost always have to provide the least expensive product. If procurement officials say "may" rather than "will" in the text of their specification, it could mean one thing to one supplier and another to the end-user. The terms "shall" or "must" are used wherever a specification expresses a requirement, and "should" or "may" are used to express non-mandatory provisions.

Technical Writing Principles and Techniques

Regardless of the types of specifications being developed, some factors will be common in the planning process. The specification writer has a tremendous responsibility to create properly designed specifications. The procedures used in writing a specification vary according to the size of the jurisdiction and the purchasing operation.

Smaller jurisdictions usually have the assigned buyer write the specifications with assistance from the end-user. Larger central purchasing operations normally have specification writers or units that exclusively deal with the development and writing of specifications.

Because there are so many areas in which expertise is needed, no central purchasing program, even the largest and most professional, has staffing that has the technical competence that is necessary to write all specifications. The end-users must provide the required assistance. However, the assigned purchasing representative should always know enough or obtain enough information from another source to be certain that the specification will fulfill all requirements. A good specification should do four things.

- Identify minimum requirements.
- Allow for competition.
- List reproducible test methods used in testing for compliance with specs.
- Provide for an equitable award.

General Form and Content

A specification should have a standard format within the jurisdiction. Government entities often use this proven outline, which is commonly used all over the country.

- Scope and Classification
- Applicable Publication(s)
- Requirements
- Sampling, Inspection and Testing Procedures
- Preparation for Delivery (packaging)
- Notes/Comments

Titles of sections should be capitalized but not underlined. The first word or words of subsections should be underlined but not capitalized. When using word processors or computers, procurement officials can use boldface to emphasize the importance of certain words. Remember that specifications should not cover requirements that belong in the General Conditions, Instructions to Bidders, and Special Conditions or Provisions sections.

Occasionally, it is difficult to determine exactly where the certain information should be placed when using Special Conditions or Provisions in conjunction with Specifications; however, one thing should be quite clear—Specifications should never be integrated with the RFP Instructions and General Terms and Conditions.

Definitions of Terms Used in Specifications

In cases where proper interpretation of a specification may be dependent upon the interpretation of terms, these terms must be clearly defined and included in the specification. The location of the definition depends on its use in the specification; however, there should be a section title to delineate its existence in the spec.

Measurements

Dimensions, gauges, capacities, size designations, volume, or temperatures should be specified in accordance with established precedent and trade practice for the particular commodity or service procurement officials are attempting to purchase. Review the document after completion.

- Make every effort to replace words with numbers. Whenever an agency goes from words to numbers, communication relating to quantity or quality is enhanced.

- Tolerances should be specified, where applicable.
- The terms "minimum" and "maximum" should be used wherever practical.

Figures and Tables

The use of figures, illustrations, tables, graphs, etc., should be maximized. Illustrations describe the item(s) more clearly and accurately than can be done through text. Graphics show relationships more clearly than text. Figures and tables should have titles and sections clearly identified and should be numbered consecutively throughout the specification. Tables should be numbered with Roman numerals and figures with Arabic numbers.

Grades, Classes, Types, Composition, Etc.

The use of grades, classes, and types should be in accordance with established precedent and trade practices for the types of equipment, materials, and supplies that procurement officials are seeking. For the purpose of preparing specifications, type, grade, class, and composition are defined as follows:

- *Type*. This term applies to differences in design, model, shape, etc., of the items.
- *Class*. This term implies differences in mechanical or other characteristics of items that do not constitute a difference in quality or grade.
- *Grade*. This term implies differences in quality of a commodity. When practicable, the first grade of a commodity should be the highest or best grade.
- *Composition*. This term is used to classify commodities that are differentiated strictly by their respective chemical compositions.
- *Other Classifications*. Classifications, such as form, weight, size, power, supply, temperature rating, condition, insulation, etc., suitable for reference for the applicable equipment or commodity item may be used.

Footnotes

Footnote references in the specification text should be used sparingly. Consecutive numerals beginning with the superior number "1" should be used for footnote references. In tables or figures, footnote references should be numbered separately for each table or figure.

Reference to Other Specifications, Standards and Publications

Including by reference the applicable specifications, standards, publications, etc., should be limited to specifications, standards, and commonly known jurisdictions, such as the Federal Government, technical societies, etc., which are widely recognized as authorities on the subject matter and accepted by the industry. Some acceptable examples include:

- American Society for Testing and Materials (ASTM),
- Canadian General Standards Board (CGSB),
- American Society of Mechanical Engineers (ASME),
- National Safety Council (NSC), and
- Underwriters Laboratory (UL).

Sampling, Inspection, and Test Procedures

Specifications should outline the ground rules for sampling, inspection, and testing. This is one of the most important sections of a specification. This often forgotten section will ensure that procurement officials purchase goods that will meet the minimum standards. The terms of the Uniform Commercial Code state that the buyer has that right before payment or acceptance to inspect. The Code further states that the cost of inspection is to be born by the buyer; however, these costs may be recovered from the seller if the goods do not conform to the specifications and are rejected.

Preparation for Delivery

Specifications should always detail how the items are to be packaged, packed, and marked. Unless other than standard commercial packaging and marking for ease of handling is required, it is better and most cost effective to use what is standard in a particular industry. If a unique situation warrants extra cost for special packaging or marking, it must be pointed out in the specification. The following are two examples of typical statements that can be used for standard packaging and marking.

Packaging/Packing. Unless otherwise stated, commercial packages and packing, suitable for the type, size, and kind of commodity, commonly used in the industry for the purpose, so constructed as to insure acceptance and safe delivery, at the lowest rate, to the point of delivery specified in the bid document is acceptable.

Marking. Unless otherwise specified, containers shall be marked with the name of the material, the class and quantity contained therein, the name of the vendor, and the number of the contract and/or purchase order number.

Notes

Unique details, which do not fit into other sections of the specifications, can be placed in this section.

Critical Ingredients of Good Specification Writing

A good specification has to be:

- consistent,
- easy to read and understand,
- easy to revise,
- formatted with good direction,
- common among agencies departments, divisions, etc.,
- categorized, and
- organized with a good numbering system.

Writing Style

Exposition is the systematic, orderly setting forth of ideas in accordance with a preconceived plan and a conscious unifying purpose with explanatory comments. It is the most appropriate and motivating writing style to use when procurement officials are preparing specifications. Primarily, exposition is concerned with the communication of ideas in a form that the reader can understand. It aims to:

- save the reader time;
- eliminate confusion; and
- help the reader gain ideas quickly and easily.

The expository style:

- is not imaginative,
- is not creative,
- sets forth a meaning or purpose,
- expounds an intent,
- is designed to convey information or explain what is difficult—explanatory, and
- presents subject matters in detail.

Active Voice

Active voice is the most simple and direct way to make statements (Table 11). Action is expressed directly, more vigorously, and makes the sentence more concise. Readers prefer the active voice because it is more direct, interesting, and descriptive.

Table 11

Examples of Passive and Active Styles

Passive Style	Active Style
• Price quotes were prepared by the offeror.	• The offeror prepared the price quotes.
• Technical assistance was provided by the offeror's engineering department.	• The offeror's engineering department provided technical assistance.

Choosing the Right Words

Agencies can make their meaning clearer by using shorter words. Shorter, more direct words get to the point, are clear-cut, and distinctive. Table 12 provides a few examples of shorter words that get to the point, and mean the same as the longer alternatives.

Table 12

Choosing the Right Words

Words that Should Not be Used	Preferred Words
consumption	use
circumvented	avoided
nevertheless	but
activate	start
cooperation	help/aid
erroneous	false
initiate	start
compensation	pay
exemplifies	show
expedite	rush
conflomeration	mixture
disseminate	spread
incinerate	burn
prioritize	rank
modification	change
necessitate	require

Use of Shorter Phrases

Long phrases should not be used when they are not necessary. Table 13 provides a few examples of preferred words that get to the point, are clear-cut, and mean the same as the longer phrases.

Table 13

Better Choice of Words or Phrases

Phrase	Preferred Words or Phrases
a great number of times	often
in most cases	usually
experience has shown	experience shows
a small number of	few
it is recommended that	we recommended
with respect to	concerning
make contact with	meet
at a later point in time	later
in consideration of the fact that	because
at your earliest convenience	soon
at regular intervals	regularly
in the normal course of	normally

Identifying the Audience

Effective communication means more than language and explanation. It also means to supply all of the information the reader needs to accomplish the purpose for which the specification is written. The audience is almost always very diversified and varied in:

- general traits and attitudes,
- educational background,
- language level,
- politics,
- authority,
- literacy, and
- specialized technical training.

Pre-Writing Checklist

Procurement officials should have a pre-writing checklist.

- They should consider whether revisions or new specifications are necessary.
- They should determine what information is needed.
- They should determine information sources.
- They should review existing related specs and standards (internal and other sources).
- They should brainstorm the proposed content with your peers.
- They should develop a conceptual specification in your mind.
- They should interview personnel in other affected departments.
- They should check to see if the RFP:
  - is within statutory and policy limits;
  - contains conflicting information; or
  - needs a detailed flow chart.

Summary

Clearly, no one type of specification is the best for all purchases. For example, a proposal for stocking and delivery of hundreds of automotive parts may be done by use of a brand name or approved equal. For the purchase of pencils, samples and trial may work best; for magnetic computer tape, qualified products list; for an X-ray machine, a modified design specification; and for an air compressor, a combination design/performance may be the best. Specifying the products or services from a required performance standpoint normally increases competition. If the product is not commercially available, has limited availability, or procurement officials have specific requirements, identifying requirements in terms of specific design features normally increases competition. (A useful checklist for writing specifications is included at the end of this chapter.)

Scope/Statement of Work

" *T*he most important section of the RFP is the Scope/Statement of Work, as it is the foundation of the development of any resulting contract" (Readey, 1999, p. 6). As shown in Figure 8, the SOW consists of not only specifications but also the procuring entities' general procurement statutes, regulations, and socio-economic policies. It covers the contractor's responsibilities, which may include, but is not limited to:

- work to be completed (specifications);
- listing of items to be furnished;
- schedule of activities;
- completion or delivery date of the item; and
- personnel to be utilized.

The range and elements of a SOW vary greatly with what is being procured. A SOW for a major system, such as a Defense weapon or for information technology, is quite long and complex, and incorporates numerous specifications (U.S. Office of Management and Budget, 1997). In contract, a SOW for an office cleaning service is relatively simple and short. It may or may not incorporate a specification. Table 14 is a listing of items that may be incorporated in a SOW.

Table 14

Items that May Be Included in a SOW

- Background;
- General scope and work/objective;
- Contractor's tasks;
- Functional/performance/design specifications;
- References to related studies, documentation, specifications, and standards;
- Data requirements;
- Support equipment for contract end items; and
- Government and contractor's furnished property, facilities, equipment, and services.

Source: Federal Acquisition Institute (1999). *The federal acquisition process* (p. 6.20). Washington, DC: Federal Acquisition Institute.

The Federal Acquisition Institute (FAI) (1999, p. 6.20) suggests that a good SOW should:

- be a clear, precise, and complete description of the work to be performed;
- make a clear-cut division of responsibility between government and contractors;
- not exceed the procurement entity's actual need;
- not be unduly restrictive; and
- be stated in terms that the market can satisfy.

Conclusion

Contract performance is entirely dependent upon the completeness and quality of the solicitation document, with emphasis on the specification or SOW. The entire document must clearly express what is wanted and the terms and conditions with which the successful offeror must comply, as it will ultimately become a part of the contract documents. The spec/SOW must be accorded the same degree of respect that is afforded the Contract documents.

References

American Bar Association (2000). *The 2000 model procurement code for state and local governments.* Chicago: American Bar Association.

Dobler, D. W., & Burt, D. N. (1996). *Purchasing and supply management* (6th ed.). New York: McGraw-Hill.

Federal Acquisition Institute (1999). *The federal acquisition process.* Washington, DC: Federal Acquisition Institute.

Nash, R. C., Jr., Cibinic, J., Jr., & O'Brien, K. R. (1999). *Competitive negotiation: The source of selection process* (2nd ed.). Washington, DC: The George Washington University, Government Contract Program.

National Institute of Governmental Purchasing, Inc. (NIGP) (1996). *Dictionary of purchasing terms.* Herndon, VA: NIGP.

National Institute of Governmental Purchasing, Inc. (NIGP) (2000). *Intermediate public procurement.* Herndon, VA: NIGP.

National Institute of Governmental Purchasing, Inc. (NIGP) (2001). *General public procurement.* Herndon, VA: NIGP.

Pettijohn, C., & Babich, K. S. (2004). *Sourcing in the public sector.* Herndon, VA: NIGP.

Readey, J. (1999). A manual for writing RFPs. A paper presented at the 1999 NIGP Annual Forum & Products Expo, Halifax, Nova Scotia.

Thai, K.V. (2004). Introduction to public procurement. Herndon, VA: National Institute of Governmental Purchasing, Inc.

U.S. Office of Management and Budget (1997). *Capital programming guide.* Washington, DC: U.S. Office of Management and Budget. Available from www.whitehouse.gov/omb.

EXAMPLE OF AN IMPROPER SPECIFICATION

Kennedy Center Granite "Equal" Improperly Rejected

Rule: The government must be reasonable in determining whether a proposed substitute item in a contract is an equal.

The government has the right to demand precisely what it wants from a vendor. But there's a twist. The material and Workmanship clause allows a contractor to provide an "or equal" product that's equal in that it functions as well in all essential respects as the designated brand-name article. The government has no right to reject an equivalent. Nor can the government's rejection be unreasonable.

Recently, granite that the contractor considered equal to what the government wanted to use on the roof of the Kennedy Center was rejected as not being equal. A board of contract appeals found the government's decision to be unreasonable.

The roof terrace at the Kennedy Center needed repairs. The specification describe the granite as "light gray/white granite: Bethel White from Rock of Ages Granite, Bethel VT." What the government really wanted was only Bethel White. Grunley Construction provided granite called Mount Airy White, which is the only granite classified as both light gray and white by the industry. When the government refused to accept Grunley's alternative, Grunley filed a claim for the additional cost it incurred buying Bethel White granite.

The government fought the claim, arguing that the colon placed before the words "Bethel White" indicated that the government wanted only that type of granite. In addition, it did not find Grunley's alternative to be "an equal" because the Mount Airy White granite was not an acceptable visual match.

The Corps of Engineers Board of Contract Appeals did not agree with the government on either of its arguments. First, the Board found the granite requirement to be ambiguous. The Board went right to the grammatical structure of the government's statement of the granite requirement. The Board interpreted the slash in the phrase "light gray/white" granite to mean that either color granite would be an acceptable alternative. Moreover, the colon before "Bethel White" gave an example of acceptable stone, "not a further and inconsistent restriction," according to the Board. The government was simply giving the contractor one acceptable choice but not the only acceptable choice. This is especially true because Bethel White was not considered a light gray granite, but rather a white granite.

Nor was the government's rejection of Mount Airy White granite reasonable. The government did not adequately tell a contractor that an equal product had to be a visual match with Bethel White. "The appearance of the stone was not listed as a salient characteristic . . . and a contractor was not put on notice of the government's strong desire to have the lightest possible granite." The government was wrong in believing that an equal had to meet both the listed salient characteristics and the "unexpressed, inherent qualities of the specified item." The Board concluded that Grunley should be paid the additional cost it incurred providing Bethel White granite.

Grunley Construction Co. Inc., ENT BCA No. 6327, Nov. 20, 1998.

Source: *Federal Acquisition Report* (1999, January). Available from Federal Acquisition Regulation Web site, *http://www.arnet.gov/far/loadmainre.html.*

SPECIFICATION WRITING CHECKLIST

1. Decide on the appropriate type of specification.

2. Include essential characteristics.

3. Exclude non-essential characteristics.

4. Clearly delineate vendor obligations by including a precise statement of:

    - the object sought;
    - the work to be performed; and
    - the items to be delivered, and when.

5. Explain terms and conditions, compliance obligations, reports, testing, etc.

6. Provide a clear, consistent, and reproducible method for determining if requirements have been met.

7. Include a clear statement of the intended use.

8. Write plainly and precisely.

    - Eliminate ambiguity.
    - Allow no room for misinterpretation.
    - Eliminate legal liabilities.
    - Use accurate technical and trade terms.
    - Use short, concise words.
    - Use phrases and words consistently.
    - Include mandatory language proper to your statutes.
    - Do not use unnecessary words.
    - Do not use words or phrases that have multiple meanings.
    - Use words in their normal, common connotation.

9. Do not put anything in the specification that is in conflict with anything else in your bid document.

10. Leave no loopholes.

11. Avoid using acronyms.

12. Avoid making assumptions.

13. Avoid the use of clichés.

CHAPTER 4

The Proposal-Handling Process

Introduction

*T*he phrase "bid opening" in traditional procurement language is typically associated with purchases via the sealed competitive bid process for commodities. Depending on the procurement method selected, "bid opening" may not be applicable. Should the method of procurement be a competitive negotiation, competitive sealed proposal, or multi-step competitive sealed proposal, the phrase "proposal handling process" would be more appropriate and would reflect the proper connotation.

The American Bar Association's (ABA) *2000 Model Procurement Code for State and Local Governments* speaks to the differences between the opening of sealed bids and the receipt of proposals. Accordingly, the Code states in Section 3-203,

> Proposals shall be opened so as to avoid disclosure of contents to competing offerors during the process of negotiation. A Register of Proposals shall be prepared in accordance with regulations promulgated by the (Policy Office) and shall be open for public inspection after contract award.

As the Code suggests, a bid opening is normally an event open to the public, unless specifically prohibited by public legislation or ordinances. It is extremely rare for bids not to be open to the general public; but, in the RFP process, the actual opening of the proposals may be deferred in certain cases. When these situations do occur, the methodology for proposal delivery and proposal opening must be clearly stated in the solicitation. The following is an example of a proposal opening notification taken from the National Institute of

Governmental Purchasing, Inc.'s (NIGP) *Contracting for Services* (1997).

> Proposals must be received by the Procurement Office no later than 2:00 p.m. on the date indicated in Section 1.C, and proposal copies are to be submitted in the enclosed envelopes. The project number and due date must appear on the outside of the proposal submission envelope. Requests for extensions beyond the date and time specified will not be granted. Late proposals, late requests for modifications, or late requests for withdrawals will not be considered. A public opening of proposals will not occur at the date and time indicated above. Proposals received will be officially recorded, and this recordation will be made available to the public. All proposals received will be turned over to the evaluation committee for opening, review, deliberation, and recommendation. Negotiations will be conducted in accordance with the procedures described in this solicitation.

The proposal-handling process varies depending on jurisdiction. The process regarding bid openings is rather clear-cut and has been in place for many years. The process of soliciting and receiving proposals and awarding contracts based on proposals received is constantly evolving. Sound public procurement policy requires that however well defined the process may be, safeguards should be in place to assure fairness and credibility. NIGP's (1997) text suggests that the following recommendations will assist the procurement official in this regard:

- Specify a date and time for receiving offers, and state that late submissions will not be accepted.

- State that a debriefing session will be afforded following a decision to award. At that time, unsuccessful offerors may inspect the responses received from the other firms and individuals who submitted competing offers.

- Due to the extensive time needed to evaluate offers and conduct negotiations, a stipulation should be included in the Scope/Statement of Work or boilerplate that pricing must be kept firm for a given period following the proposal due date and may be extended by mutual written agreement. The suggested period would be between 120 and 180 days.

- Rather than a formal bid opening, invite all proposers to attend a "public recording of sealed offers." On the time and date that offers are due, a member of the procurement office, along with an administrative assistant who will serve as a witness, will record the offers received in a public forum. Public recording may include the name of the offeror, verification that price or Technical Proposals were submitted, and a sign-in sheet for those in attendance. At this time, it should be stated that there will be no questions taken from those in attendance and that questions or inquiries regarding the offers submitted will not be entertained during the evaluation process, with the exception of formal negotiations as specified in the RFP.

- All offers received should be time and date stamped, as it would normally be done with sealed competitive bids.

- If only price proposals are being asked for, consideration may be given to a public opening of price proposals, which may be subject to further negotiation. Prices may be recorded on a spreadsheet and read aloud. Any tabulation made during the public recordation may be available within a reasonable time.

Proposal Receipt

*P*roposers expect the purchasing organization to safeguard their response submission prior to the designated closing date and time. The organization is obligated to retain all responses in a safe, secure, and confidential manner. Some organizations use a locked drop-box, while others use a locked file cabinet, and some use a locked room with shelves indicating the solicitation reference number.

NIGP's (2000) text, *Competitive Sealed Proposal/Competitive Negotiation* states that as proposals arrive at the place designated in the solicitation, a receiving official should take steps to secure proposals.

- Time-stamp proposals.
- Record receipt of proposals in the log.
- Secure proposals in a locked box or safe with the log.
- Leave proposals unopened.
- Provide information to jurisdiction employees only on a need-to-know basis.

Envelopes that are not marked or are marked as proposals, but do not identify the offeror or the solicitation, may be opened solely for identification. In these cases, the envelope shall include the opener's signature and title and shall be delivered to the designated procurement official. This official shall immediately write on the envelope an explanation of the opening.

The procurement official should then immediately sign and reseal the envelope. No information contained in the envelope shall be discussed before the time set for receipt of offers.

Safeguarding Confidential Information Contained in Proposals

*U*nlike sealed bidding, in a negotiated procurement, most information concerning the proposals received should be made available only to jurisdiction employees having a legitimate interest (Federal Acquisition Regulation [FAR] 15.413). The information that procurement officials should safeguard includes the following:

- number of proposals received,
- identity of offerors, information contained in the proposals, and
- any restriction placed on disclosure and use of data by an offeror. (NIGP's text on *Competitive Negotiations* is available from http://www. nigp.org/).

Sometimes, offerors may submit proposals with descriptive literature and material or special technical data in which they have a proprietary interest. Typically, they do not want this information disclosed to the public or used by the procurement official for any purpose other than the evaluation of their offers. Offerors may mark each sheet of technical data they wish to restrict with the following legend:

> This proposal contains data that shall not be disclosed outside the [procurement agency] and shall not be duplicated, used, or disclosed—in whole or in part—for any purpose other than to evaluate this proposal. If, however, a contract is awarded to this offeror as a result of or in conjunction with the submission of this data, the [procurement agency] shall have the right to duplicate, use, or disclose the data to the extent provided in the resulting contract. This restriction does not limit the [procurement agency's] right to use information contained in this data if it is obtained from another source without restriction. The data subject to this restriction are contained in sheets (insert numbers or other identification of sheets) (FAR 52.215-12).

Procurement personnel may not refuse to consider any proposal merely because the data submitted with it are marked in this way.

Proposal Handling

*T*he goal of the RFP process is to utilize a procurement process that will afford an agency the benefits of constructive vendor or consultant thinking and also provide the best procurement value for the taxpayers. Value is an integration of quality with price, and an RFP recognizes that there are different needs and different priorities in buying decisions. Further, RFPs recognize that there may be more than one solution to a problem and that each solution may carry a different price tag.

Sequence of Proposal Receipt and Processing

*T*here are several methods of processing the receipt of proposals, which are described in the following scenarios. The scenarios are not intended to be a discussion of evaluation methods that follow later on in this text but are intended to describe some of the possible variations in handling proposals.

Scenario I

The Q&E factor is solicited through the methods normally utilized by the jurisdiction. These submittals by the respondents are sometimes called "Letters of Interest" or "Statements of Qualification." The team may use specially developed or standardized forms, e.g., the U.S. Federal Forms 254, 255 and 330, to obtain this information or have the vendor/consultant submit the data in their own format. It is highly recommended that the team clearly tell the proposer community how it wants the information submitted. This will facilitate the evaluation.

After evaluation of these submittals, the Evaluation Team develops a list of those firms that they have determined posses the capabilities of best satisfying the agency's needs. Detailed Technical Proposals (Section 2) are solicited from these firms (Scenario 1A), or Technical and Cost Proposals (Sections 2 and 3) are solicited from these firms (Scenario 1B).

Scenario 1A

The technical factor is received from the highest ranked firms and the Technical Proposals evaluated and ranked. After ranking, the Evaluation Team negotiates the final Scope of Work (SOW) and cost of the project with the highest ranked firm. If agreement cannot be reached, then negotiation with the number 2 firm will follow. This procedure will continue until a successful agreement is reached with one of the highest ranked firms.

Scenario 1B

The technical and cost factors are received from the highest ranked firms. The combination of the two is then evaluated together according to the method described in the RFP, and an award is made to the firm offering the greatest value.

Scenario 2

The Q&E and technical factors are received from all respondents. These are evaluated and the proposals ranked. No cost information is received at this stage.

Scenario 2A

After ranking, the Evaluation Team negotiates the final SOW and cost of the project with the highest ranked firm. If agreement cannot be reached, then negotiation with the number 2 firm will follow. This procedure will continue until a successful agreement is reached with one of the highest-ranked firms. This is the same methodology discussed in Scenario 1A, the difference being when Section 2 was received.

Scenario 2B

The cost factor is received from the highest ranked firms. The combination of the technical merits of the proposal along with the costs are then evaluated according to the method described in the RFP, and an award is made to the firm offering the greatest value. This is the same methodology discussed in Scenario 1B, the difference being when Section 2 was received.

Scenario 2C

This scenario is sometimes referred to as a "two-step" or "hybrid" RFP. It combines elements of both processes. In this scenario, the Q&E and technical factors of the proposals are received, evaluated, and the firms ranked based on their submittals. This is not too different from establishing a "pre-qualified list." A revised SOW or specification is sent only to the highest ranked firms that then submit a price based on 100% compliance with the revised specifications or SOW. No deviations are permitted at this point. Award is made to the lowest responsive bid proposer.

Scenario 3

In this scenario, all three factors—Q&E, Technical, and Cost—of the proposal are received at the same time. This is the most commonly followed practice. The cost factor may be included with Sections 1 and 2, or it may be in a separate package that remains closed and unopened until a later stage in the process (Scenario 3A.)

Scenario 3A

Sections 1 and 2 (Q&E and Technical) are evaluated and the firms ranked based on these two sections. The Cost Sections from only the highest ranked firms are opened for evaluation. Two alternatives are now available to us. If the cost of the highest ranked firm falls within the project estimates, one alternative is to accept this proposal. Another alternative is to combine the technical merits of the proposal along with the costs and then evaluate them together according to the method described in the RFP, and an award is made to the firm offering the greatest value.

Scenario 3B

All three factors—Q&E, Technical, and Cost—of the proposal are received at the same time. The combination of all three factors is then evaluated according to method described in the RFP, and an award is made to the firm offering the greatest value.

Conclusion

*T*he way the Evaluation Team handles the receipt of a proposal differs significantly from the way the receipt of a bid is handled, including the terminology used. Typically, bids have opening times and dates, whereas proposals have closing times and dates. Generally, bid openings are public with prices being read out loud. Most jurisdictions will read only the names of proposers upon the receipt of the offers. Some jurisdictions do not reveal the names of offerors until after an award is made. There is considerable variation from jurisdiction to jurisdiction. New York City rules even allow a three-hour window in which late proposal submittals can be accepted.

The way a jurisdiction handles the submittals after receipt depends upon the evaluation method the jurisdiction has selected for the specific procurement. In some instances, prices are an integral part of the proposal; while, in other cases, they may be received separately. The important thing is that the process is consistent, fair, and easily understood.

References

American Bar Association (2000). *The 2000 model procurement code for state and local governments.* Chicago: American Bar Association.

Federal Acquisition Regulation Web site, http://www.arnet.gov/far/loadmainre. html.

National Institute of Governmental Purchasing, Inc. (NIGP) (1997). *Contracting for services.* Herndon, VA: NIGP.

National Institute of Governmental Purchasing, Inc. (NIGP) (2000). *Competitive sealed proposal/competitive negotiations.* Herndon, VA: NIGP.

CHAPTER 5

The Evaluation Process and Selection of the Right Offeror

Introduction

*E*valuation is probably the most critical phase in any Request for Proposal (RFP) process. If the evaluation is not conducted appropriately, the procurement official (PO) may face many problems ranging from possible protests to unsatisfactory performance. As the public procurement process must seek transparency, it is important that a committee fairly weigh many factors that are constantly described in the RFP and that also exist explicitly in the jurisdiction's law and regulations, such as preferential treatments. As opposed to the Request for Bids (RFB) procurement method, when using the RFP method, the contract is not awarded purely on price received from the lowest responsive and responsible offeror, but to the vendor making the best offer as determined by various criteria., such as experience, staff, and prior history with the jurisdiction.

Evaluation Committee

Concept or Purpose

It is standard policy in most jurisdictions to establish a formal selection committee to evaluate proposals. This is necessary due to the sophistication and complexity of this type of procurement. A committee should be comprised of broad-based representation that merges a variety of separate disciplinary skills needed to perform this type of proposal evaluation. Remember that the committee in actuality is a team and must be treated as such.

Committee/Team Composition

The make-up of the Evaluation Committee varies from jurisdiction to jurisdiction and depends on the size and complexity of the procurement. The procurement official, a representative of the end-user, and a technical expert normally form the foundation of the team. While the head of the requesting jurisdiction may be ultimately responsible for the source selection, the Director of the Central Purchasing Authority or the Director's designee should approve appointment of Evaluation Committee members. Typically, the Committee consists of three individuals. In those cases where the procurement official is not considered to be a voting member of the committee, there may be four members.

The Evaluation Committee should include members from all functional areas in the jurisdiction in order to utilize the best-qualified individuals. Not only should they be technically qualified, they also should be free of bias or conflict of interest. The number of voting members need not be limited; however, the more members, the more difficult it becomes to manage the group. There are always competing priorities and schedules with which the Chair will have to deal. The number of voting members should always be an odd number to avoid the possibility of a tie vote, although split decisions usually are rare.

In addition to the members appointed from the jurisdiction itself, there might be other members who are experienced in the same or similar field to which the proposal applies chosen from other governmental agencies or universities. The nominees must be individuals who will not participate in the project under evaluation and must be considered completely impartial in making an award recommendation.

Depending on the complexity and technical requirements of the RFP, procurement officials may want to request the assistance of a specialist in one or more discipline (Pettijohn & Babich, 2004).

- Technical
- Engineering
- Legal
- Contract Administration
- Contract Pricing
- Financial
- Information Technology
- Audit

- Procurement
- Other

This varied talent combination is required on the Evaluation Committee because the mission of the Committee is to recommend the most economical proposal, which is expected to fully meet the jurisdiction's needs and have the highest probability for successful project completion. The evaluators must exercise judgment and be as impartial as possible in evaluating the relative merits of each proposal. Occasionally, the Committee should consider and involve, when appropriate, any of the above individuals to assist in making the final recommendation.

The Committee may receive advice or recommendations from other knowledgeable sources such as Consultants. The others need not be voting or actual Committee members. Committees should include one or more representatives from the end-user, the procurement department and from other functions such as legal or any of the other areas of expertise previously discussed.

Committee Functions

- Apply Evaluation Criteria
- Evaluate Proposals Individually and/or Discuss
- Rank and/or Develop a Shortlist
- Interview/Obtain Clarifications and Negotiate Finalize Contract Terms with Selected Vendor
- Recommend Award

The initial tasks of an Evaluation Committee are to review the Statement of Work (SOW) or purchase description and develop evaluation criteria that will establish the standards that measure how well an offeror's approach meets the needs of the requesting jurisdiction or the RFP's performance requirements. The establishment of these criteria is critical, since only those standards established in the RFP can be considered in the evaluation of competing offers.

The second major task of the Evaluation Committee is to agree on a scoring method to rate or rank the offers. Once a scoring system has been devised, it must be impartially applied to each proposal (Harney, p. 101).

The Evaluation Committee Roles

Once the Evaluation Committee has been assembled, each member's role on the Committee/Team must be determined, a work plan established and a schedule and milestone dates set. The Committee must then review procedures that will be used during the process and review the solicitation document, or RFP. The purchasing representative will always serve as the Committee Chair or Team Leader.

The procurement department representative serving as the Chair of the Evaluation Committee is charged with the responsibility of assuring that the Committee's actions are in accordance with good, sound procurement policies and applicable guidelines. The Chair establishes a timetable for evaluation activities and assumes the responsibility for keeping activities on schedule. If necessary, intervention by management to assist in enforcing the completion of scheduled events can be solicited.

The Chair is responsible for scheduling and coordinating the activities of the Evaluation Committee; however, these efforts can be negated if other Committee members are not cooperative and do not make the required time commitment to Committee activities. Participation on an Evaluation Committee is a priority effort. Committee members should work out an acceptable workload arrangement with their supervisor in order to allow the proper time for Evaluation Committee activities. Management must be supportive of these arrangements so that Committee members can adequately fulfill their evaluation duties.

The Chair also arranges the time; date and place for any oral sessions that the Committee feels are necessary and notifies the firms. These firms are individually scheduled to appear before the Committee; and all other firms are normally barred from attendance unless prohibited by law, as is the case in the State of Florida. It is customary for the Committee to ask a certain set of questions that apply to all the firms invited to oral sessions in addition to specific questions that are directed to specific firms. For informational purposes, the Chair also arranges for all proceedings to be recorded (tape or transcription) and available to all firms upon request, normally after award of the contract.

Purchasing Representative's Role

- Serves as Committee Chair (Administrative)
- Votes, if voting member
- Insures integrity of procurement system
- Insures compliance with RFP requirements
- Schedules Committee meetings
- Schedules vendor interviews
- Keeps minutes and files
- Corresponds with RFP respondents
- Negotiates financial issues

User Jurisdiction Representative and Other Technical Parties' Roles

- Develop SOW and Technical Requirements
- Develop Budget Estimates
- Develop Technical Questions for Orals
- Negotiate Technical RFP Aspects
- Provide Overall Technical Input

Evaluation Committee Code of Conduct

Committee membership obligates the individual to both a commitment of judgment as well as time. A participant serving on a committee that is evaluating proposals is morally bound to be as objective and fair as possible, since these decisions impact the expenditure of public funds and the business livelihood of the submitting firms in the private sector. An Evaluation Committee member should also be prepared to make a priority commitment of time, since a timely turnaround on award recommendation is important. Management must recognize and support the need for a priority commitment of time for Evaluation Committee activities.

When individuals sign their names to an Evaluation Committee Selection Report, they represent themselves, their individual jurisdictions, and *the* jurisdiction. Individual Committee members are responsible for defending their own vote. A voting Committee member is charged with recommending the award of a contract to the proposer who offers the best proposal response to the jurisdiction's RFP.

Committee members are expected to conduct themselves in a professional manner at all times, whether with each other, with proposers, or the public. Internal Committee deliberations over the merits of proposals should be constructive discussions. Members have the right to voice their opinions to either make or refute a point.

Inherent in committee membership is a trust that requires that all proceedings be held in confidence until final contract award is made a matter of public record. The only information that a committee member is obligated to divulge to an outside party is a reconfirmation of the contents of the Evaluation Committee Selection Report. This document is the official statement of the deliberations and decision-making process within any committee. In practice, all outside questions relating to any area of the procurement process shall be referred to the Committee Chair (Purchase Jurisdiction Representative).

Evaluation Committee members are expected to conduct themselves in a professional manner at all tines when dealing with prospective proposers, actual proposers, or the general public. The opportunities for outside interaction can present themselves a number of times. Pre-Solicitation Conferences, proposal openings, and oral presentations are typical examples of outside interaction. In addition, there is always the possibility of having to appear at administrative hearings if an official award protest is registered.

Evaluation Committee members should always be courteous and professional when dealing with the public. A Committee member should exhibit a competent, non-authoritarian, attitude in representing the jurisdiction's position on any particular procurement. There should be a strong resolution as to the needs and interests of the jurisdiction from the very beginning of the procurement. Committee members should be reasonable, open-minded, and willing to entertain and consider suggestions and compromises that could ultimately result in a better contract for the jurisdiction.

Committee members are encouraged to take as many notes as they feel necessary when reading through proposals. Not only does it help them to mentally organize the information, but also aids in any recap required to come up with final scoring. In addition, the notes become a quick reference tool to an individual when the Committee meets as a group to discuss each proposal.

The number of proposals to be evaluated from interested respondents for any open-competitive procurement can theoretically range from a single submittal to an indefinite number. A committee can conceivably be formed to review just one proposal. For example, a firm may be the sole source vendor for the particular goods or services required; or only a few submittals are received in response to an open-competitive RFP and all but one firm has to be automatically rejected for mandatory requirements (e.g., signature, bid bond, insurance, etc.).

Depending on the number of proposals to be evaluated for the project, the Committee members must be prepared to budget the time and make the necessary commitment to read and evaluate proposals in a timely fashion. When the Committee members have completed their individual reading and scoring of proposals, the Chair assembles the Committee as a group.

These group/team meetings are the center points of the evaluation process. The discussions on each proposal and the resulting deliberations are the means by which the Committee can ultimately arrive at a collective decision. At this stage, the Committee process is dynamic; it is designed to solicit the perspectives and opinions of all voting members. What one Committee member may have understood about a certain concept or approach may differ from what another member may have perceived. A Committee can go back and forth until all members are convinced of their choices and the rationale behind then.

Depending upon the degree of agreement/disagreement within the Committee, the Chair may deem it necessary to end the present Committee meeting and reconvene the group for another meeting at a later date. In the interim, Committee members may choose to re-read certain proposals or sections of proposals in order to confirm their particular convictions or to verify the positions of other Committee members. Once the Committee has met several times as a group, it is hoped that a unanimous decision on award recommendation can be made. However, when it is clear that only a consensus opinion has resulted, then the Committee should go forward with both a majority and minority report.

Evaluation Committee Guidelines

Tables 15 and 16 exhibit excerpts from State Evaluation Committee Guidelines.

Table 15

State of Pennsylvania Evaluation Committee Guidelines

It is recommended the Evaluation Committee be composed of five to seven individuals who possess the technical and managerial expertise in the appropriate field, as well as those with experience. As appropriate, individuals from other agencies of the Commonwealth should be given the opportunity to participate as voting members or observers on all Committees. While an agency is required to invite its comptroller to participate as a nonvoting member of the Committee, agencies should also consider asking its comptroller to participate as a voting member. Once appointed to the Committee, neither the chairman nor members may meet with offerors or discuss the RFP or related matters with them except in formal, scheduled meetings of the Committee or as directed by the Committee.

Duties of the Committee are to:

(1) Establish checklist identifying mandatory requirements and assure qualitative evaluation criteria contained in the RFP have been reduced to weighted checklists.

(2) Arrange for determination of offeror and subcontractors responsibility in accordance with Management Directive 215.9.

(3) Screen all proposals to determine which of them meet mandatory requirements. Committee members should be given adequate time to review each proposal.

(4) Evaluate remaining proposals and rank them in order of merit based on evaluation criteria as contained in the RFP.

(5) Recommend proposal selection. The proposals should not be disclosed or discussed with anyone, including other Commonwealth employees, except agency counsel or agency comptroller.

Source: Pennsylvania Department of General Services (2001, March). *Field procurement handbook*. Available from www.dgs.state.pa.us/site/default.asp, p. 28.

Table 16

State of New Mexico Evaluation Committee Guidelines

There are several key points regarding the organization of the Evaluation Committee as follows:

- The Committee size should be manageable. Five voting members are recommended. Three voting members are the recommended minimum, and seven voting members are the recommended maximum. Experience has shown that larger Committees lengthen the procurement process unnecessarily and reduce the quality of the process.

- The members of the Committee should be identified as early as possible. Ideally, the entire Evaluation Committee would have participated in some of the pre-procurement activities. The Committee must be in place prior to the pre-proposal conference.

- The Evaluation Committee composition should represent a cross section, including agency management, user management and technical support. The correct mix depends on the type of procurement. If the procurement is for an application system, there should be sufficient user representation to cover the functional areas of the application. If it is a technical procurement, the majority of the Committee should be composed of technically qualified members.

- The Evaluation Committee members must make time in their individual schedules, and workloads may have to be adjusted to provide time for the members to complete document drafting and the evaluation.

- The Procurement Manager may or may not be a voting member of the Evaluation Committee at the discretion of the Procurement Manager.

Source: State of New Mexico (1999, July). *Request for proposals procurement guide*. Available from www.state.nm.us/clients/spd/rfpdevel.html.

Upon formation of the Evaluation Committee, the procurement representative should convene a meeting to provide instructions and direction on the process, role, responsibilities and requirements of the Committee/Team. Typically, the representative and the end-user determine the composition of the Committee. To ensure integrity in the process as well as fair and open competition, the Committee members should be instructed to retain all evaluation documents, including worksheets, evaluation forms, and notes during the evaluation. These should be returned to purchasing for future reference and referral. Committee members should also be instructed to individually and independently evaluate, score, and rank proposals by applying the same objective criteria and to refrain from discussions with any other member during the evaluation process.

During the evaluation process, if additional information or clarification is required, it should be directed to the purchasing official, who will seek the response and distribute the related information to all Committee members. Committee members should also be instructed not to make contact with any of the offerors or proponents but, rather, direct inquiries to the purchasing officer. Similarly, if a site visit, demonstration, or further presentation is required, it should be coordinated, established, and arranged through purchasing.

Evaluation Plan

The first step in developing the evaluation plan is to identify the parameters that will be used in the solicitation method to measure both the technical competence of the offerors and the financial value of their particular proposals. Rating factors are then assigned to the evaluation. The rating factors must reflect the relative importance of the evaluation criteria. By reviewing the proposed weighting at this stage, purchasing can help the end-user ensure that the significant factors drive the choice of the recommended offeror. Again, the relative weighting of each component will change for each RFP issuance. Finally, the plan must indicate the offeror selection method that will be used.

The evaluation factors and procedures must be completed prior to issuing the proposals.

To establish the evaluation plan, considerable collaboration with and input from the end-user must be secured. There must be consensus among all interested parties as to the manner in which proposals will be evaluated, as well as the process and methods used prior to the commencement of the solicitation.

The purpose of the evaluation process is to identify the most responsive proposal and ensure that there is sufficient accurate information to make a sound decision. A well-defined and thorough RFP will result in a contract with multiple responses. There are some ground rules for defining a proper evaluation process.

The evaluation factors and procedures must be completed prior to issuing the proposals. An Evaluation Committee should be appointed and given an orientation as to their role in the selection process. Should the evaluation process not be clearly established prior to the Committee receiving the proposals, disgruntled offerors may (and probably will) argue that the Committee acted improperly.

Thus, it is important to make it known how the RFP Evaluation Committee is going to conduct the evaluation and include the process as part of the RFP documentation before the Evaluation Committee reviews submitted proposals.

Evaluation Criteria

As mentioned in Chapter 3, RFP award decisions are based on the proposal affording the best value—in other words, not only on the price but also on technical quality and other factors of the proposal. Thus, fair evaluation based on clearly defined evaluation criteria is very important. These criteria, including price and non-price, factors, weights and values by category, minimum upset score by category, where appropriate, and the evaluation matrix, should appear in the RFP document. At a minimum, the order of importance of the criteria should be stated.

Steps in the Evaluation Process

The evaluation process is slightly different in every RFP, and these processes vary from jurisdiction to jurisdiction. For example, the State of Pennsylvania's (Pennsylvania Department of General Services, 2001) evaluation process consists of five steps.

- Mandatory requirements
- Discussions for clarification
- Preliminary evaluation
- Tentative cost evaluation
- Discussion with responsible offerors for best and final offers

While every entity is fully able to enact home-rule provisions, there is a strong similarity between evaluation procedures in all jurisdictions using RFPs. The process in Cincinnati is not very different from the one used by the State of Montana, and that process is very similar to the process used in Iqaluit—the capital of Canada's newest northern territory. Regardless of the entity type or location, it is the best practice to develop and finalize the evaluation procedure prior to opening the proposals.

Once the deadline for receipt of proposals arrives, proposals are copied and distributed to the Evaluation Committee. Generally, each Committee member will review a proposal in its entirety. Occasionally, a subject matter expert will do a special review of a particular section. Scores received from these individuals are incorporated into the final scoring matrix.

Review Proposals for Completeness (Determination of Responsiveness)

When procurement officials undertake a Competitive Negotiation Acquisition, any and all contractual terms and provisions may be subject to negotiation. Accordingly, the jurisdiction is permitted greater latitude in considering proposals that fail to conform to the requirements of the solicitation or which qualify their response or suggest alternatives to the jurisdiction's stated requirements. It is the procurement official's responsibility to review all timely proposals to identify (Federal Acquisition Regulation [FAR] 412):

- any minor irregularities and informalities; and
- any substantive differences between the RFP and the proposal's terms and conditions, or inconsistencies and errors in quantitative or other reasoning.

Examples of minor irregularities and informalities include but are not limited to the failure of an offeror to (FAR 412):

- provide information concerning the number of its employees;
- return the number of copies of signed offers required by solicitation; and
- furnish affidavits concerning parent company and affiliates.

The jurisdiction or the offeror may initiate clarifications to eliminate minor irregularities or apparent clerical mistakes. However it is the procurement official's responsibility to verify any variances between the offeror's proposal and the RFP.

The jurisdiction has the right to reject proposals that cannot be made responsive. Although the jurisdiction has greater flexibility in the case of RFPs than in the case of bids, certain mandatory requirements may be essential to the performance of the contract. This includes insurance requirements, license requirements, and certain types of certifications for both the offeror as a jurisdiction and their personnel as well as the need for specialized equipment. The determination of responsiveness must consider whether the offeror is capable of meeting these requirements in an acceptable time frame prior to any contract award.

In addition to the general standards of responsibility that all prospective contractors must possess, the requesting jurisdiction may determine that there are special standards of responsibility and related technical/business management factors that must be met to ensure satisfactory contract performance (FAR 9.104-2).

Evaluation Process

Processing Proposals

Proposals received before the closing date should be secured, unopened, in a locked file. Should electronic proposals be accepted, they should be stored in a secured restricted-access electronic offer box. As soon as possible after the due date, the procurement official and a witness should open and record the proposals.

Screening Proposals for Compliance with Mandatory Requirements

The purchasing official should screen all proposals received for compliance with mandatory requirements. Any discrepancies should be noted, along with proposals that are non-conforming, once the initial review is complete. Each Evaluation Committee member should review the proposals and score them based on the matrix provided. When preparing an RFP document, it is important to anticipate every aspect of the requirements definition or manner and content of response submission from each offeror. RFP documents should make provision for the jurisdiction to have adequate discretion in the receipt, evaluation, recommendation, and award decision to account for minor informalities and irregularities. The Evaluation Committee must be careful to not inadvertently waive any irregularities that would create an unfair advantage to another offeror and alienate a good offeror. A few examples of minor irregularities that may be waived include the following:

- There is no material variation from the original requirements definition, specifications, and SOW or deliverable.

- The variation, as previously noted, has no impact on quality, delivery, quantity, performance, price or the proposer's ability to comply with the fulfillment conditions.

- The variation would not restrict or impact the open, fair and competitive nature of the acquisition.

Table 17 provides examples of minor irregularities that may be waived. The National Institute of Governmental Purchasing, Inc.'s (NIGP) (2004) LEAP text, Sourcing in the Public Sector, contains extensive discussion on bidding irregularities.

Table 17

Examples of Minor Irregularities That May Be Waived

- Failure to sign all sections of a response submission, when it is clear from the documentation submitted in the response that the bidder and proponent intended to submit the response and that not executing or signing all the stipulated sections of the response was an oversight by the proposer.

- Failure to submit with a response submission certain required documents or forms regarding the proposer's qualifications or ability to perform. Examples are submission of financial statements, execution of non-collusion affidavits, etc. These can be provided prior to award of the contract.

- Failure to submit with a response submission an executed acknowledgement of receipt of Addenda form. As long as the bidder and proponent materially comply with all aspects of the Scope of Work and deliverables, the return of this from is immaterial in the firm's ability to perform.

- Failure to provide with a response submission adequate description catalogues or brochures for the products being acquired.

- Failure to return the number of executed response submissions.

- Failure to return response submissions to the specified location, but received on time at the official location through secondary delivery (mail room or delivery service).

If the offeror provides sufficient evidence within their response submission that it intends to comply with all mandatory terms and conditions prior to award of contract, the Evaluation Committee should waive these minor irregularities. It is highly unusual for a proposal not to comply with mandatory requirements. An offeror who fails to meet a mandatory submittal requirement is usually eliminated from further consideration with regard to the RFP. The decision to eliminate a proposal submission must be thoroughly documented to justify the Committee's decision.

Mandatory requirements are clearly stated in the RFP. These requirements may be administrative, such as, "Proposals are due by August 15 and must be received no later than 5:00 p.m. at the specified location." These requirements may be technical in nature, identifying a critical feature or functional capability. For RFPs with mandatory requirements, the evaluation process should be a two-step process. In this type of process, the Committee first examines each offeror's stated ability to satisfy the mandatory requirements. Suppliers who are unable to meet these standards are eliminated from further consideration. Once compliance is determined, the evaluators assign a score to each proposal based on the evaluation criteria defined in the RFP.

A mandatory condition is a requirement that must be met without alteration. One example is the submission of the proposal by a specified time. If it is late, it is usually returned to the supplier unopened. Another example is a requirement that the offeror must provide 24-hour emergency service. To ensure that offerors do not miss mandatory requirements scattered throughout the RFP, all of the mandatory requirements should be identified in one section of the RFP. Many evaluators can be uncomfortable eliminating an offeror from further consideration for failure to satisfy a mandatory condition, especially when the purchasing officer deems the requirement to be only highly desirable. It is incumbent upon purchasing to ensure that mandatory requirements are precisely defined and must be essential elements for the success of the project.

A mandatory condition is a requirement that must be met without alteration.

The process of proposal rejection is awkward, risky, and sometimes embarrassing when the mandatory requirements are unclear and could be interpreted in several ways. In order to compensate for error, purchasing officers may declare all proposals responsive, examine the actual requirement more closely, and seek clarification from the proposers. Committee members should evaluate each proposal on its merits. Failing to deal properly with mandatory requirements may lead to litigation. The procurement official must be careful to be very clear when specifying mandatory requirements.

In practice, however, most are vague and compliance may be subjective. The use of the word "may" rather than "must" allows for the waiver of mandatory conditions which some proposers failed to meet. They can also waive mandatory conditions, which, on close examination during the evaluation process, have proven to be ambiguous. When "may" is used, the principle of treating each proposal fairly must prevail. Evaluators should expect complaints and protests from offerors that were eliminated for failure to comply with a mandatory condition that was ambiguous or not an essential part of the solution.

As a result of this process, each proposal is declared to be either responsive or non-responsive. Responsive proposals are evaluated further. Non-responsive proposals are removed from further review after preparing a memo for the project file and senior management (in anticipation of a protest).

To ensure that proposers understand the significance of key words such as "mandatory," many RFPs define the term and indicate that it will be synonymous with the word "must." Tables 18 and 19 offer examples of mandatory requirements and/or circumstances, which may result in elimination of the proposal. The jurisdiction or the offeror may initiate clarifications to eliminate minor irregularities or apparent clerical mistakes; however, it is the procurement official's responsibility to verify any variances between the offeror's proposal and the RFP.

Table 18

Examples of Mandatory Requirements

Definitions of Key Words Used in the RFP

"Shall" or "Must" indicates a mandatory requirement. Failure to meet mandatory requirements may result in the rejection of a proposal as non-responsive.

"Should" indicates something that is recommended but not mandatory. If the offeror fails to provide recommended information, the State may, at its sole option, ask the offeror to provide the information or evaluate the proposal without the information.

"May" indicates something that is not mandatory, but permissible.

Table 19

*Circumstances That May Result in Elimination
of the Proposal*

Mandatory Requirement Defined

A mandatory requirement (MR) is an essential need that must be met by the proposer. The Department of Labor and Industries (L&I) may eliminate from the evaluation process any vendor not fulfilling all mandatory requirements.

Failure to meet a mandatory requirement (ground for disqualification) shall be established by any of the following conditions:

- The vendor states that a mandatory requirement cannot or will not be met.

- The vendor presents the information requested by this RFP in a manner inconsistent with the instructions stated in any part of the RFP.

- Customer references report the proposer's inability to provide average (satisfactory) service or to comply with one or more of the mandatory requirements.

- The proposer's references fail to send the customer reference forms as required and/or by the time required.

- The proposer fails to include information requested by a mandatory requirement.

Source: Information Technology Professional Services, State of Washington Department of Labor and Industries (1997, March 7). *Request for proposal* (p. 28). Available from http://www.Ini.wa.gov/.

The jurisdiction has the right to reject proposals that cannot be made responsive. Although the jurisdiction has greater flexibility in the case of RFPs than in the case of bids, certain mandatory requirements may be essential to the performance of the contract. This includes insurance requirements, license requirements, and certain types of certifications for both the offeror as a jurisdiction and their personnel as well as the need for specialized equipment. Prior to any contract award and determination of responsiveness, it must be considered whether the offeror is capable of meeting these requirements in an acceptable time frame.

In addition to the general standards of responsibility that all prospective contractors must possess, the requesting jurisdiction may determine that there are special standards of responsibility and related technical/business management factors that must be met to ensure satisfactory contract performance (FAR 9.104-2).

The language used in solicitation documents may cause many of the difficulties that procurement officials experience. If procurement officials use mandatory language, such as "must" or "shall," procurement officials will be faced with making a determination of the offeror's responsiveness. An example is the requirement for the submission of samples. If our documents use language such as "the bidder must submit a sample of the product with the bid," then failure to do so could result in a judgment of non-responsiveness. A more desirable approach might be to use non-mandatory language such as "the bidder should submit" or even requesting that samples be submitted "when the procurement official requests them." Consideration of the terminology will go a long way toward reducing problems in proposal evaluation.

Procurement professionals should make a common practice of summarizing all mandatory terms (Table 20) on one page of the RFP with further reference to the pages, which describe each of the requirements in more detail. This is an additional aid to proposers.

Table 20
Mandatory Criteria

All mandatory requirements should be shown here, even if they are introduced elsewhere. The number of mandatory requirements should be kept to a minimum. Any proposal not meeting all of the mandatory criteria cannot be evaluated; it must be rejected. It is important, therefore, that mandatory criteria not be too restrictive or difficult to meet, and most should be critical to the success of the project. Whether each criterion is met should be readily determined by a "yes" or "no." The following are examples:

a) At least one member of the project team must be a registered clinical psychologist.

b) The proposed mode of transportation must be able to accommodate at least six adult clients.

c) The proposed software must be compatible with Microsoft products, including Microsoft Windows, Word, Excel, and PowerPoint.

This section could begin: "The following are mandatory requirements. Proposals not meeting them, or not clearly demonstrating that they meet them in a substantially unaltered form, will receive no further consideration during the evaluation process."

Source: Government of Nova Scotia Procurement Branch (March 2002). *Departmental guide to the preparation of a request for proposal.* Available from www.gov.ns.ca/fina/ptns.

Highly Desirable versus Mandatory Requirements

The State of Connecticut issued an RFP to "outsource all IT services . . . so that such Agencies can completely exit the business of providing IT services and focus on their core function—the business of government." The state only

wanted large, world-class corporations to bid. Rather than imposing a mandatory condition such as revenue of more than $1 billion per year, a condition
that could be seen as restricting competition, they simply told their story in the
RFP and defined the characteristics of the winner as highly desirable. Table 21
reflects the wording found in the RFP.

Table 21
Desirable v. Mandatory Requirements

While Connecticut will take receipt of and evaluate all Proposals complying
with the RFP requirements, it is unlikely that a Proposal from other than a
world-class IT services provider will be considered Acceptable or Potentially
Acceptable, as described in Section 1.4. Your organization is discouraged
from submitting a Proposal unless it meets each of the following criteria:

   (a) Your organization, either alone or teaming with other entities, has
       entered into at least one IT services contract for the provision of IT
       services where the annual contract value exceeded $50,000,000;

   (b) Your organization, either alone or teaming with other entities, has pro-
       vided services in at least six of the eight services categories described
       in Section 4.5 of the RFP; and

   (c) Your organization has had average gross annual revenues in excess of
       $1 billion over its three latest fiscal years.

Source: State of Connecticut. Available from http://www.ct.gov/.

Selecting a Right Offeror: Performance Evaluation

Two terms that are used extensively by procurement professionals are "responsive" and "responsible." They appear in almost all of our solicitation documents. Typically, the solicitation documents provide that an award be made to
the low responsive and responsible bidder. Determination of responsiveness
takes place at the time of bid opening and evaluation. When bids are submitted, the procurement official determines whether or not the bids are responsive
to the solicitation documents.

NIGP's (1996) *Dictionary of Purchasing Terms* offers the following definitions:

   • *Responsive Bidder:* a vendor who has submitted a bid, which conforms
     in all material respects to the requirements, stated in the IFB. The
     notation "see informality" follows the definition.

   • *Informality:* a minor or immaterial defect in a bid that is a matter of
     form rather than of substance; a variation of a bid or proposal from
     the exact requirements of the IFB or RFP, which can be corrected or

waived without being prejudicial to other bidders, and has no material effect on the price, quality, quantity, or delivery schedule for the goods, services, or construction being procured. The notation "see waiver of mistake or informality" follows the definition.

- *Waiver of Mistake or Informality:* the act of disregarding minor informalities, errors, or technical non-conformities in the bid that will not adversely affect the competition adversely or prejudice one bidder in favor of another.

Determination of Responsiveness

Determination of a proposal's responsiveness is a judgment call by the procurement official. The procurement official must determine whether or not the omission of any requirement of the solicitation document or a modification thereof is material. Such a determination cannot be made without considering the possibility of waiving these deviations as possible minor technicalities. Differences in procurement policies in different jurisdictions will result in different interpretations being made that are based on the professional judgment of the procurement officials in conjunction with their end-users and legal departments.

Generally, proposals will be deemed to be non-responsive if they:

- substitute their standard terms and conditions for those included in the solicitation document;
- qualify their offers in such a manner as to nullify or limit their liability to the jurisdiction;
- offer an all-or-none proposal;
- fail to conform with required delivery schedules as set forth in the solicitation or the permissible alternatives;
- qualify their prices in such a manner that the proposal price cannot be determined;
- make the proposal contingent upon the receipt of other awards currently under consideration;
- make the purchasing authority responsible for determining that the offeror's products or services conform to the specifications;
- limit the rights of the contracting authority under any contract clause;
- fail to provide required bonds.

Examples of minor irregularities may include:

- failure to furnish with the proposal certain required information regarding the firm's qualifications to perform the contract, such as financial statements;

- failure to submit required descriptive information on the product offered;

- failure to provide requested samples;

- failure to return the proper number (copies) of executed documents or attachments, including certifications and affidavits;

- failure to return the proposal addendum or amendment, if on the face of the offeror's submittal, it is apparent to the procurement official that the offeror was aware of the addendum and their proposal was submitted in accordance therewith;

- failure to sign off on the proposal when evidence is submitted with the documents that clearly shows that this proposal was the one intended to bind the offeror and failure to sign was strictly an oversight; or

- failure to provide required insurance documents.

Judgment calls are influenced by interpretation of the word "material" in the definition of responsive proposer. As a general rule, procurement officials should consider the impact of omission or errors in the proposal. Were they merely matters of fact that are not subject to change with time, such as descriptive literature or samples? Correction of this type of omission generally will not afford the offeror an unfair advantage or opportunity to change their bid/proposal and, in effect, get a second bite at the apple. Certainly, failing to supply the requested number of copies does not impact the offeror's price or afford the offeror an advantage over competitors.

How to Select the Right/Best-Value Offer

Offeror selection is becoming more critical as procurement officials develop innovative ways of doing business. If procurement officials are going to practice stockless purchasing or use a just-in-time delivery schedule, the dependency upon a given offeror becomes even more critical. The offeror becomes an integral part of the jurisdiction's overall operation—the offeror becomes a partner. Selecting the right offeror requires more intensive evaluation than a simple determination of who is the lowest responsive and responsible bidder.

A good procurement official-offeror relationship makes it easier to realize superior performance and extra service from a given offeror. The goal should be to establish mutual trust and confidence between the offeror and the jurisdiction. Procurement officials must take six important offeror-oriented actions in order to satisfy their responsibility for selection and management of the right offerors (Dobler & Burt, 1996). Procurement officials should:

- develop and maintain a viable offeror base;
- address the appropriate strategic and tactical issues;
- ensure that potential offerors are evaluated carefully and that they have the potential to be satisfactory supply partners;
- decide whether to use competitive bidding or negotiation as the basis for the source selection;
- select the appropriate source or be the team leader responsible for this task; and
- manage the selected offeror to ensure timely delivery of the required quality at the right price.

The process starts with the development of offeror goodwill. The business sector has long recognized that customer good will has value and constitutes a valuable asset. Government procurement officials are now beginning to realize that offeror goodwill is equally important. If procurement officials are to develop a base of firms who are interested in pursuing government business, procurement officials must create an attractive business atmosphere for them. This includes making them aware of jurisdiction's procurement policies, rules, and procedures. Procurement officials must provide them with a manual or other written document that provides information on how to do business with the jurisdiction. They have a right to know how procurement officials select vendors and how their performance is evaluated. The forms and solicitation documents should be simple. Procurement officials should make prompt payments and have uniform contract administration procedures so that the potential offeror world is convinced that procurement officials do business in a fair and equitable way.

Ethics is a major issue in the selection of offerors. Jurisdictions try to avoid doing business with any offerors that are known to have questionable business ethics. Procurement officials do not wish to be tainted by associating with such firms. On the contrary, ethical firms may be discouraged from competing if they believe procurement officials conduct RFPs in an unethical way (NIGP, 2001). Ethics also involve procurement officials' personal behaviors. Procurement officials need to be aware of and avoid potential conflicts of interest or the appearance of such potential conflicts. For example, procurement officials should disqualify themselves from being the individuals evaluating bids and awarding contracts to firms by which procurement officials may gain or appear to gain some reward.

Effective competition does not necessarily mean a large mailing list of potential vendors, but it does mean a list of dependable, competent offerors. An adequate offeror base is essential for the well-being of any jurisdiction. The determination of the optimal number of offerors is a critical and strategic issue. Recent tendencies in the private sector have been to reduce the number of offerors that a company maintains. Quality, rather than quantity, seems to be yielding the greatest benefits. The argument in favor of one offeror is that better pricing will result from a higher dollar volume contract and that the procurement official will have more influence with the offeror. Additionally, lower administrative costs may result.

An argument in favor of dual or multiple sources of supplies is that protection will be afforded to the company or the jurisdiction in the event some problem occurs with the single offeror. Many firms maintain two suppliers: a primary supplier and a secondary back-up. In the event the primary offeror does not perform well, the customer can order additional supplies from the backup or secondary offeror. This keeps all of the offerors on their toes.

The world keeps shrinking. International trade treaties, such as the North American Free Trade Agreement (NAFTA), have influenced the amount of foreign goods purchased by procurement officials. Much of foreign purchasing makes good economic sense. Procurement professionals in the new millennium will have to consider possible offerors from foreign sources as well as from national and/or local sources. Foreign purchasing involves new methodologies and risks. Procurement officials have to decide whether to purchase directly or through local distributors. Deliveries, lead times, and payment procedures play a role in the decision-making process as well. Certainly, evaluating foreign offerors is much more difficult than evaluating local offerors.

Political and socioeconomic considerations also enter into the deliberations in the selection of a vendor. Consideration must be given to environmental issues, local preferences, and preferences for traditionally underutilized, discriminated against, and disadvantaged groups. The selection of the offeror may not always be a simple low bidder award.

Other factors that will enhance the number of responses from the vendor community to solicitations are the contract types that procurement officials choose to use. Although many jurisdictions do not currently allow long-term contracts, governmental entities are becoming more aware that the ultimate benefit available to the jurisdiction of good quality goods and services at a reasonable price depends upon the offerors' ability to make process changes that would lower their and the jurisdiction's costs. This may require that longer-term contracts be permitted. If the procurement officials are going to offer incentives to offerors, longer-term contracts may be more desirable than short-term financial rewards. This is especially true when procurement officials look to privatization of specific governmental functions and expect that the contracted offeror will have to make some initial investments. Industry has long practiced this concept of partnering.

Conclusion

The new millennium offers the procurement professional new challenges and opportunities. Procurement officials will have to embrace many new concepts, especially as they impact the relationships procurement officials have and will develop with offerors. The new relationships will be based on the premise that procurement officials and reputable suppliers are dependent upon each other and both stand to gain from this relationship. Procurement officials will seek out qualified offerors in much the same way that offerors are currently seeking customers.

Offerors will be selected carefully on the basis of their management philosophies, company ethics, reputation, prior performance record, innovation, delivery capabilities, service, and financial considerations. Procurement officials will appreciate the fact that most offerors are experts at what they do and traditionally have been the leaders in new product and service development. Competition is really all about who can build a better mousetrap. Why shouldn't procurement officials as guardians of the public trust take advantage of these opportunities for the benefit of their jurisdictions?

As professionals, procurement officials know market conditions and will pick the best time to obtain competitive proposals. Procurement officials will develop a mutually acceptable contract that will be fair to both the jurisdictions and offerors. The true professionals will be able to evaluate vendors to determine if the offerors are capable of providing the needed goods or services (responsible) and have addressed the material requirements of the solicitation (responsive). Having the knowledge to make price and cost analyses, procurement officials will successfully complete the process by negotiating fair contracts. Procurement officials will not hesitate to make recommendations to elected officials to make legislative changes to create situations where jurisdictions are assured of quality offerors, products, and services at a cost the taxpayers will appreciate.

References

Dobler, D. W., & Burt, D. N. (1996). *Purchasing and supply management* (6ᵗʰ ed.). New York: McGraw-Hill.

Cavinato, J. L., & Kauffman, R. G. (2000). *The purchasing handbook: A guide for the purchasing and supply professional* (6th ed.). New York: McGraw-Hill Companies, Inc.

Fearon, H. E., Dobler, D. W., & Killen, K. H. (2000). *The purchasing handbook* (5ᵗʰ ed). New York: McGraw-Hill Companies, Inc.

Federal Acquisition Institute (1999). *The federal acquisition process.* Washington, DC: Federal Acquisition Institute.

Federal Acquisition Regulation Web site, http://www.arnet.gov/far/loadmainre. html.

Government of Nova Scotia Procurement Branch (2002, March). *Departmental guide to the preparation of a request for proposal.* Halifax, Nova Scotia: Government of Nova Scotia.

Harney, D. F. (1992). *Service contracting: A local government guide.* Washington, DC: International City Management Association.

National Association of State Purchasing Officials (NASPO) (1997). *State and local government purchasing principles and practices* (5th ed.). Lexington, KY: NASPO.

National Institute of Governmental Purchasing, Inc. (NIGP) (1996). *Dictionary of purchasing terms* (5th ed.). Herndon, VA: NIGP.

National Institute of Governmental Purchasing, Inc. (NIGP) (2001). *Advanced public procurement.* Herndon, VA: NIGP.

National Institute of Governmental Purchasing, Inc. (NIGP) (2004). *Sourcing in the public sector.* Herndon, VA: NIGP.

Pennsylvania Department of General Services (2001, March). *Field procurement handbook.* Harrisburg, PA: Commonwealth of Pennsylvania.

Pettijohn, C., & Babich, K.S. (2004). *Sourcing in the public sector.* Herndon, VA: NIGP

State of New Mexico, Department of Health (1999, July). *Request for proposal procurement guide.* Santa Fe, NM: State of New Mexico.

State of Washington Department of Labor and Industries. Information Technology Professional Services (1997, March 7). *Request for proposal.* Available from http//www.pbs3.gsa.gov/vendor.htm (Federal Government Forms 254 and 255).

Young, R. R. (2000). Managing residual disposition: Achieving economy, environmental responsibility, and competitive advantage using the supply chain framework. *Journal of Supply Chain Management, 12,* 57-66.

CHAPTER 6

Evaluation Methodologies

Introduction

*E*valuation is very important in the RFP process. There are major differences between Invitation for Bids (IFB) and Request for Proposal (RFP) processes. Table 22 and Figure 9 illustrate some of the major differences in the evaluation techniques between bids and requests for proposals.

Table 22

Evaluation Differences between IFB and RFP

IFB	RFP
Normally carried out by procurement official with technical approval from end-user	Always a team effort by the Evaluation Committee
Vendors are compared to the spec. only and either pass or fail	Vendors are compared to the spec. and are scored comparison to each other

Source: Corwin, S. (1999). *How to handle competitive negotiations.* A paper presented at the Annual Forum of the National Institute of Governmental Purchasing, Inc., Halifax, Canada.

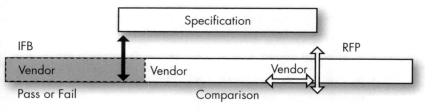

Figure 9 - *Evaluation differences between RFP and IFB.*

Initiating Evaluation

Once responsiveness has been determined by procurement, Technical Proposals are forwarded to the evaluation team. Price proposals may be assigned to specialists in the contracting office for evaluation and may also be furnished in part or in whole to technical evaluators for determining whether the technical approach and price are consistent and represent a reasonable amount of risk (i.e., for cost realism analyses). If field pricing support or audit is required, copies of the proposals will be furnished to the appropriate organizations. When distributing copies, procurement is charged with safeguarding the proposals, other proprietary information, and source selection information against unauthorized disclosure.

Technical Evaluation by Committee

The technical evaluation review should take the following into account.

- The requirements documents and related aspects of the RFP;
- The solicitation's stated evaluation factors, along with any special standards of responsibility;
- Instructions for proposal preparation;
- Oral presentations, when the solicitation provides for oral proposals as supplements to written proposals; and
- The written language of the quotations or proposals.

The technical evaluation is important because it will:

- determine whether the proposals or quotations are technically acceptable and in compliance with the intent of the documents;
- allow for the inclusion of non-price evaluation factors, such as past performance, and justify the rankings;
- review the proposed labor mix, hours of direct labor, material mix and quantities to support the analysis of proposed costs;
- determine the need and prepare for communication/fact-finding prior to discussions;
- establish the competitive range (or select proposers, if any, for negotiations of quotations);
- identify and support technical negotiation objectives; and
- provide constructive information to unsuccessful offerors regarding their Technical Proposals (debriefings).

Determination of Responsibility

The National Institute of Governmental Purchasing, Inc.'s (NIGP) (1996) *Dictionary of Purchasing Terms* defines a responsible bidder or offeror as "a bidder or offeror who has the capability in all respects to perform fully the contract requirements, and the experience, integrity, perseverance, reliability, capacity, facilities, equipment, and credit that will assure good faith performance" (p. 73). Note that the definition allows for the use of criteria dealing with the management of the firm, financial strength, ethics, and past performance as well as the technical capabilities of the supplier.

The determination of the offeror's responsibility need not be made at the time of the bid/proposal opening, but this must occur during the evaluation process by one or all of the Evaluation Team members. Procurement officials can make this determination at any time up to the actual award of the contract. The determination should be as objective as possible. The definition suggests that the following factors be reviewed as part of a proposal's analysis:

- *Experience:* determined by examining vendor files, which indicate how the supplier performed in the past, and by making reference checks that will tell how the supplier has performed for others.

- *Integrity, Perseverance, and Reliability:* determined by conducting an in-depth evaluation of the management of the firm, its philosophies, policies, reputation in the industry, and the company's quality control programs.

- *Capacity, Facilities, and Equipment:* determined by information submitted by the proposer or by plant visits, if deemed appropriate.

- *Credit:* determined by an investigation of the firm's financial statements and/or credit reports as well as bonding capabilities.

- *Supplier Experience:* evaluation of the supplier's past experience by reviewing the vendor/supplier files or conducting reference checks.

- *Reference Checks:* The information obtained from reference checks is highly dependent upon the questions asked. In today's society, people are reluctant to make negative comments about anyone for fear of possible litigation. The Committee should develop questions that can be answered objectively and simply and should be written in a specific format. Furthermore, it is a good idea for only one person (whenever practical) to call all of the references, as it can be assured that the questions are being asked in the same voice modulation, sequence, selection of words, and without differences in mannerisms that might influence the response.

The following is a list of representative questions that could be asked. Each Evaluation Team should make appropriate modifications to suit its specific needs. Note that these questions attempt to solicit factual statements.

- Who was the firm's project manager?
- How was he/she to work with?
- How many times was the proposer late with deliveries?
- Were there any contracting issues that were difficult to resolve?
- Was the project manager easy to contact?
- How quickly did he/she return your phone calls?
- Were there any quality questions or issues to resolve?
- Did the company handle complaints quickly and efficiently?
- Did the company change any prices during the life of the contract?
- Were shipments properly marked?

What to Look For in Terms of Management, Quality Control, Ethics, Facilities, and Financial Evaluation

Management

A well-managed firm seldom experiences the instability that results from continuing labor problems and financial difficulties. The selected firm should always strive to reduce its operating costs and enhance its quality-control programs and the service it renders to its client base. Technical competency alone does not assure that a firm will be a good supplier of goods and services. It is the firm's technical competency, financial strength and, most important, its management philosophy that will determine how a potential supplier will ultimately perform. Management is responsible for determining the attitudes and stability of the workforce, the morale of all personnel, the firm's service policies and, above all, its ethical behavior. Management will set the tone for the firm's business behavior that will be followed throughout the life of the contract.

Quality Control

It is becoming more common for firms in the private sector and many governmental jurisdictions to do business, if not exclusively, at least preferentially, with firms that have made a commitment to Total Quality Management (TQM). Procurement officials should be looking to select firms that have made the commitment to total quality as the company's way of life. This is demonstrated by the education and training of its employees, the use of the quality methods and especially by listening to their customers. It must be determined if the firm has adopted Quality Assurance/Quality Control (QA/QC) measures. Are they International Organization for Standardization (ISO) 9000 certified? Do they require similar assurances from their subcontractors?

Ethics

What is the reputation of the firm? Would doing business with them in any way create negative impressions of the jurisdiction? Does the firm have its own Code of Ethics? Very often, the behavior a firm expects from its purchasing and administrative personnel will be a clue to what procurement officials can expect from its sales and service people.

Facilities

To determine a firm's manufacturing, warehousing, or distribution capabilities, the Committee may rely on the written information supplied; or, in some cases, the Committee may choose to visit the site. Desirable firms will have modern, suitable equipment and enough of it to meet the quantity requirements anticipated in the contract. The firm should have sufficient staff that possess the right skills. As the facility is checked, Committee members can talk to the labor force and get impressions about the relationship between management and the workforce, the attitude of the workforce, and possibly some of their QC procedures. When necessary, determine if adequate storage is available and an appropriate level of inventory maintained, especially if any sort of a just-in-time contract is being considered.

Financial Evaluation

A qualified expert from the finance department should conduct an investigation of the prospective vendor's financial condition. While not mandatory, procurement officials should be able to interpret financial statements and make meaningful comparisons.

Typically, the financial information required will be found in *Dunn & Bradstreet Business Reports, Moody's Industrials*, and other financial publications. A review of financial statements and credit reports can reveal if a potential supplier is completely incapable of performing satisfactorily. Financial stability is essential for firms to assure continuity of supplies and reliability of product quality. Imagine the difficulty of working with:

- a financially weak firm that cannot maintain quality;
- a firm that does not have sufficient working capital to settle an expensive claim; or
- a financially unsound supplier that cannot afford overtime to meet a promised delivery date.

Usually, financially sound companies are also well managed (Dobler & Burt, 1996, p. 242).

Table 23 is a summary, or directional flow chart, that points the Evaluation Team to the different methodologies that should be used in evaluating proposals. The different methodologies are designed to apply to the different scenarios that the Evaluation Team chose in the RFP. These scenarios are described in Chapter 4.

Table 23

Methodology Flowchart

Issue RFP with Description of Process Scenario and Evaluation Criteria		
Select Scenario 1A or 1B	Select Scenario 2A, 2B or 2C	Select Scenario 3A or 3B
Scenario 1A Award	Scenario 2A Award	Scenario 3A Award
Scenario 1B Award	Scenario 2B Award	
• Award to lowest priced acceptable proposal	• Award to lowest priced acceptable proposal	• Open prices only from highest technically ranked firms
• Award to highest technically ranked firm in competitive range, or best value	• Award to highest technically ranked firm in competitive range, or best value	• Award to highest technically ranked firm in competitive range, or best value
	Scenario 2C Award	Scenario 3B Award
	• "Two-step or hybrid"	• See best value award methodologies

Verbal Evaluations

Evaluations need not always be numerical, but can be verbal as well. The following are some of the verbal descriptions used.

- Go, No Go
- Priority statements

- Decisional Rule
- Tradeoff Analysis
- Lowest Price Acceptable
- Air Force Color System
- Adjective Ratings

Go, No-Go

Another system for evaluating proposals is known as go, no-go. It can be applied to major areas and elements of management, operational suitability and other criteria, when identified for evaluation. This procedure is frequently used in situations in which the product is subjected to testing. Management may be utilized as an instrument for evaluation on the basis of go, no-go, providing the offeror proposes a management plan that supports the promises made in their proposal. This plan must adequately meet the requirements of management. In evaluation, the proposal is either adequate—go—or inadequate—no-go. If it is inadequate, the Evaluation Team may solicit from the offeror a revised proposal designed to make management adequate for the task at hand. In a "go" situation, the element will not be further scored or summarized.

If a factor is scored "adequate," it is no longer relevant in the evaluation process, and the award is made on the basis of the other criteria. An "adequate" score in an area is a minimum requirement for selection. The RFP may provide for award to the offeror with the lowest overall price among those offers found acceptable in the technical and management areas. Technical and management criteria are scored on a go, no-go basis.

Tradeoff Analysis

This approach requires the Evaluation Team to evaluate the value of technical differences between proposals in order to determine if these differences justify paying the cost or price differential. Cost/technical tradeoffs may be made at the discretion of the Evaluation Team, subject to the test of rationality and consistency with the established evaluation criteria. The Evaluation Team may recommend an award to offerors with higher technical scores and higher costs if the result is consistent with the evaluation criteria and if it is determined that the technical difference outweighs the cost difference. Tradeoff analysis is a system that requires the Evaluation Team to evaluate the value of technical differences among proposals in order to determine if these differences justify paying the cost or price differential. Technical criteria are point-scored, with technical differences being of more relative importance than price.

The Evaluation Team has a great deal of discretion when using tradeoff analysis. In competitive negotiation, purchasing regulations do not require that awards be made on the basis of lowest cost. Where a solicitation does not mention the relative importance of cost, cost and technical considerations are given equal merit. The Evaluation Team has broad discretion in determining the manner and extent to which it will utilize technical and cost evaluation results. Costs/technical tradeoffs may be made, administered only by the test of rationality and consistency, with the established evaluation criteria.

The Evaluation Team may choose to use a fixed weight method or a variable weight method.

A purchasing jurisdiction may award offerors with higher technical scores and higher costs if the result is consistent with the evaluation criteria and if it is determined that the technical difference outweighs the cost difference. When tradeoff analysis is used, the RFP must inform offerors that the procurement official will determine the weight to be accorded cost criteria after determining the relative merits of the Technical Proposals. Cost factors are not scored because the weight to be accorded them can only be judged after the relative merits of the proposals have been determined from a technical standpoint.

Lowest Priced Acceptable Proposal

The lowest-priced acceptable proposal is an alternative method that entails awarding to the lowest priced proposal among all proposals found acceptable in the technical and management areas. All evaluation criteria except price are scored on a go, no-go basis. Technically unacceptable proposals may still be included in the competitive range if they are capable of being made acceptable. For instance, an award on a fixed-price contract can be made to the lowest-priced offeror meeting the RFP's technical specifications. An award may also be made to the technically acceptable proposal with the lowest total discounted life cycle cost.

Color Coding

Four levels of ratings are used that are defined prior to evaluation, e.g., blue: exceptional, exceeds specified performance or capability; green: acceptable, meets standards, good probability of success; yellow: marginal, weak, low probability of success but correctable; and red: unacceptable, not minimally acceptable. Whatever rating or scoring system is used, it is important to ensure that the descriptions permit significant differences in order to prevent leveling of evaluations.

Adjective Ratings

Terms such as Excellent, Good, Average or Above Normal, Normal and Below Normal are used. Variations of these adjectival words can be used. Each adjective must also contain the standard that must be met to achieve that weight.

Numerical System of Evaluation

Points are assigned to factors and can be further broken down to the sub-factor level. The more important the factor or sub-factor, the higher the number of points assigned to that factor or sub-factor. The Evaluation Team may choose to use a **fixed weight method** or a **variable weight method**.

Fixed Weights

The most commonly used system is fixed weights. This is a simple mathematical weighting system. The Evaluation Team assigns weight to each evaluation criteria by percentage distribution. Weights may be distributed in the major criteria based on 100%. Within the criteria, a 100% distribution may be used again to fix the relative importance of each criterion. A similar method is to determine the relative value of the criteria according to their expected impact on the life cycle cost of the item being procured.

Variable Weights

In many cases, the Evaluation Team will determine that fixed weights should not control the source selection in all situations. The most common instance in which this occurs is where the jurisdiction determines that cost/price should become more important when Technical Proposals are of relative equal merit. For instance, the RFP may state that the degree of importance of cost as a factor could become greater, depending upon the equality of the proposals evaluated for other criteria evaluated.

Evaluation Methodologies for Scenario 1

Evaluation for proposals in this scenario is straightforward. In scenario 1A, the Evaluation Team evaluates the Q&E Statements and selects firms that they believe are capable of carrying out the proposed work. The Team then solicits Technical Proposals from these firms and then ranks them. The evaluation may be either verbal or numerical, although numerical is generally more accepted. The Evaluation Team then negotiates with the highest ranked firm, as will be discussed under Scenario 2A.

If the Evaluation Team chooses to follow Scenario 2B, it solicits both Technical and Cost proposals from the firms chosen as in Scenario 1A—the difference being that the Team receives Cost Proposals at the same time they receive Technical Proposals. The Team would then evaluate the proposals using the methodologies described under Scenario 3.

Evaluation Methodologies for Scenario 2

Score Sheet Development

There are several ways to develop and use score sheets. They can vary from simple to complex. The score sheet selected by the Evaluation Team will depend upon the complexity of the solicitation. Table 24 provides a sample of a relatively simplistic score sheet.

Table 24

Simplistic Score Sheet

Criteria	Weight	Firm #1	Firm #2	Firm #3
Q&E	50% or 50	Each firm is evaluated in each sub-category and is awarded points ranging zero (0) up to fifty (50)		
Technical	50% or 50			
Total	100% or 100			

Source: Corwin, S. (1999). *How to handle competitive negotiations*. A paper presented at the Annual Forum of the National Institute of Governmental Purchasing, Inc., Halifax, Canada.

Each of the factors shown above may be subdivided into several sub-factors. The division of evaluation factors between Q&E and Technical need not be 50/50. Any combination of the two is permissible. The Evaluation Team determines this when the criteria are developed. A more refined score sheet is shown in Table 25.

Table 25

Complex Score Sheet

Criteria	Weight	Firm #1	Firm #2	Firm #3
Q&E	50			
Firm Exp.	25			
Facilities	25			
Technical	50			
Schedule	25			
Work Plan	25			
Grand Total	100			

Each firm is evaluated in each sub-category and is awarded points ranging from (0) up to twenty-five (25).

Source: Corwin, S. (1999). *How to handle competitive negotiations.* A paper presented at the Annual Forum of the National Institute of Governmental Purchasing, Inc., Halifax, Canada.

At this point the Evaluation Team has ranked the firms from a Q&E and Technical standpoint. The Team must now make the selection. If the evaluation Team follows the scenario 2A procedure, it negotiates with the highest ranked firm. If the Team cannot come to an agreement with this firm, it ends the negotiation process and goes to the second choice. This process may continue until the Team has a satisfactory agreement with a qualified firm that can perform the work in a satisfactory manner.

If the Evaluation Team follows the Scenario 2B procedure, it will get prices from the highest ranked firms (sometimes called the "shortlist"). Be careful when developing the Solicitation Document not to specify a specific number of firms to be included on the "short list." Experience has shown that when the Evaluation Team lists all of the firms with their mathematical scores (either committee-average or committee-cumulative), a natural break point occurs. This is where the point score spread is significant and meaningful.

This is where the verbal evaluation methods are of benefit to the Evaluation Team. The Team can apply any either of the following techniques to make a professional judgment.

- Tradeoff analysis among the highest ranked firms only; or
- Lowest price acceptable among the highest ranked firms only.

Dollar ($) Per Point

In this methodology, the Evaluation Team divides the price of the proposal by the number of points awarded to the firms on the short list for their combined technical and Q&E portion of their proposal. For example:

- Firm #1 received 850 points (average of the Committee), and their proposal was ultimately priced at $450,000. Therefore, their proposal had a cost per point of $529.41 ($450,000 divided by 850).

- Firm #2 received 950 points (average of the Committee) and their proposal was ultimately priced at $650,000. Therefore, their proposal had a cost per point of $684.21 ($650,000 divided by 950).

Firm #1 is, therefore, deemed to offer the greatest value. Although Firm #2 may have been ranked higher from a Q&E/Technical standpoint, the difference in cost cannot be justified.

Scenario 2C is really a hybrid between an RFP and a bid. It has elements of both procurement methodologies. Step 1 in this process is to get the Q&E/Technical portions of the offerors' proposals as the Evaluation Team did in Scenarios 2A and 2B. A short list is developed. The Team reviews the best suggestions taken from the highest ranked firms and our own judgment as to what will best satisfy our needs. The Team then issues a revised SOW to only the short-listed firms. These firms will then submit prices based on the revised SOW, with the award being made to the lowest priced submittal (or the Team can even call it a bid).

Evaluation Methodologies for Scenario 3

Each of the factors shown in Table 26 may be subdivided into several subfactors. The distribution of evaluation factors among Q&E, Technical, and Cost need not be 40/40/20. Any combination of the three is permissible. The Evaluation Team determines this when developing the criteria. A more refined score-sheet would look like Table 27.

Table 26
Simple Score Sheet

Criteria	Weight	Firm #1	Firm #2	Firm #3
Q&E	40% or 40	Each firm is evaluated in each sub-category and is awarded points ranging from (0) up to forty (40).		
Technical	40% or 40			
Cost	20% or 20	Each firm is awarded up to 20 points.		
Total	100% or 100			

Source: Corwin, S. (1999). *How to handle competitive negotiations.* A paper presented at the Annual Forum of the National Institute of Governmental Purchasing, Inc., Halifax, Canada.

Table 27
Refined Score Sheet

Criteria	Weight	Firm #1	Firm #2	Firm #3
Q&E	40			
Firm Exp.	20	Each firm is evaluated in each sub-category and is awarded points ranging from (0) up to twenty (20).		
Facilities	20			
Technical	40			
Schedule	20			
Work Plan	20			
Cost	20	Each firm is awarded up to 20 points.		
Grand Total	100			

Source: Corwin, S. (1999). *How to handle competitive negotiations.* A paper presented at the Annual Forum of the National Institute of Governmental Purchasing, Inc., Halifax, Canada.

There are two basic methods used to integrate the offerors' costs with their Q&E/Technical scores. One is to award the low price with the maximum number of points, and the other is to award the average price with the maximum points. In the case of the latter method, the reason is to discourage offerors from submitting low-ball prices and to discourage unreasonably high costs.

Reward Low Price

In this scenario, assume the Evaluation Team has received three proposals: Firm #1 with a price of $400,000; Firm #2 with a price of $600,000; and Firm #3 with a price of $800,000.

- Firm #1 would receive the maximum of 20 points.
- Firm #2 would receive $400,000 divided by $600,000 or 67% of the 20 maximum allowable points =13.3 points (or 13 for ease of math).
- Firm #3 would receive $400,000 divided by $800,000 or 50% of the 20 maximum allowable points = 10 points.

Reward Average Price

The data in this scenario is the same as in Scenario 3. The Evaluation Team received the following costs from the three firms.

- Firm #1 = $400,000
- Firm #2 = $600,000
- Firm #3 = $800,000

In this case, the average cost is $600,000, and the Team would award Firm #2 the 20 maximum allowable points and Firm #1 and Firm #3 a lesser number of points, depending on the formula the selected. An example of this type of evaluation is exhibited at the end of this chapter. A more sophisticated or detailed breakdown of evaluation criteria is shown in Table 28.

Table 28

Detailed Numerical Evaluation Sheet

Criteria	Weight	Outstanding (10 pts.)	Adequate to Good (6-8 pts.)	Marginally Acceptable (3 or 4 pts.)	Unacceptable (0 pts.)	Su
Technical	40					
Q&E	40					
Cost	20					
Grand Total	100					

Grading:

Outstanding = 10. There is no 9 as a score.
Adequate to Good = 6, 7 or 8. There is no 5 as a score.
Marginally Acceptable = 3 or 4. There is no 1 or 2 as a score.
Unacceptable = 0.

The Evaluation Team should use a separate score sheet for each offeror. Based on their professional evaluation, Team members individually assign a score to each evaluation criterion, multiply the score by weight to obtain the sub-total and add the sub-total columns to obtain the grand total score for firm. The maximum score achievable will be equal to 1,000. This can be broken down into further sub-factors, as previously discussed.

Each of these factors may be subdivided into several sub-factors. The distribution among Q&E, Technical, and Cost need not be 40/40/20. Any combination of the 3 is permissible. The Evaluation Team determines this when the criteria are developed.

Each rating criterion is given a weight factor, which when multiplied by the points assigned by the Committee in its evaluation, results in the total weighted points for each criterion. These weight factors are determined based on prior work experience as the appropriate emphasis to be placed on each evaluation criterion in order to successfully carry out the needed tasks. These weight factors are included in the RFP.

Each Team member evaluates each proposal for jurisdictional support (including personnel), experience, proposal requirements (**Q&E Section**) and the **Technical Approach**. Each factor or sub-factor is awarded 0 to 10 points as follows:

Unacceptable: (0) Points. Zero (0) points are awarded to firms in any category in which they either fail to respond, fail to provide any information, or provide information which cannot be understood.

Marginal: 3 or 4 Points. 3 or 4 points are awarded to responses considered to be marginally acceptable. For example:

- The proposal reiterated a requirement, but offered no explanation of how or what was to be accomplished in the Technical Scope of Work.
- The proposal offered an explanation of how or what was to be accomplished in the Technical Scope of Work but may have contained inaccurate statements or references which impacted their approach but did not totally negate the technical approach.
- The proposal referred to the quality of their jurisdiction, but the vendor did not supply adequate descriptions of its past experience/personnel or provided resumes of people and/or case histories of work experience that was not relevant.

The Team cannot award 1, 2 or 5 points. The purpose is to create differences among the scores awarded in order to separate the vendors and help create meaningful rankings.

Adequate to Good: 6, 7 or 8 Points.

- Varying amounts of points are awarded if the jurisdictional, personnel and experience (**Q&E**) section of the proposal satisfies the requirement and provides information on the company's capabilities, personal resumes, and case history reports on prior similar types of efforts in clear detail, including job names, job responsibilities, and types of assignments, and the jurisdiction personnel and experience are adequate to good for the job.

- Varying amounts of points are awarded if the Technical Proposal satisfies the requirement and describes specifically how and/or what is to be accomplished in clear detail, including sample products and illustrative materials (i.e., in diagrams, charts, graphs, etc.).

You cannot award 9 points as per above discussion.

Outstanding: 10 Points. 10 points are awarded if the proposal satisfies the requirements and describes specifically how and what will be accomplished in a superior manner, both quantitatively and qualitatively for their technical approach and the quantity and quality of their previous similar jobs and the experience and training of their personnel (Corwin, 1999).

Cost and Price Analysis

Price Analysis

Prior to the negotiation component of review and award, procurement officials need to establish, through price and cost analyses, a price objective, i.e., the final expected fair price. In developing such objectives, the primary goal is to negotiate a fair and reasonable price, as shown in Table 29.

Table 29

What is a Fair and Reasonable Price?

In pricing a contract, the Purchasing Official's most important objective is to balance the contract type, cost, and profit or fee negotiated to achieve a total result and price fair and reasonable to both the buyer (i.e., the Government) and the seller (i.e., the contractor).

"Fair to the buyer" means a price that is in line with (or below) either of the following:

- The fair market value of the contract deliverable. "Fair market value" is the price that procurement officials should expect to pay given the prices of bona fide sales between informed buyers and informed sellers under like market conditions in competitive markets for deliverables of like type, quality, and quantity.

- The (1) total allowable cost of providing the contract deliverable that would have been incurred by a well managed, responsible firm using reasonably efficient and economical methods of performance + (2) a reasonable profit.

Can a firm fixed price be considered "fair," even if the seller's actual costs exceed the price?

Yes, if the high costs result from slipshod management, obsolete tooling, and other such causes. The question is how the firm fixed price compares to what the work ought to have cost.

"Fair" to the seller means a price that is realistic in terms of the seller's ability to satisfy the terms and conditions of the contract. Why should the Purchasing Official care if a low offer is realistic? Because an unrealistic price puts both parties at risk. The risk to the Government is that the seller to cut its losses might:

- cut corners on product quality;
- deliver late;
- default, forcing a time-consuming reprocurement;
- refuse to deal with the jurisdiction in the future; or
- be forced out of business entirely.

Source: Federal Acquisition Institute (1999). *The federal acquisition process* (p. 7.28). Washington, DC: Federal Acquisition Institute.

No matter which evaluation methodology the Evaluation Team chooses, at some point in the evaluation process the Team will be required to determine or evaluate the reasonableness of the price requested by some or all of the offerors or possibly only a single price by the successful offeror. There are only two ways to accomplish this. The first method is price analysis, which is an examination and comparison of offerors' price proposals or bids to one another and to the buyer's estimate of reasonable price. It does not include examination and evaluation of separate elements of cost and profit.

Price analysis is defined as the examination of a seller's price, bid, or proposal by comparison with reasonable price benchmarks without examination and evaluation of the cost elements and the profit making up the price. Typically, the buyer uses four ways to perform this analysis (Dobler & Burt, 1996, p. 305):

- Review the competitive price proposals.
- Compare with catalog or published price data.
- Compare with historical prices.
- Obtain data from other jurisdictions that have purchased the same product.

The second method is cost analysis, which is a review and evaluation of actual or anticipated cost data. The data includes labor, material, overhead, and general and administrative costs. It involves applying experience, knowledge, and judgment to data in an attempt to discern reasonable estimated costs.

NIGP (1996) defines price analysis as "the process of examining and evaluating price data without evaluating separate cost elements or proposed profit (as is done in cost analysis) to assist in arriving at prices to be paid and costs to be reimbursed" (p. 62).

When negotiating, price analysis or cost analysis is required to arrive at a satisfactory contract. There are times when cost analysis would be more useful, and the procurement officer will have to determine when to use which method or analytical approach. Price analysis negotiation (often referred to simply as price negotiation) is the most commonly used technique when negotiating for price. Contract negotiation based on a price analysis may offer several advantages over cost analysis negotiation, including:

- the shortened time of negotiation;
- the procurement official is able to conduct these negotiations without technical assistance; and
- the fact that the price data is much easier to obtain than cost data (Dobler & Burt, 1996, p. 377).

The most commonly used method of price analysis is the comparison of prices received in response to the RFP. This system works well when reviewing responses to solicitations that are independently submitted and the offers are each responsive to the requirements. Procurement officials should always be convinced that the price is fair and reasonable, when awarding a contract and especially so when only one proposal is received or when negotiating a sole-source solicitation contract.

The second most common method of price analysis is that of looking at histori-cal prices. An historical comparison is a review of the pricing received today as compared to the prices received last year or when the agency last received quotations. Consideration must be given as to whether there have been any changes in the economic climate that have caused a price deviation greater than expected. If lower prices are received, reviewers should be looking to determine if new players have entered the marketplace or if new technologies have caused the price to decrease.

Vendor Files

Constant record keeping and maintenance of databases is required to protect meaningful data. Good files must include, at a minimum, commodity, end-user, and vendor files. Computerization is a must. Vendor files are critical to providing information regarding suppliers. These files include the amount of money expended with a supplier, the types of services or commodities pur-chased, and the number of complaints and difficulties with the vendor that have been noted. Vendor files are developed and maintained by the jurisdic-tion and are the most meaningful. Some of the information in a vendor file of this type provides an objective, personal, and well-documented history. An evaluation works well with vendors who have worked for the jurisdiction, but it does not address those vendors who have never worked for the jurisdiction or provided services and commodities. For these vendors, thorough reference checks or other inquiries need to be made by Team members.

Other means of determining the reasonableness of a price is to research cata-logues, published price lists, and current industry publications that provide the latest price information. Examples include the *Oil and Drug Reporter*, publications by the American and Canadian oil and the gas industries, the American Metal Market, the Official Board Market, and various commercial services in Canada and the United States that track detailed prices paid for technical items, alternate sources, and parts breakdowns for major equipment and raw materials.

Procurement officials must become aware of current trends in the marketplace and should be fully aware of all conditions that can impact the price of a commodity or service. Salespeople often provide data that is useful in understanding current market trends. For example, changes in the applicable Minimum Wage Act can significantly impact those service contracts where lower paid laborers are typically employed. Is the vendor entitled to a contract modification? The procurement official should be able to assess the reasonableness of the request. Being aware of and being able to use all of these tools, either by themselves or in combination, should provide procurement officials with the information they need to make sound, professional judgments.

Cost Analysis

The evolution of highly complex technical systems and increasing dependence upon external service contracts has created a dramatic change in contracting approaches. This tendency will probably continue at an accelerated pace during the 21st Century. As procurement officials turn more and more to longer-term contracts, the use of cost-reimbursement contracts is becoming more prevalent.

We cannot always determine what prices might be in the future and, therefore, have to rely on subsequent negotiations with our suppliers at some future date to determine fair and reasonable prices. For example, in a long-term contract for the design and installation of a computer network system, procurement officials cannot know what equipment may be available in the future or its possible price because of the rapidly changing marketplace. Nor can procurement officials anticipate the possible software needs, modifications, or additional services that may be required. The more familiar procurement officials are with cost analysis, the better negotiations they will be able to conduct.

Cost-reimbursement contracts have several distinct features.

- The contractor is reimbursed all allowable applicable costs incurred during performance of the contract.
- The contractor commits to making the best effort to complete all of the work.
- The total amount to be paid to the contractor is not fixed at the outset of the project.
- The jurisdiction assumes most of the risk.
- The jurisdiction has greater contract administration responsibility.

The need to be aware of cost principles and how to use them in price evaluation is obviously very critical to the success of the contracting process and the economic well-being of the jurisdiction. NIGP (1996) defines cost analysis as "the review and evaluation of cost data for the purpose of arriving at costs actually incurred or estimates of costs to be incurred, prices to be paid, and costs to be reimbursed." "This analysis involves the application of experience, knowledge, and judgment to data in an attempt to project reasonable estimated contract costs. Estimated costs serve as the basis for buyer-seller negotiations to arrive at mutually agreeable contract prices" (Dobler & Burt, 1996, p. 313).

Generally, costs have been divided into six categories, while these include variable costs, fixed costs and semi-variable costs, total costs, direct costs, and indirect costs (Dobler & Burt, 1996, p. 301).

- *Variable Costs* vary directly and proportionally to the production quantity of a particular item. Variable costs include direct labor wages, the cost of materials, and a small number of overhead costs that the supplier incurs in filling an order.

- *Fixed Costs* do not vary with the volume of production but, rather, change over time. Fixed costs are costs that sellers must pay simply because they are in business. They are a function of time and not influenced by the volume of production.

- *Semi-variable Costs* are those that do not fall easily into either of the above categories. Costs such as maintenance, utilities, and postage are partly variable and partly fixed. Each is like a fixed cost, because its total cannot be tied directly to a particular unit of production, yet there are times when they can fluctuate based on production quantities and are then defined as variable costs.

- *Total Costs* are the sum of the variable, fixed, and semi-variable costs.

Because it is difficult to specifically allocate costs as fixed, variable, and semi-variable, accountants generally classify costs in two other categories: direct costs and indirect costs.

- *Direct Costs* are labor and/or material costs that are directly related to or caused by a specific project. Two techniques are available for determination of the direct labor cost. The first is to use the actual salaries of the specific employees who are working on the project. The second is to utilize an average rate for the overall categories of the employees doing the work. Suppliers prefer to use the method that affords them the highest billing rate, and buyers prefer to use the method that affords them the lowest billing rate. The hourly rate, weekly rate, or any other appropriate labor rate is, therefore, a subject of negotiation between the supplier and the buyer. Material costs are easier to determine. Invoices that the supplier is able to produce can indicate actual costs that can be easily verified.

- *Indirect Costs,* commonly referred to as overhead, are typically made up of two components. One is known as the burden or load, and the other is known as general sales and administrative expenses (GS&A). The burden or load component of the overhead refers to the additional expenses associated with basic labor costs. It includes items such as vacation, sick leave, insurance costs, and taxes. GS&A covers other overhead items, such as rent, telephone, equipment leases, etc.

The overhead factor requested by a supplier might include the costs that are incurred for the company as a whole or may include only costs for a specific operating unit. Many corporations have several divisions, and their overhead factors may vary from one to another. Some companies have various branch offices, and the overhead rates may be different in each of the branch offices, as opposed to the corporation as a whole. As was the case with labor rates previously discussed, suppliers would like to charge the highest possible overhead factor, and buyers prefer to pay the lowest overhead factor. This becomes a subject of negotiation.

Negotiations between the supplier and the seller result in a determination of allocable costs. An allocable cost is "a cost that can be assigned or charged as an item of cost to one or more cost objectives, in accordance with the terms of the contract and applicable laws and regulations" (NIGP, 1996, p. 4). Both direct and indirect costs submitted by the vendor need to be examined to determine if they should be allocated to the project. Agreement of both parties is needed if procurement officials are to have a mutually satisfactory and beneficial relationship. The same process of negotiation determines what are known as allowable costs, costs that are "reasonable, allocable to the given cost objective . . . in accordance with the terms of the contract and not prohibited by law or regulation" (p. 4).

Because a cost may be allocable does not necessarily make it allowable. Allocable simply means that a cost can be traced to a specific function or project. This does not mean that the buyer should pay for it. The buyer must first make a determination that the cost is justifiable and appropriate. If the buyer reaches this decision, then the cost becomes allowable.

Buyers should be aware that while labor and material costs may be available from objective references such as published labor rates and industry publications on material costs, procurement officials are dependent upon the overhead information furnished by their suppliers. The best information is obtained from suppliers when they believe that procurement officials are working in a partnership and not an adversarial relationship. Buyers must also understand that costs and overhead may vary from one firm to another. Although procurement officials should examine each firm individually, data obtained from other suppliers can be very useful when discussing the reasonableness of a firm's costs and projected prices.

Value Analysis

Life-cycle Costing/Total Cost of Ownership

Life-cycle cost is defined as "the total cost of ownership; the total cost of acquiring, operating, maintaining, supporting, and (if applicable) disposing of an item" (NIGP, 1996, p. 46). Life-cycle costing focuses on the total cost of ownership rather than merely the initial acquisition cost. It attempts to estimate all of the costs, including acquiring, installing, maintaining, and eventually disposing of the commodity. Some private sector estimates indicate that initial acquisition costs are usually less than 50% of the total cost of capital equipment.

Table 30 is an example of the application of life cycle costing to compare the ownership costs of a new and used vehicle, based upon the following assumptions:

- MSRP for the new vehicle is $20,000.00.
- This is a 6-cylinder vehicle getting 20 miles/gallon at $1.00/gallon.
- Insurance costs are lower for older vehicles.
- Routine maintenance includes anticipated replacement of known wearable items, such as oil changes, brakes, tires, etc.
- Major repairs are estimates for repairs or replacement of major components, such as transmission, a/c system, exhaust system, electrical, etc.
- The car will be driven for four years and 50,000 miles in each case.
- The costs indicated are for the four-year period.

Table 30

Life Cycle Costing

	New Car	Used Car
Acquisition Cost	$20,000.00	$12,000.00
Fuel Estimate	$2,500.00	$2,500.00
Insurance Estimate	$4,000.00	$3,200.00
Routine Maintenance Estimate	$1,300.00	$1,300.00
Major Repairs (Estimated)	None	2,000.00
Sub-Total = All Estimated Costs	$25,300.00	$21,000.00
Less Estimated Residual Value	-$12,000.00	-$8,000.00
Total Cost of Ownership for Four Years	$13,300.00	$13,000.00

Table 30 indicates that there is very little difference in actual costs (dollars) between purchasing a new car or a used car. However, if procurement officials perform a value analysis, they may make the determination that the money saved with the purchase of the used car is not justified because of the downtime for the additional repair work. In the value analysis process, procurement officials would also look at leasing costs.

The procedure followed in conducting a life cycle cost analysis is summarized as follows (Dobler & Burt, 1996, p. 392):

- Determine the operating cycle for the equipment: types of operation, routine maintenance, overhaul sequence, and so on, detailing how the machine functions or what will be done in each step of this cycle.

- Identify and quantify the factors that affect costs: power consumption and rates at various levels of operation, labor requirements and rates, maintenance requirements and rates, average time between failures, time between overhauls, average downtime costs, and so on.

- Calculate all costs at current rates and prices.

- Project costs to the future date at which they will be incurred: adjust for expected inflation or deflation; consider estimated salvage value; and complete the life cycle cost matrix.
- Discount all future costs and benefits to their present values.
- Sum all costs and benefits to obtain the total life cycle cost, expressed in present value terms.

Note that all of the costs are brought back to year one by using present value factors directly related to the jurisdiction's cost.

Scoring the Proposals

Total Cost of Ownership

While the concept of life cycle costing applies most frequently to the purchase life of capital equipment, it is also applicable to other items as well. There is an increasing tendency in both private industry and government entities to make decisions based on total costs rather than on initial acquisition costs alone. Procurement officials should learn to develop a total cost model (TCM) that can lead to decisions that may not be initially obvious. For example, when purchasing high technology equipment, the buyer should consider The following items:

- acquisition price (including shipping);
- cost of future upgrades;
- licensing fees;
- maintenance costs;
- site-preparation costs;
- training costs;
- cost of supplies and operating manuals;
- security costs;
- utility and insurance costs; and
- installation costs.

Buyers must develop the skills to practice the concept of total cost of ownership whenever possible. They should strive to make user agencies aware of the benefit the agency will receive.

In most evaluation processes, scoring is performed as the second task, immediately following the determination of responsiveness. Most proposals require that the financial information be provided separately. This is to ensure that the technical evaluators have no knowledge of the pricing proposal. This avoids the debate over whether knowledge of the pricing proposal influenced an evaluator's assessment of technical factors.

Developing a Short List

Once an overall evaluation score has been determined for each proposal, the next step is to reduce the number of proposals to be further evaluated. Consider this example: eight proposals were reviewed and these scores were assigned: 82, 80, 78, 72, 65, 63, 50, and 48. The higher the numerical score, the better the proposal.

A short list for further review must be developed. First, divide the scores into groups. A group consists of proposals with similar scores. The first group could be 82, 80, and 78. There may be questions as to in which group the proposal scoring 72 should be. It is always easier to justify keeping a proposal in the competition than removing it. Since 72 is midway between 78 and 65, the safest approach is to place the proposal with the score of 72 in the first group. The next two groups are easier to classify: one being 65 and 63; the other, 50 and 48.

A typical short list consists of three to four proposals.

A typical short list consists of three to four proposals. Inclusion or exclusion of proposals is often tied to the agency policy guidelines. It is neither fair nor defensible to eliminate a proposal that scored better than one that has been kept in. For example, procurement officials cannot drop the proposal with the score of 72 if procurement officials keep the one with the score of 65. If the proposal with the score of 72 was clearly inferior to the proposal with the score of 65, then the evaluation process was flawed. The proposal with the score of 65 is in fifth place; and, most likely, there is little chance that it will emerge as the winner. If it becomes necessary to disqualify this proposal, procurement officials must have documented justification for their activities. In some jurisdictions, each major criterion has a lowest acceptable score that must be exceeded to remain in the competition.

In some jurisdictions, the point scores may not strictly bind the Committee. The Project Manager has the discretionary power to declare whether a one- or two-point difference in scores represents a significant difference in the quality of the proposed solutions.

Interviewing Suppliers

This step usually occurs after the initial evaluation. The interview may, in fact, be a presentation, a demonstration of software, or a question-and-answer session. During these sessions, information is obtained to clarify the supplier's proposal but not to modify the proposal. These sessions are not an opportunity for the purchaser to change the requirements or the RFP terms, or for the supplier to submit major modifications. They are not negotiation sessions.

Sometimes, the sessions are simply to clarify information and to permit the evaluators to complete the scoring of the written RFP. At other times, these sessions are scored as a separate part of the evaluation. Whether or not a score is assigned, a face-to-face meeting with supplier personnel or a demonstration of a system often results in significant changes in scoring.

Checking References

There are two common approaches to incorporating references into the evaluation process: award points, or simply use the references to confirm the winner's capabilities.

Using References to Confirm a Selection

Proponent references are usually used to confirm the selection rather than as an evaluation criterion. In many cases, only the references of the winning proponent are checked. If several proponents are close in the final evaluation, references may be used to help choose among them. The interview should be conducted using predetermined, consistent questions in order to receive reliable and objective information about service, support, reliability, etc.

Assigning Points to References

Some organizations assign a score to the references and include the points in the overall evaluation. Sometimes, there is a minimum acceptable score, say 12 out of 20. Firms receiving 12 or fewer points would be eliminated from further consideration. Typically, references are worth between 5% and 25% of the total points. The references for the "winner" or the "finalists" are contacted; the information is obtained using a checklist or questionnaire, and a score is assigned.

Establishing the Competitive Range

The competitive range is determined on the basis of cost or price analysis and other factors that were stated in the RFP and should include all proposals that have a reasonable chance of being selected for award. Determining the competitive range accomplishes the following:

- Eliminates offers that do not have a reasonable chance of selection for award; and

- Prevents the entity and the offeror from spending time and money on negotiations that have no reasonable expectation of leading to selection and award.

Determining which offers fall within the competitive range is important. If the Evaluation Team does not award on initial proposals, the Team should have oral or written communications with offerors in the competitive range (FAR 15.610). The competitive range is established by comparing the submitted proposals with each other and the jurisdiction's requirements. A proposal that might be capable of meeting the jurisdiction's requirements, if it is significantly revised, may be excluded from the competitive range. Or if, based on the array of technical scores or prices of all offerors, the proposal clearly does not have a real chance of being selected for award, it can also be excluded. This can occur if, for example, its technical score is far lower than that of the next higher-scoring offeror and its price is higher than that of any of the offers in the competitive range.

Steps in determining the competitive range include:

- Identify offers that are outside the technical range. Since oral discussions or written communications provide an opportunity for clarification and proposal modifications (sometimes referred to as correction of deficiencies in FARS), the Evaluation Team should not exclude a proposal from discussions solely because it fails to conform to the solicitation. The Team may omit offers that require major modifications or revisions and, therefore, exclude from the competitive range any proposal that is considered non-responsive, or grossly deficient. That is, it is rated so low that any attempt to upgrade it to an acceptable level would require an unreasonable and unfair degree of assistance on the part of the procurement jurisdiction. A technically unacceptable proposal may be excluded from the competitive range regardless of its low offered price.

- Identify offers whose evaluated prices are outside the price range. The Evaluation Team may determine a technically acceptable proposal to be outside the competitive range if the evaluated price exceeds the highest reasonable price and the Team believes that it could not be reduced sufficiently without detracting from its technical acceptability. Proposals that are significantly beneath the lowest reasonable price may also be excluded from the competitive range if the proposal is judged technically unacceptable.

- When making a selection based on best value, exclude offers that rank well behind other proposals, having accounted for all evaluation factors, including price.

Determining Basis of Award

There are two basic approaches for evaluating proposals that are appropriate for use in conjunction with selecting a source: lowest price and best value (FAR 15.605).

In the **lowest-price approach** to source selection, technical evaluation factors are applied only on a go, no-go basis to identify technically acceptable proposals. Unacceptable proposals are removed from consideration. Price and price-related factors alone are applied to rank the proposals and select the proposal in line for award. The lowest-price-acceptable approach is similar to Two-Step Sealed Bidding; however, when the negotiated method of procurement is used, discussions or negotiations may or may not be conducted not only regarding Technical Proposals, but also for price.

In the **best-value approach** to source selection, weighted technical evaluation factors are applied to rate proposals. Best value is a process used in competitive negotiated contracting to select the most advantageous offer by evaluating and comparing factors in addition to cost or price. Unacceptable proposals are removed from further consideration.

Award is made to the offeror whose proposal represents the best value to the jurisdiction, as defined by all factors. As a consequence, the proposal in line for award will not necessarily be the proposal with the lowest evaluated price or the lowest estimated total cost. If the award goes to a proposal with a higher price, source selection officials must document the value analysis that justifies the expenditure of additional funds. When selecting on best value, some technical factors may be applied only in determining the competitive range (i.e., on a go, no-go basis). Others factors may be applied only in ranking proposals within the competitive range. Still, other factors may serve both purposes. The best value approach provides the jurisdiction with the greatest amount of flexibility in selecting the offeror whose performance is expected to best meet the stated jurisdiction requirements. This approach should be used where the technical expertise of the contractor is of particular importance.

Use the best value approach when it is essential to evaluate and compare factors in addition to cost in order to identify and select the most advantageous offer (NIGP, 1997).

- Always include cost or price as an evaluation factor.
- Include the offeror's relevant past performance as an evaluation factor, unless it would clearly serve no useful purpose.
- Structure evaluation criteria and their relative order of importance to clearly reflect the jurisdiction's need, and facilitate preparation of proposals that best satisfy that need.
- Limit evaluation criteria to those areas that will reveal substantive differences or risk levels among competing offers.
- Clearly state in the solicitation the basis upon which the jurisdiction will make the best value decision.
- Request only the information needed to evaluate proposals against the evaluation criteria.
- Ensure consistency among the objectives of the acquisition, the contracting strategy, the plan for selecting a source, the solicitation, and the evaluation and selection.

Best and Final Offers

Once all proposals have been reviewed and a short list of suppliers has been developed, a best and final offer (BAFO) can be requested from each of the vendors appearing on the list. Most often during the extensive review process, and as a result of the questions and clarifications received from the procuring jurisdiction, vendors submitting proposals realize that they may have overestimated the quantity of work or materials needed to complete the work associated with the RFP. A BAFO is a recognized tool in the RFP process which allows a price change after proposal receipt. Note that BAFOs are not requested for SOWs or specifications that differ from those initially issued in the RFP. A BAFO is issued for revised pricing related to the original RFP. Any substantive changes to the specs or SOW of an RFP must be re-bid to avoid possible protests from non-short-listed suppliers and from others that did not submit bids on the first solicitation due to the originally specified (un-changed) item. BAFOs are ranked on the matrix issued with the RFP for both technical evaluation and price-related factors, mirroring the evaluation of the first round of review.

Decision to Award without Oral Discussions or Written Communications

Upon the completion of initial technical and cost evaluations, the Evaluation Team must first decide whether to make a contract award without oral discussions or written communications or to establish a short list and conduct such discussions. The Team would generally award on initial proposals when the lowest priced, responsive proposal from a responsible offeror:

- offers a price that is fixed by law or regulation;
- provides a fair and reasonable price; and
- is priced at or near the procurement jurisdiction's most optimistic pre-negotiation position on price.

Even though the above criteria may be met, the Evaluation Team always has the discretion to proceed to oral or written discussions. It is not automatic. The Team should not make an award without further exploration and discussion when:

- there is uncertainty about the pricing or technical aspects of any proposals; and
- when the competition, including the pattern of prices obtained, reasonably puts the evaluation team on notice that award on the basis of initial proposals may not result in the lowest overall cost to the purchasing jurisdiction.

Alternative Evaluation Procedures

In Scenario 3B, all three components—Q&E, Technical, and Cost—of the proposal are received at the same time. An exceedingly simple way to award the contract is to make the award to the lowest priced firm whose Q&E/ Technical parts of the proposal have been deemed acceptable (not necessarily highest ranked). Here, again, verbal evaluations are enough to judge the offerors' submittals.

If desired, the Evaluation Team may do a Q&E/Technical evaluation and ranking. This will result in a short list. The award may be made to the lowest priced firm on the short list. The award may also be made to the highest ranked firm that is within the budget.

Level or Even Cost Process. Tell the RFP respondents what the project budget is. They will all submit proposals for that specific dollar amount. The Evaluation Team will determine who offered the most in terms of quality and approach. This will be an evaluation of the Q&E and Technical approach. Award will be made to that firm. No price negotiations are needed. The advantage of this method is that the selection of a contractor will be based exclusively on their qualifications and technical expertise without the need to make any price comparisons. Care must be exercised by the awarding jurisdiction not to commit all of their available funds in case a change order may be required later on.

Conclusion

*T*here are many ways and different methodologies that a jurisdiction could use to evaluate proposals. The focus should be on developing a methodology that affords the maximum opportunity to make the optimum objective selection. The evaluation criteria should reflect the needs of the project being procured. The members of the evaluation team should have expertise pertinent to aspects of the project, understand team dynamics, and commit the resources needed to complete the evaluation process on time. The potential respondents should be made aware of the evaluation criteria and, at a minimum, their relative importance. Ethics play a critical role in the process. Evaluation Team members should maintain confidentiality regarding deliberation and avoid speaking with respondents and other interested parties. The outcome must be considered fair and equitable to all respondents. Unsuccessful offerors should be debriefed after award to educate them and enlist their continued interest in the jurisdiction's solicitations.

References

American Bar Association (2000). *The 2000 model procurement code for state and local governments.* Chicago: American Bar Association.

Cibinic, J., Jr., & Nash, R. C., Jr. (1998). *Formation of government contracts* (3rd ed.). Washington, DC: George Washington University, Government Contracts Program.

Corwin, S. (1999). *How to handle competitive negotiations.* A paper presented at the Annual Forum of the National Institute of Governmental Purchasing, Inc., Halifax, Canada.

Dobler, D. W., & Burt, D. N. (1996). *Purchasing and supply management* (6th ed.). New York: McGraw-Hill Companies, Inc.

Fearon, H. E., Dobler, D. W., & Killen, K. H. (2000). *The purchasing handbook* (5th ed). New York: McGraw-Hill Companies, Inc.

Federal Acquisition Regulation Web site, http://www.arnet.gov/far/loadmainre.html.

Harney, D. F. (1992). *Service contracting: A local government guide.* Washington, DC: International City Management Association.

Nash, R. C., Jr., Cibinic, J., Jr., & O'Brien, K. R. (1999). *Competitive negotiation: The source of selection process* (2nd ed.). Washington, DC: The George Washington University, Government Contract Program.

National Institute of Governmental Purchasing, Inc. (NIGP) (1996). *Dictionary of purchasing terms* (5th ed.). Herndon, VA: NIGP.

National Institute of Governmental Purchasing, Inc. (NIGP) (1997). *Contracting for services.* Herndon, VA: NIGP.

National Institute of Governmental Purchasing, Inc. (NIGP) (2000). *Competitive sealed proposal/competitive negotiations.* Herndon, VA: NIGP.

SCADA SYSTEM SUPPLIER SELECTION PROCESS FOR COMPETITIVE BIDDING*

Timothy J. O'Neil, Steve Corwin, Ronald Eyma and Chris Helfrich

(*Reproduced with authors' permission)

Abstract

The City of Sunrise in Broward County, Florida, has approximately 170 public wastewater lift stations and three potable water storage sites with repumping facilities in their service area. These remote wastewater and water sites are currently controlled by local pump control panels. Monitoring of the site is based on a regular maintenance schedule and occasionally by notification from nearby residents should they see or hear something unusual. The City's desire is to control and monitor these sites by using a Supervisory Control and Data Acquisition (SCADA) system. One primary concern the City expressed was who would be responsible for providing and installing the SCADA system. The City wanted a system supplier who had the financial and technical resources to provide and install the SCADA system, and provide warranty service for several years after installation. The process of selecting a group of system suppliers who would competitively bid on the SCADA project is the focus of this paper.

Selecting a group of system suppliers begins with assembling an Evaluation Committee. The Evaluation Committee then determines the basis on which the system suppliers should be selected such as experience, capabilities, services to be provided, completeness of proposal, and price. A score sheet with the evaluation criteria categories is prepared. Each basis or category is then broken down into subcategories and given predetermined weight factors. An advertisement for Request for Proposal (RFP) is issued and a pre-proposals meeting is held. The Evaluation Committee evaluates qualification submittals from interested system suppliers and pre-qualifies a group of system suppliers. Finally, a Request for Proposals is issued to pre-qualified system suppliers interested in providing a SCADA system based on the final scope developed by the City.

Background

In 1992, the City of Sunrise advertised for system suppliers to submit a proposal for a SCADA system package for the City's service area. The proposal scope was more performance based than detailed design. There were submittals employing different technologies which made their evaluation difficult. As is the case with SCADA systems, the options and variations from one SCADA system to the next can be numerous and overwhelming to comprehend. Therefore, the project was placed on hold.

In 1995, the City of Sunrise revisited the process and embarked on a revised SCADA project where the guidelines or general scope of the SCADA system were more defined with the guidance of a consultant prior to advertising the RFP. The predetermined general scope enabled system suppliers to ascertain their ability to deliver the type of SCADA system the City desired.

General Scope Defined

In order to select qualified system suppliers who would be invited to submit proposals on the finalized SCADA project, the general scope of the project is first defined. Typical general scopes would include method of communication (e.g., frequency) from the remote site to the home site, proprietary versus non-proprietary software, open architectural versus closed architectural computer hardware, and digital versus programmable logic controls. The City of Sunrise's SCADA project defined the general scope to include a remote terminal unit (RTU) with programmable logic controller (PLC), spread spectrum, 902-928 MHZ band width radio communication, Reduced Instruction Set Computing (RISC)-based computer processor, and Windows NT software operating system with Cimplicity graphic software as the operator to machine interface (OMI) software.

Integral to defining the general scope of the SCADA system is the method of communication from the individual remote sites back to the home site. A service area that includes a maximum of nine miles between remote and home site prompted the selection of radio frequency communication over hard wire communication. A radio frequency propagation survey led to the use of the spread spectrum band width (902-928 MHz) for the City's site-specific conditions. Latitude and longitude, signal strength, recommended antenna height, recommended communication path, and recommended radio hardware were incorporated in the radio frequency survey which was included with the RFP.

Concurrent to the radio survey was the electrical evaluation of each water and wastewater site. This is critical to a successful SCADA project because the data transmitted must be electronically available to the RTU in order for it to be evaluated and/or transmit the Station's status. A survey of station electrical controls is labor intensive and requires scheduling between consultant and City staff. Pictures of electrical controls at each site provide valuable reference information and reduced the number of repeat site visits during final design.

In addition to the radio survey and electrical survey, an area map indicating the home site location along with the remote site locations accompanies the RFP. A system block diagram is useful in conveying pictorially the general project scope.

Basis of Selection

An evaluation of the qualifications of the system suppliers who would be invited to submit proposals on the final design is the second part of a two-part process for a successful project. Qualifications such as experience, capability, services to be provided, completeness of proposal, and price can be further broken down into subcategories. For example, experience could contain subcategories such as length of time in business, wastewater collection system experience, and/or water repump system experience. The next step is to assign a weight factor to each category and subcategory. The weight factor is a method by which a category or subcategory is given priority over other categories or subcategories. For example, completeness of a proposal may not be as much of a concern as the system supplier's overall experience. In this example, the experience may carry a weight factor of 30 percent and completeness of proposal may carry a weight factor of 5 percent. Attachment B presents a copy of the Scoring Sheet developed for the City of Sunrise SCADA project.

Request for Proposal Package

The RFP incorporates the general scope, the radio survey, the electrical survey, the area map, and system block diagram. The City's front-end documents such as a Non-Collusion Affidavit, Drug-Free Workplace, and Qualification Statement forms are included. The City also included an initial price sheet which solicited a budget cost to provide the SCADA system based on the general scope provided. The lowest price was not ranked the highest at this point since the City's objective was to confirm the budget cost for the work. The City's basis for selecting a group of system suppliers, which includes the qualification categories and subcategories, is incorporated into the RFP. The City held a pre-submittal conference which indicated the level of interest in this project by system suppliers and allowed system suppliers to request clarifications prior to submitting their proposal.

Evaluation Committee

The Evaluation Committee consisted of voting and non-voting members. The voting members comprised an odd-numbered group so as to avoid tie votes. The voting members originated from various departments within the City. For example, the Utilities Department (with functionality and usability concerns), the Engineering Department (with technical concerns), and the Purchasing Department (with funding and procurement concerns) would each have one representative. The non-voting members consisted of the consultant and other City staff who would assist the Evaluation Committee with answering technical questions. The consultant's presence during the evaluation process allowed for first-hand knowledge of the City's technical and non-technical desires and concerns. This first-hand knowledge assisted the consultant in providing the Client with their desired final design.

Pre-Qualifications

The City received eight proposals from interested system suppliers. The City's Evaluation Committee reviewed each proposal to ascertain the system suppliers' qualifications. Four of the eight system suppliers were invited to give a 30-minute presentation, which includes a question and answer period, so the City could further define their qualifications. The Evaluation Committee met 10 times over a 3-month period. The Evaluation Committee's scoring sheet ranged in total points from 226 to 769. The City's Evaluation Committee ultimately selected two system suppliers to competitively bid on the City's final design of the SCADA system.

Final Scope and Bidding

Following the pre-qualification steps, a detailed design package consisting of drawings and technical specifications based on the final scope was prepared. The final design included several of the recommendations suggested by the various system suppliers at their presentations. Once the design was completed, competitive proposals were obtained from the two pre-qualified system suppliers. The City held a mandatory pre-bid conference and site(s) visit. The contract was awarded to the lowest bidder.

In conclusion, the process of selecting a group of system suppliers who would competitively propose on the final design was a fair process and met the City's objectives.

CHAPTER 7

Contract Negotiations

Introduction

*A*s the purchasing profession continues to evolve and mature, procurement officials increasingly are called upon to chair a committee or participate in negotiations that can range from simple to complex, including:

- Sensitive discussions with irate vendors who may or may not file protests;

- Complex negotiations with offerors during the evaluation of proposals;

- Complex negotiations with a vendor that has been selected to provide a service as a result of a Request for Proposal (RFP) process;

- Negotiations with sole sources of supply; and

- Negotiations after contract awards in the contract administration phase with change orders and dispute resolution.

The use of more multi-year and evergreen (automatically renew unless one party notifies the other 90-120 days prior to expiration) contracts, or partnership oriented relationships, provides additional challenges for ongoing negotiations and makes the more traditional, adversarial approaches to vendor relationships increasingly harmful. It is incumbent upon the procurement official to ensure that the potential supplier in negotiations is treated fairly, including not revealing pricing or technical aspects of potential supplier proposals during the solicitation process. The procurement process also requires that public money be spent transparently when negotiations are completed. Records must be complete to show that public interest is protected.

For example, the City of Fort Collins, Colorado, recently enacted legislation allowing for direct negotiations with potential suppliers in certain situations involving the electric utility. As deregulation proceeds, it is imperative to have a mechanism to effectively compete in the marketplace. In addition to supplying electricity, the utility has the opportunity to offer an increased array of additional services, such as long-distance phone service, Internet access and cable television. A new process was proposed by the procurement department and adopted by the City Council that allowed potential suppliers to be approached privately and asked to provide proposals so as not to give away competitive advantage. No publicly advertised notice was required. Negotiations could take place with the potential supplier(s) whose proposal was evaluated to be the best based on the evaluation criteria. It was imperative that the details of any potential suppliers' proposals not be revealed to other vendors. Confidentiality was also tantamount in assuring the public, including the City Council, that public funds were being protected. The contract for and record of any procurement made as a result of this special negotiation method would be available for public inspection and a report made in open session to the City Council, once award was made.

...procurement officials are called upon daily to negotiate contract amendments and change orders.

The State of Florida has also added a process for competitive negotiation (CN) to its selection methods. In competitive negotiations, allowance is made for the negotiation of highly technical commodities/services, terms, pricing, and conditions of performance. Examples include contracts for computer programming, telephone system maintenance, medical services, and social service contracts that provide counseling to clients. Competitive negotiations is allowed when:

- The invitation to bid or request for proposal processes will not provide the solution needed by the jurisdiction;
- The qualifications of a potential supplier or the terms of the working relationship required to achieve the goal of the contract are more critical to the success of the program than the price; and
- A single source exists for the good or service needed (Barker, 1998).

On the other end of the negotiating perspective, procurement officials are called upon daily to negotiate contract amendments and change orders. For example, a construction contract may require the addition of another rest-room to meet revised staffing estimates. Here, the procurement official takes an active role in ensuring that the additional amounts paid are in line with project estimates. Conversely, the contractor may propose a contract change order to allow for a substitute heating system. The procurement official must be involved with the negotiation of this change order to ensure that the original intent of the specifications is being met and that the negotiated price is proper. Another common example is a consultant's request that a contract be amended to allow for additional time to complete a study. The procurement official must ensure that the consultant is meeting the requirements of the agreement and that any contract extensions are in the agency's best interests.

Although all aspects of the offer are negotiable, the amount of effort applied to each negotiation situation will depend on the importance of the issue and the relative importance of the particular procurement. The larger the dollar amount, the more important the negotiation becomes. Procurement officials may run through a quick, intuitive Pareto (80/20) analysis to ensure that they direct their energy toward more important items of an agreement. Another factor that will also affect the negotiation is the degree of competition available. The more competition there is, the more comfortable the procurement official may be that the market has set a reasonable price. The negotiating techniques used are similar in every situation. They reflect the essential elements of fairness, transparency, and ethical treatment. (A "negotiation checklist" is included at the end of this chapter.)

Planning for Negotiations

Why do procurement officials need to be good negotiators? It is reported that 60 to 70 percent of the benefits of negotiation go to the more skilled negotiator (Dobler & Burt, 1996, p. 376). One of the best ways to become a more proficient negotiator is to plan and prepare for the negotiation. Government personnel must be trained in negotiation techniques, and the team chosen for a specific project must receive specialized training for that individual undertaking.

The procurement official alone may handle simple negotiations. Such minor points as firming up delivery, ensuring final pricing, or determining minor contract changes are usually handled directly by the procurement official involved with the purchase of a product or service.

If the negotiations will result from proposals received through an RFP process, an Evaluation Committee must review the proposals. Procurement officials may decide to award a contract without discussion or establish a price range within which negotiations might not be required. Competitive range is used to describe those proposals that have a reasonable chance of being selected for award. A comparison of the proposals received and the procurement official's estimate of what the service should cost establishes the competitive range. Proposals must also be capable of meeting the technical requirements of the service needed. Most of the time, the highest ranked proposal will be the one chosen for negotiations. A Negotiating Team will be selected for a major acquisition that may include some or all members of the Evaluation Committee.

Negotiating Team

A team of negotiators rather than a single person is important in more complex procurements because of the synergistic nature of teams.

Synergy is the action of separate forces that together produce an effect greater than that of any force alone. For example, the procurement official has a good understanding of the importance of procurement to the agency and has knowledge of the past performance of a vendor. An engineering representative has the technical knowledge of how a vendor would perform a desired service or produce a desired product. In more concrete terms, the procurement official may know that a vendor has a history of late deliveries on certain items, while the engineering representative knows the vendor's manufacturing capability to produce the item currently being negotiated. When their knowledge is combined, they can negotiate an effective contract with performance guarantees. If the procurement official had negotiated the contract alone, the vendor might not have been awarded the contract at all. If engineering had negotiated the contract alone, performance guarantees might not have been sought.

Teams should be more creative than an individual. Team members challenge each other's assumptions. They are less apt to overlook details and, therefore, to plan and think better. Teams "take greater risks in setting higher targets"; and yet, if the risks of loss are large, teams are more conservative. After an agreement is reached, the Team can also help sell the agreement to others in organization (Karrass, 1998a). However, while teams provide many advantages, they must guard against groupthink—the belief that the Team is infallible or even the tendency for members to seek consensus so strongly that they lose the willingness and ability to evaluate one another's ideas critically (Northcraft & Neale, 1994).

In general, negotiating teams should be limited to those members who have essential skills or knowledge necessary to reach a sound agreement. The complexity of the negotiation will determine the size of the Team, but it should be noted that the larger the Team, the more difficult it is to reach an agreement (Fuller, 1991). The make-up of the Negotiating Team will vary, but a typical team should include a procurement official, project manager, technical staff, financial analyst, and legal expert.

Procurement Official

The procurement official is an integral part of the Team and should take the lead role. Often, the procurement official is the one representative of the jurisdiction to have the overall objective of the negotiation in view. Where other departments may be focused on particular areas of expertise, the procurement official can look at the business issues and the project as a whole. It has been stated that the most successful negotiators look at the good of the whole organization versus any one functional area. It should be noted that, "A firm's negotiating position is always strengthened when the company has a clear policy that permits only members of its purchasing department to discuss pricing, timing, and other contractual terms with sellers" (Dobler & Burt, 1996, p. 365). It is also useful to point out that negotiations are inherently subjective processes, and an essential role of the procurement official is to ensure the good of the whole organization while protecting the public interest by keeping the process fair and transparent.

Project Manager

Other team members include the project manager, or a representative of the department needing the item or service being negotiated. This person provides the end-user or operational perspective to the negotiation. In some instances, the end-users may be included in planning but not in the actual negotiation sessions (Fuller, 1991, p. 31).

Technical Experts

Various technical experts may be needed on the Team. These experts can be engineers or other specialists who have information needed by the Negotiating Team. The jurisdiction may hire outside consultants or expert staff from other jurisdictions. One caution is to ensure that there is no real or perceived link between the expert and a preferred vendor. Technical experts are a source of power (which will be discussed later) for the Team.

Financial Analyst

A price and cost analyst is needed to perform a financial analysis unless this skill rests with other members of the Team. These specialists may come from the jurisdiction's financial or budget departments, or they may be experts from the outside or other jurisdictions. These members are responsible for obtaining the cost and pricing data needed to analyze the proposal (TCI, Inc., 1984, p. 116).

Legal Expert

Legal representation is needed in varying degrees, either as an integral part of the Team or on an as-needed basis. Legal review is required for complex contract negotiations.

Team Leader

The preferred Team Leader in most negotiations is the procurement official. It is important for the Team Leader to possess a range of skills, including:

- the ability to make sound decisions under pressure;
- tact and an ability to build consensus;
- an even temper;
- flexibility;
- confidence and trustworthiness;
- the ability to reason; and
- the confidence of superiors who have veto power over negotiations (Fuller, 1991, pp. 32-33).

Team Leaders must have the full support of the Team and the organization. If the other side thinks it can go "over the head" of the negotiation team and appeal, the negotiation position is permanently weakened (Fuller, 1991, p. 33). It is important that agency managers and governing bodies refer any questions from the other side to the Negotiating Team.

Responsibilities

The Team Leader has some essential responsibilities.

- Act as the spokesperson for the Team;
- Make and respond to all offers;
- Plans, strategies, and objectives;
- Set the timetable for pre-negotiation work;

- Control the comments at the sessions;
- Assign team member roles;
- Obtain technical representation, as needed; and
- Interacts with the other side before the negotiations start to agree on team size and other logistical items (Fuller, 1991, pp. 34-35).

The Team should be briefed on the background and history of the particular procurement as well as the importance of the procurement to the organization. This initial briefing is critical so that all members can be briefed on why the Team is being created; to allow time to get acquainted; and to learn the skills of each Team member. The first Team meeting sets the structure for teamwork and how the Team will achieve its goals. This is extremely important with a Negotiating Team that may be together for only one negotiation. When it understands the procurement, the Team can determine:

- the most appropriate type of contract;
- terms of the contract;
- any special warranty or delivery provisions;
- the manufacturing or service delivery process involved;
- technical and engineering specifications;
- the subcontractors needed;
- problems that can be anticipated with product or service delivery; and
- the competitive range (TCI, 1984, p. 115).

Ground Rules

The next step is to review the ground rules with the Team and the importance of each member's role. The ground rules require that the Team present a united front in the negotiations. The Team Leader must control the flow of discussion at meetings, including who can speak and when. An inadvertent comment can reveal too much information to the other side and weaken the Team's negotiating position (Karrass, 1998a, p. 24). Team members must be informed in how to call for a caucus when negotiations are in progress. The Team Leader also creates the timetable for pre-negotiation work and assigns roles to team members, including taking minutes of negotiations, noting which tactics the other side is using and alerting the Team, and attending the actual negotiations or standing by to provide information. The Team Leader must determine if any of the Team members have an abrasive or other type of personality that does not lend itself to teamwork. If so, the member should be used as a resource outside of the actual negotiation sessions (Fuller, 1991, p. 29). It is worth pointing out that Negotiating Teams have two faces—inward and outward. Team members may well (and should) contribute, argue, and debate when within the family, but must present a unified approach when dealing with contractors. In public procurement, it is of paramount importance that all negotiations be fair and ethical. No information from competing proposals should be shared. No information about the public agency's negotiation positions should be shared with the contractor. Presenting a united front will increase the power of the Team and avoid the other side's tactic of trying to divide and conquer.

Factors in Selecting Contract Types

There are different types of contracts that can be considered for each type of procurement projects. There are many factors that should be considered in selecting and negotiating the contract type. They include the following (Federal Acquisition Regulation [FAR] 16.194):

- *Price Competition.* Normally, effective price competition results in realistic pricing, and a fixed-price contract is ordinarily in the Government's interest.

- *Price Analysis.* Price analysis, with or without competition, may provide a basis for selecting the contract type. The degree to which price analysis can provide a realistic pricing standard should be carefully considered.

- *Cost Analysis.* In the absence of effective price competition and if price analysis is not sufficient, the cost estimates of the offeror and the jurisdiction provide the basis for negotiating contract-pricing arrangements. It is essential that the uncertainties involved in performance and their possible impact upon costs be identified and evaluated, so that a contract type that places a reasonable degree of cost responsibility upon the contractor can be negotiated.

- *Type and Complexity of the Requirement.* Complex requirements, particularly those unique to the Government, usually result in greater risk assumption by the jurisdiction. This is especially true for complex research and development contracts, when performance uncertainties or the likelihood of changes make it difficult to estimate performance costs in advance. As a requirement recurs or as quantity production begins, the cost risk should shift to the contractor, and a fixed-price contract should be considered.

- *Urgency of the Requirement.* If urgency is a primary factor, the jurisdiction may choose to assume a greater proportion of risk or it may offer incentives to ensure timely contract performance.

- *Period of Performance or Length of Production Run.* In times of economic uncertainty, contracts extending over a relatively long period may require economic price adjustment terms.

- *Adequacy of the Contractor's Accounting System.* Before agreeing on a contract type other than firm-fixed-price, the contracting officer shall ensure that the contractor's accounting system will permit timely development of all necessary cost data in the form required by the proposed contract type. This factor may be critical when the contract type requires price revision while performance is in progress, or when a cost-reimbursement contract is being considered and all current or past experience with the contractor has been on a fixed-price basis.

- *Concurrent Contracts.* If performance under the proposed contract involves concurrent operations under other contracts, the impact of those contracts, including their pricing arrangements, should be considered.

- *Extent and Nature of Proposed Subcontracting.* If the contractor proposes extensive subcontracting, a contract type reflecting the actual risks to the prime contractor should be selected.

- *Acquisition History.* Contractor risk usually decreases as the requirement is repetitively acquired. Also, product descriptions or descriptions of services to be performed can be defined more clearly.

Negotiation Process

The negotiation process consists of three major phases: preparation, negotiations, and agreement.

Preparation

The majority of time in a negotiation should be spent in the preparation phase. Preparation includes gaining a technical understanding of what is being negotiated and performing an analysis of each side's negotiating positions. This begins with a review of the proposal. What are the technical strengths of the proposal? What is the price or components of the cost proposal? The Team must consider the other side's motivation: How badly does the vendor want the contract? How confident is the potential supplier? How much time is available to reach an acceptable agreement (Dobler & Burt, 1996, p. 364)?

Procurement officials must determine how much competition there is to provide a particular product or service. The Team Leader must ensure that a thorough cost and price analysis is prepared. For every term and condition to be negotiated, an objective minimum and maximum negotiating goal should be prepared (Dobler & Burt, 1996, p. 366). The Team must anticipate the tactics that will be used by the other side and prepare responses.

Negotiation Targets

The object of the negotiation must be identified. Negotiations can clarify price, terms and conditions, quality, performance of the contract, or any other aspect of the procurement (Dobler & Burt, 1996). Negotiating targets can be divided into substantive and relationship issues (Fischer & Ury, 1991, p. 158). These issues demand different approaches and tactics to reach a satisfactory outcome. It is, therefore, important to know these issues as they relate to the specific procurement.

Substantive Issues

Substantive issues include, but are not limited to:

- terms,
- conditions,
- prices,
- dates,
- numbers, and
- liabilities.

Substantive issues also include the technical aspects of the item or service. Is the agency receiving the most current release of the product? Are the components being used actually going to function in the way the jurisdiction requires? The technical targets will require the technical representative's input.

Price and Cost Analyses will be needed to determine the fairness of any amounts due under a contract. Are the overhead rates reasonable? Is the amount of direct and indirect labor reasonable? How do the prices compare to other commodity indexes? Know what is included in averages, standard costs, overhead rates, administrative expenses, and profit margins. Do all of these items apply to your particular purchase (Karrass, 1998)?

Relationship Issues

Relationship issues can affect the outcome of negotiations and include:

- balance of emotion and reason;
- ease of communication, degree of trust and reliability;
- attitude of acceptance (or rejection);
- relative emphasis on persuasion (or coercion); and
- degree of mutual understanding (Karrass, 1998a, p. 158).

Relationship issues are important to all agreements but are even more important when a jurisdiction enters into a long-term relationship with a potential supplier. Can the contractor be relied upon to make delivery? Will the jurisdiction be notified of potential problems? Is there a degree of mutual understanding of each party's goals? The balance of relationship and substantive issues can work together to produce a mutually beneficial agreement. The Team must understand their counterpart's personal decision-making and business-decision processes in order to choose the appropriate tactic to gain concessions in negotiations (Fearon, Dobler, & Killen, 1993, p. 242).

Rehearsal

A list of questions must be developed that the other side may raise and responses formulated. The Team must also ask its own questions about the other side in the negotiation and decide what concessions it is willing to make in order to reach an agreement (Fuller, 1991). A list of items that are sacred to the Negotiating Team and cannot be compromised must be developed. The Team should establish alternatives and agree on a worst-case scenario, including a best alternative if a negotiated agreement cannot be reached (Fischer & Ury, 1991). Negotiators should never accept an agreement that is not in the jurisdiction's interests. The goal of negotiation is to reach an agreement that is as beneficial as possible to both sides (p. 97).

One technique to use when the Team Leader believes the Team is ready for negotiations is to perform a mock negotiation in front of jurisdictional personnel (sometimes known as *Murder Boards*) who are knowledgeable about the procurement. These personnel can challenge the Team and point out weak points in its arguments (Dobler & Burt, 1996, p. 371).

When all is seemingly ready, a detailed agenda should be prepared before the negotiating session (Fuller, 1991, p. 130). The date, time, and location need to be agreed upon. The names and responsibilities of each side's attendees should be determined, and this will serve as a valuable aid in determining what personnel resources the Negotiating Team needs. For example, if the potential supplier is bringing legal counsel, it will be necessary for a member of the jurisdiction's legal department to attend as well. If it is necessary for the contractor's and jurisdiction's teams to break into subgroups to discuss technical or cost analysis, it will be helpful to know with whom the members will be meeting.

Power

Negotiators must recognize and be able to use various power and negotiation tactics. "Power is the ability to influence someone else's behavior" (Fearon et al., 1993, p. 238). Team members must be skilled in presenting options that allow both parties to get as close as possible to their goals.

There are several sources of power in negotiation, including reward, punishment, information, legitimacy, expertise, referent, choices, and counter (Fearon et al., 1993, pp. 239-240). It is an important part of the planning process to identify the sources of power accruing to both teams. Negotiating parties often underestimate their own power and overestimate the opponent's power. The perception of power is relative and shifts as perceptions shift (pp. 240-241). That is, if the Team thinks it has power, it will. If the Team has power today, they may not have it tomorrow; once the Team shows their power to their opponent, the opponent may make a counteroffer that will diminish the Team's perceived power. Understanding the strengths of both negotiating sides' positions is vital to a successful negotiation (pp. 239-241).

- *Reward.* This power is the ability to do something for someone. It can be both tangible and intangible. Issuing a purchase order is tangible. A positive remark—saying buyers are glad to see sellers—is intangible.

- *Punishment.* This source of power is the ability to inflict pain or cause negative consequences. Procurement officials have the ability to debar vendors who do not perform. The potential supplier may have the ability to go the jurisdiction's chief executive or to elected officials if the procurement divisions are not cooperative.

- *Information.* Information is very powerful. If the Team knows something the counterpart does not, it gives the Team power in the negotiation. Another source of power comes from a Negotiating Team presenting a united front. That is why this aspect of team preparation is so important. Each member of the Team knows when and how to respond in a unified voice.

- *Legitimacy.* The right to have compliance with a request conveys legitimacy. This is especially powerful in public procurement. Contractors must comply with procurement regulations and laws. Using standard contract forms approved by legal counsel gives legitimacy to demands that certain provisions are not negotiable.

- *Expertise.* Groups acknowledge the power of experts. Experts are rarely required to show proof of their opinions; it is assumed they know what they are talking about. That is why it is so important to have the required technical experts on the Negotiating Team.

- *Referent Power.* Referent power is based on the personal qualities of an individual. This may have come from past experience with the person as fair and open-minded. It also emanates from the appearance and interpersonal behavior of the person. People comply with requests from people with referent power because they identify compliance with being like the person having referent power.

- *Choices.* The number of choices available to any one party in a negotiation conveys power. The party with the most choices and options for reaching an agreement has more power than one who has fewer options for give-and-take in reaching an agreement. If the Team has no flexibility on when they can take delivery, they will be at the mercy of an opponent who may force the Team to accept higher pricing or other concessions.

- *Counter Power.* Counter power comes from the ability to counteract the power of an opponent. If the Team has many of the powers already mentioned, they will have a greater ability to refuse requests made by the vendor. For example, experts on the Team may justify the technical requirements of an agreement.

Logistics

The venue where negotiations are to be held has psychological implications. The Team must decide whether to meet at their office, the potential supplier's location, or on neutral ground. There are advantages and disadvantages to each choice (Fischer & Ury, 1991, p. 134). If negotiations are conducted on the jurisdiction's home ground, the Team will maintain the advantage of logistical support and psychological benefits. The Evaluation Team has control over the room, seating, timing of breaks, etc. There are no potential travel problems or undue personnel burdens; technical support is always available, and interruption ploys by the other side are avoided (Fuller, 1991).

Meeting at the proposer's site may be advantageous if there is a need to review plant facilities. In addition, there is an opportunity for delay tactics in order to get additional information from your home location or to break off negotiations, if necessary (Fuller, 1991). Be sure to avoid undue dependence on the other party in the negotiation by arranging for the jurisdiction team's own transportation and support services.

Neutral sites may be needed if the teams cannot agree on whose site to use. A neutral site may also be advantageous if the negotiations are anticipated to be very acrimonious. As shown in Table 31, negotiation location selections depends on negotiation issues.

Table 31

Where Should Procurement Officials Negotiate?

Issue	Jurisdiction Place	Vendor Place	Neutral Site
Control of Room, etc.	x		
Technical Support	x		
Ease of Walking Out		x	x
Acrimonious Situations			x
Travel Ease	x		
Facility Review		x	
Delaying Tactics		x	
No Agreement on Site			x
Control Interruptions	x		

The Room

The negotiating room should have comfortable seating and lighting and be neither too hot nor too cold. The Team Advisor should be seated next to the Team Leader. Some team leaders prefer a command location at the head of the table, but others prefer to sit side-by-side with the other party. Name cards for seating can preclude seat shuffling and are also a good way to identify the parties. Try to arrive first at any location so that your team may choose their seating before the other side arrives (Fuller, 1991, p. 127).

Verbal and Non-Verbal Clues

Negotiators must recognize the verbal and non-verbal clues that indicate attitudes and perceptions of an opponent, including attitude, appearance, facial expressions, gestures, and tone of voice (Fuller, 1991).

Attitude

What is the attitude of the other party? Are they aggressive, friendly, aloof? Initial attitude may yield clues to where the other party is coming from and what the tone of the negotiations will be. A relaxed, friendly attitude may indicate that the other party is in a problem-solving mode. However, attitude must be monitored throughout the negotiations and verified against the actions of the other party.

Appearance

First appearances may be lasting ones in negotiating as well as in other life situations. Is the appearance of the vendor in keeping with the normal business practices in the area? Are they neat, well kept? If the proposer's appearance is out of the ordinary, it should be read in conjunction with other signals to see if something is not right. It might indicate that the vendor has no intention of serious negotiation, or it may simply reflect lack of preparation.

Because of the importance of non-verbal clues, face-to-face discussions are the preferred method of negotiation. Telephone negotiations may be necessary to iron out minor points or to negotiate simple agreements; however, most non-verbal clues are lost in telephone exchanges.

Facial Expressions

Smiles, frowns, grimaces, or signs of boredom given through the facial expression need to be examined to see if the Team's points are getting across. The agency's negotiation team should be aware that facial expressions might prematurely give away their position. The non-verbal signals that team members send should reinforce the Team's negotiating position. Team members must also know that experienced negotiators may try to give the leader false signals with facial expressions. Grimacing at a counteroffer may be a ploy to persuade others to raise the offer or accept a concession.

Gestures

Gestures and body language are another source of information. Is the reason the other side is sitting rigid because they are hard to deal with, or did they hurt their back the day before?

Tone of Voice

Tone of voice is also an important signal. Is the supplier agreeing with the negotiator in a condescending or sarcastic tone of voice? The negotiator must read this in conjunction with other signals to clearly understand what is being communicated.

Negotiation Approaches

In *Getting to Yes*, Fischer and Ury (1991) suggest that negotiators:

- separate people from the problem;
- focus on interest not positions;
- create a variety of options before deciding which to pursue; and
- insist on objective criteria.

People

Each side in a negotiation perceives the negotiation differently. The perception of the negotiation is the reality as each side sees it. It is important for negotiators to view any problem from the opposite perspective. How can the Negotiating Team get to know the other side? Most procurement officials are adverse to lunch and dinner exchanges; however, the Team can be the first to arrive for the negotiations and stay after the negotiations for conversation. Each side has certain emotions vested in the resolution of the negotiation. It is very important to understand both sides' emotions. Is anyone on either side's job on the line with this negotiation? To be successful in negotiations, the Team must look at their counterparts as having the same goal—a mutually acceptable solution to the issues.

Interests

Most negotiations have several positions that can satisfy the different interests of the parties. Negotiators need to explore the compatible and conflicting interests behind positions, because both shared and differing but complementary interests are the building blocks of wise agreements. Suppose the other side's interest is in increasing sales by $100,000. The agency, on the other hand, needs a lower price to meet budget. If the other side only focuses on the $100,000 in sales, the entity may have a hard time reaching an agreement.

However, if the Team proposes a long-term contract that meets the goal of a lower price, the negotiation team may be able to meet the other side's goal of increased sales over a longer period of time, thus reaching a mutually satisfying agreement. If the focus is on only one sale for $100,000, negotiations are likely to break down and no agreement will be reached.

Options

Once the other side's interests have been determined, the Negotiation Team should prioritize potential solutions that will satisfy those interests according to those most acceptable within the entity's priorities. It is important to avoid focusing on one solution and to remain open to options that may satisfy both sides' interests. Some inhibitors to developing options are:

- premature judgment;
- searching for one answer;
- assuming there is a fixed pie to be split; and
- taking the position that solving their problem is their problem.

Fischer and Ury (1991) propose a four-step process of reviewing the problem, analyzing the problem, and developing approaches and possible action ideas, as shown in Table 32. Once the Team has a number of options, it is possible to find one or more which meets the objective of a solution that is low cost to the agency but of high benefit to them.

Table 32

Four-Step Process of Reviewing the Problem

Steps in the Negotiation Process	Issues that Should Be Addressed
Step 1. Identifying Problems	• What's wrong? • What are the current symptoms? • What are disliked facts contrasted with a preferred situation?
Step 2. Diagnosing Problems	• Sorting symptoms into categories • Suggesting causes • Observing what is lacking • Noting barriers to resolving the problem
Step 3. Searching for Alternatives	• What are possible strategies or prescriptions? • What are some theoretical cures? • Generate broad ideas about what might be done
Step 4. Suggested Action Ideas	• What might be done? • What specific steps might be taken to deal with the problem?

Criteria

How can the Team develop objective criteria to judge the negotiation? One way is to check with their peer network. This is one advantage of governmental purchasing, as information about contracts, prices, and successes and failures in negotiations is publicly shared. How did the city in the next state fare during software negotiations with Vapor Ware, Incorporated? In addition, an agreement that allows for future price increases can be negotiated to follow the objective criteria of a commodity price index. It is important to find independent criteria that both sides can agree upon and can be based on market value (the commodity index), a precedent, or some professional standards. Negotiators can use several techniques to reach agreement on objective criteria from the other side.

- Framing the issue as a joint search for the right criteria;
- Presenting justification for which standards are appropriate and how they should be applied;
- Never yielding to pressure that is not based on objective criteria (Fischer & Ury, 1991, p. 88). (When pressure is applied, invite the other side to state its reasoning and what objective criteria apply; do not move unless the reason is reasonable.)

Negotiation Tactics

*P*ublic purchasing requires that all parties to the negotiation be treated fairly, and the results of the negotiation must be able to withstand public scrutiny. The Team members must always exhibit the highest ethical conduct.

Negotiators must be able to recognize various negotiation tactics and be able to use them in ways that meet the ethical conduct test. Several common negotiation tactics are discussed below.

Win/Win

Win/win is the goal of a principled negotiation, whereby the interests of both parties are satisfied. The premise is that the parties are best served by working together. The dilemma with this strategy is that there is a problem if one side reveals its options and the other side does not reciprocate. In addition, it is often difficult to find objective criteria that will establish the right price and terms for both parties. If both sides are willing to work in this mode, it is the best approach for the agency. For example, a professional service provider is anxious to begin a working relationship with a jurisdiction. The proposal sub-mitted is judged to be technically competent, in the competitive range, and is the highest rated proposal. The potential consultant has given very competitive pricing to begin the relationship. The jurisdiction in the negotiations knows the pricing is very competitive but also needs to ensure that it is adequate to provide for the services needed and is not just an introductory loss leader rate to be recouped by possible change orders. Both sides have open and honest discussions of their interests. A mutual agreement that prices are reasonable for this work is reached.

Stonewalling

Stonewalling occurs when one side has no intention of reaching an agreement unless there is an irresistible offer. The hope of the stonewaller is that the tactic will cause the opposition to better each successive offer, or become frustrated and make a mistake. Another reason for stonewalling is that some negotiators believe the best offers are received only when talks are on the verge of break-ing down completely. Stonewalling is sometimes used as a stalling tactic if the other side thinks the agency has a deadline that will cause the Team to make a better offer. Counter tactics include:

- breaking off negotiations, and
- setting a deadline beyond which the agency will not continue if there is no evidence of good-faith negotiating (Fischer & Ury, 1991).

A major reason for the use of stonewalling by the other side is simply that the more time and effort involved in the negotiation, the more reluctant the Team is to quit without an agreement. In the public sector, stonewalling may prompt more senior or elected officials to become involved and, consequently, the Team loses control over the negotiations. It is very important to know when this tactic is being used and to initiate counter tactics. It is also important to have briefed senior jurisdictional officials thoroughly on what is expected in the negotiations.

Good Samaritan

This is the tactic used by the other side when it acts as if it is doing the agency a favor or making a great sacrifice with its offer in order to put the Team off guard and persuade negotiators to accept it without determining whether it is actually in their best interest (Fischer & Ury, 1991, pp. 90-91). The counter tactic is to continue to work toward a discussion of the facts of the deal. If the Team can never get to the facts, the negotiations should be terminated.

Take It or Leave It

The other side has made its final offer and says it will no longer negotiate. The common counter tactic is to continue negotiating regardless. What are your alternatives? Can your team initiate negotiations with other competitors who want your business? If the other side does not actually break off the negotiations, the negotiators will have called its bluff. When the Team has indeed made its own final offer to the other side, a more tactful approach is needed to let the other side know that negotiations have ended (Fischer & Ury, 1991, p. 142).

Splitting the Difference

Splitting the difference involves an offer to cut the dollar difference in half, thus avoiding discussion of the details of the deal. This ploy may be used when positions are weak. It is also easy for the Team to agree to this if it has not done its homework. Counter tactics include questioning from what baseline the split is proposed. Never agree to a split if it is above the highest price your team is willing to pay when negotiations started. Always avoid even dollar splits because these tend to favor those offering the split. Try to offer an uneven split. For example, an agency is at $1,100,000, they are at $1,300,000; and offer to split the $200,000 difference, making the offer $1,200,000. The Team should counter with $1,185,000. If accepted, the Team has saved $15,000. Another counter is to come back to discussions of non-dollar issues with the hope of gaining concessions on those if your team cannot get concessions on the dollars. As negotiation involves the entire agreement, a difference splitter may not only simply haggle over price but also try to avoid discussing other areas of the agreement and refuse to delve into the cost/price analysis of the proposed offer.

Nickel and Dime

In this case, the other side wants to negotiate each and every point (Fischer & Ury, 1991, p. 94). This tactic may narrow disagreements but makes it harder to reach a final agreement when, for example, the Team thinks it has an agreement on price and moves on to who will pay for delivery; the other side objects to being asked to pay for delivery because it insists that price has already been negotiated. The final contract must be clear and precise on the nature of the business deal.

Good Cop/Bad Cop

From television to the negotiating table, everyone has seen the good cop/bad cop tactic played out. This tactic tries to elicit feelings of sympathy and understanding in order to get concessions (Fischer & Ury, 1991, pp. 102-103). The counter tactic is to insist on discussing the facts of the proposal with the "good cop" just as the Team does with the "bad cop."

Pity Me

This ploy is designed to play on the sense of fair play and to make it hard for the Team to walk away. The counter tactic is to keep insisting on discussing facts rather than emotion.

Piece By Piece

This tactic is used to negotiate each item of a contract. If all works well, the agency will get maximum value for concessions made. It also lessens the probability that the negotiators will give up something unnecessarily during the negotiation process. However, this tactic increases the time needed to reach an agreement and also increases the likelihood that some impasse will be encountered that will cause negotiations to break down.

Total Package

Total package offers are acceptable when only one or two major elements need to be negotiated. This can avoid the frustrations and problems of the piece-by-piece tactic. However, there may be items that should be negotiated which might be overlooked when a total package offer is accepted.

Refusal to Negotiate

Another negotiating ploy is a refusal to negotiate. The other side wants a concession even to talk. This technique was used successfully by the Soviet Union in many negotiations with the United States (Whitaker, Cullen, Whitmore, & Doherty, 1984, pp. 26-27). The Team must decide if there is something it wants to concede just to talk.

Status

Sometimes the party the evaluation team is negotiating with is perceived to have a higher status, such as when the president of a company personally negotiates with the Team. The better prepared the Team, the less status matters. In fact, higher-level executives may not be as well prepared for negotiations as your team, so do not be intimidated (Karrass, 1998a, p. 26).

Other Tactics

Other ploys may involve the use of extreme or escalating demands, divide-and-conquer tactics, and power plays. Sometimes the other side will make extreme demands in order to get the Team to lower its expectations for a final agreement (Fischer & Ury, 1991, pp. 139-142). Escalating demands appear when the other side keeps raising what they want as the negotiation progresses. This ploy is designed to get your side to come to agreement before demand rises again.

Divide-and-conquer tactics are used to persuade various members of the Team to accept the opposition's position. This can occur in side conversations during breaks or openly in the negotiating room with comments directed to specific team members. A lead negotiator can lose control of a negotiation when their agency's attorney fails to present a united front with the procurement official as the leader of the Negotiating Team. For example, the attorney proceeded to make business decisions instead of providing strictly legal advice. The other side picked up on this wrestling of the leadership role from the procurement official. Proposals were directed to the attorney and accepted. Consequently, an agreement that failed to include all the negotiating targets of the Team was accepted, to the detriment of the agency. It cannot be emphasized enough that the Team Leader must be in charge and that the entire Team presents a united front.

Power plays occur in several forms, but the most common one is to try to go over the head of the agency's Team Leader to the senior executives of the jurisdiction. It is important to keep senior management and elected officials informed of the detrimental consequences of these ploys. There are appropriate times when one must go over the head of the party with whom they are negotiating. If one is at an impasse because their counterpart does not have the delegated authority to proceed, it is necessary to get other parties involved. This can be accomplished by acknowledging in a non-threatening way that it is apparent that others must be brought into the negotiation before any progress can be made. For example, one agency was negotiating with a software provider. Withholding payments was under discussion. It became apparent to the procurement official that the standard provisions of the software agreement would not allow for this and the company representative had no authority to alter the software agreement. The solution was to ask for the involvement of the software company's vice-president of governmental operations and their legal department. The vice-president was able to incorporate a rarely made change into the agreement. Without involving the vice-president, the negotiations would have broken off. Make sure that negotiations take place only if the potential supplier's representatives have the authority to make a binding commitment. Never negotiate if the other side must go back to higher authorities for approvals. It has been recommended that the other side, prior to negotiations, submit a formal letter of authorization.

Defense

You or your adversary may use the tactic of trying to keep the other side on the defensive. This is done in several ways.

- Ignore what is said by the other side and focus on your own strengths.
- Attack adversary's weaknesses.
- Bluff. This will work as long as it is not challenged. Most negotiators make a point of challenging all bluffs. The evaluation team must always be prepared to call a bluff and back up its position with facts. Remember, if you bluff, you will probably be called on to produce your supporting evidence as well.
- Create an illusion of power. An example of this is the contractor who tries to force you into making a hasty decision by stating they have another offer to buy their product or service (Fischer & Ury, 1991, p. 27).
- A good negotiator needs to be able to recognize the tactics discussed above. The evaluation team can then decide if they want to let the other side know that they are aware they are being used. Remember that a clever tactic by either side will not make up for poor preparation (Fischer & Ury, 1991, p. 27).

It is important to note that once negative tactics are detected, they lose their power. These tactics can be effective against unskilled, unprepared, and tired negotiators. The Team Leader must assign someone the task of monitoring negative tactics and alerting the rest of the Team. This will allow the Team to thoughtfully respond. The lead negotiator should not use negative tactics. It is important to note that they often work when not detected but, when detected, send a negative message about the party using the tactic (Fearon et al., 1993, p. 239).

Effective Negotiators

*E*ffective negotiators have the ability to listen, question, and maintain control of their emotions.

Listening

A good negotiator must also be a good listener. Essential listening skills include:

- paying attention to what the other side is saying;
- maintaining good eye contact;
- questioning in a non-threatening manner;
- watching for the non-verbal signs of the other party;
- not interrupting;
- requesting clarification of any items you do not understand;
- showing patience and empathy for the other side's position; and
- looking for areas of agreement (Fuller, 1991, pp. 55-58).

Silence

During negotiations, silence may be to the evaluation team's advantage. Silence can keep the other side talking. Silence can show displeasure. Silence can add emphasis to what the evaluation team has to say (Fuller, 1991, pp. 55-56). Use silence when presented with an unreasonable demand. The opposition may think they have to break the silence by asking another question or suggesting an alternate plan or option (Fischer & Ury, 1991, pp. 139-142).

Emotions

Team members must never lose their tempers during negotiations. They may acknowledge their anger but should try not to vent it because anger can lead to mistakes. If the other side gets angry, they should be particularly alert to any mistakes they may make that the Team can use to its advantage. At the same time, the Team should try not to take the other side's anger personally.

Questions

Questioning is an effective way to gain information and clarification in negotiations. Avoid questions that can be answered with a simple yes or no. Formulate a series of questions to probe complex and tough issues. Use follow-up questions to further explore the answers given (Fuller, 1991, pp. 65-68). When offering an answer to a question from the other side, put the issue before the answer—clarify the interest and the reason for the question before presenting the solution. For example, "We know we are both concerned with the escalating cost of raw materials. We would like to offer the following _____ as a possible solution to slow down this growth in costs" Fischer & Ury, 1991, p. 53). Or,

We know we both want this project completed in a timely manner and that the weather has been less than desirable. But my review of your request for additional time shows that your request for 20 additional weather days does not meet the criteria for a weather delay. I show that inclement weather with temperatures below 10 degrees only occurred on 12 days (Fischer & Ury, 1991, p. 53).

If there is an issue that the Team does not understand, keep asking for clarification. Do not move forward until the Team has an understanding or, at the minimum, there is an agreement to come back and discuss the issue. Additionally, it is helpful to discuss only one item at a time (Karrass, 1998a, p. 26).

Questioning is also effective when pressure is applied by the other side. They should be invited to state their reasoning and the objective criteria behind their position. Again, do not move forward unless the answers given are reasonable.

Offers and Concessions

It is preferable that the other side makes the first offer. Sometimes, a preliminary discussion of the background of the procurement and other items may be necessary before either side will feel comfortable in making an offer. Many negotiations resulting from an RFP process will have a price or cost basis from which to begin the negotiations.

When it comes to making concessions, the advice is to concede a little at a time over a long period of time. Always try to get something in return. Never make a concession without getting one in return. This applies to even the low dollar and seemingly trivial issues. Good planning should make the Team aware of what the other side is capable of and willing to concede as well as to those items on which that they cannot make any concessions. Minutes of the negotiations should note what was given away so that all will clearly understand who is being more responsive in the negotiations. It is important not to concede a point too quickly because the other side is likely to believe that it may have settled for too little (Karrass, 1998a, p. 21). It will be assumed that the Team has something left to concede; therefore, it is advisable to take longer to make concessions and to concede less as the negotiations progress. Knowing when and how to make concessions is one of the more difficult skills to acquire (Fearon et al., 1993, p. 247).

Documenting the Negotiation

The Team Leader must ensure that the negotiation is documented in order to record the negotiation targets and demonstrate that a fair and reasonable price was obtained. It also demonstrates that the Team made a conscientious effort. This documentation begins in the pre-planning stage with the recording of the various negotiation targets and options for meeting the other side's perceived issues. Documentation continues with the minutes of each negotiation session. Eventually, these notes are used to draw up the agreement between the parties. A complete negotiation record protects the public's trust and can also be used to interpret the agreement in the event of a dispute. In addition, the negotiation record may lay the foundation for future negotiations. For example, if the evaluation team has agreed to pay start-up costs in a contract and later negotiate subsequent work; these costs will be eliminated because the evaluation team can demonstrate that they were paid in the original contract.

The negotiation is not complete until the contract is written and executed.

The negotiation is not complete until the contract is written and executed. Care should be taken to insure that all terms of the agreement are included and the specific performance required by both parties is stated. Definite start, completion, and delivery dates should be detailed to include late payment provisions and how the agreement can be modified. Standard boilerplate provisions should also be reviewed to ensure that they are relevant to the specific agreement. A check of any referenced documents must also be made to verify that the contents do not contradict the agreement (Fuller, 1991, pp. 260-261).

It is highly recommended that the jurisdiction act as the official recorder or secretary of the negotiation sessions. In this way, the jurisdiction can be assured that all of its concerns are addressed, noted and incorporated into the final contract itself.

It has been stated that a negotiation can be judged by three criteria: Did it produce a wise agreement? Does it improve or at least not damage the relationship? Is it efficient (Fischer & Ury, 1991)?

Special Factors

International Negotiation

With the increase in the global economy, it is likely that many jurisdictions will be involved in negotiations with other countries. It is easy to see how one's normal thought processes might work against clear communication when different cultures are involved. This is especially true when the subject of the communication or negotiation is abstract and complex. Decision- making styles of the culture must be reviewed. The United States and Canada have a business culture that assumes that unless an action or agreement is restricted by law, it is permitted; while nations of the former Soviet Union assume that nothing is permitted unless expressly allowed by the law. Japan is one of many nations that has a collective decision-making business process. It is unreasonable to expect a negotiator from such a culture to immediately agree to a change in negotiating position.

When embarking on international negotiations, two questions should be considered:

- How does the nature of a given nation's institutional culture produce a unique pattern of collective decision-making?
- In what way does a local culture affect an individual's decision-making style (Fisher, 1980, p. 29)?

Some other common factors to be considered are how women are looked upon as business equals, gestures, facial expressions, and possible verbal expressions. Be Careful! Not all cultures have the same sense of humor. It is better to omit rather than do something that may be misunderstood.

The consensus process is slow in getting an agreement, but it leads to quicker implementation of the agreement, as all parties have been involved in the decision. By contrast, those from the United States or Canada may reach a negotiated agreement sooner but be slower in carrying it out because consensus is often built after the fact.

Other cross-cultural differences, such as normal speaking distance between people, must be recognized to avoid insulting the other party. Some cross-cultural differences that can lead to inadvertent insults include slouching, displaying the soles of one's shoes, forgetting to address the other party by the appropriate title, inappropriate dress, speaking volume, tipping too much, and manner of approaching the opposite sex. Negotiators with limited international experience will likely experience problems in these areas. For example, many Japanese use silence as an integral part of normal conversation, but many Americans may interpret silence to mean anger or disapproval. Many languages use both a formal and informal form of "you." Using the inappropriate form when addressing a counterpart can lead to misunderstanding or insult.

Similarly, the use of interpreters presents its own problems. There are some ideas and situations that are not common to every culture and are, therefore, difficult to translate. Often, the effectiveness of international agreements is directly related to the way they are understood following negotiation. Translators should be aware of the subjective understanding of both sides in agreement. For example, the concept of "individualistic" has a positive connotation in the United States but a negative one in Japan. The words "fair play" in English have no direct translation to other languages. Communication is further complicated by words with more than one meaning, tones of voice, and gestures (Fisher, 1980, p. 63). While English is becoming a business lingua franca (a common language used by speakers of different languages) for much of the world, negotiators must be cognizant that attempting to communicate in the other party's language can be a barrier to true communication when it is beyond the ability of the speaker.

Negotiating with Multiple Offerors

There are occasions when a jurisdiction may embark on simultaneous negotiations with more than one vendor, thus multiplying the difficulties of preparing separate negotiating strategies. It is extremely important not to share information learned from one offeror in negotiations with another, including technical information and pricing. It is highly unethical to auction off the agreement—"I have a price of X from vendor Y. Are you willing to beat it?" As with any procurement process all vendors, must be treated fairly and as equal as possible.

Conclusion

Agencies are increasingly called upon to negotiate various agreements. How much time and effort is expended on negotiation depends on the strategic importance of the procurement, the amount of money involved, the time available, and the degree of competition. Procurement officials must take an active role in negotiations, and enough time must be delegated to pre-negotiation strategy and preparation. Effective negotiators must have a thorough grasp of tactics and communication techniques in order to be effective.

References

Barker, H. P., Jr. (1998, July). *Competitive negotiations*. Paper presented at the NIGP Forum, Phoenix, Arizona.

Dobler, D. W., & Burt, D. N. (1996). *Purchasing and supply management* (6th ed.). New York: McGraw-Hill Companies, Inc.

Fearon, H. E., Dobler, D. W., & Killen, K. K. (1993). *The purchasing handbook* (5th ed.). New York: McGraw-Hill Companies, Inc.

Fischer, R., & Ury, W. (1991). *Getting to yes: Negotiating agreement without giving in* (2nd ed.). New York: Penguin Books.

Fisher, G. (1980). *International negotiation*. New York: Intercultural Press, Inc.

Fuller, G. (1991). *The negotiator's handbook*. Englewood Cliffs, NJ: Prentice Hall.

Karrass, C. L. (1996, April 11). Five ways to make concessions. *Purchasing Magazine*, 120 (5), 21.

Karrass, C. L. (1998, December 10). Tips for team negotiators. *Purchasing Magazine*, 125 (9), 24.

Karrass, C. L. (1998, April 9). Averages are fair game for skeptics. *Purchasing Magazine*, 124 (5), 24.

National Institute of Governmental Purchasing, Inc. (NIGP) (1996). *Dictionary of purchasing terms* (5th ed.). Herndon, VA: NIGP.

National Institute of Governmental Purchasing, Inc. (NIGP) (2001). *Advanced public procurement*. Herndon, VA: NIGP.

Northcraft, G. B., & Neale, M. A. (1994). *Organizational behavior: A management challenge* (2nd ed.). Fort Worth, TX: The Dryden Press, Harcourt Brace College Publishers.

TCI, Inc. (1984). *Cost and price analysis and contract negotiations*. Emsherst, MA: Urban Mass Transportation Administration, Office of Administration.

Whitaker, M., Cullen, R., Whitmore, J., & Doherty, S. (1984, October 1). The Gromyko method. *Newsweek*.

Negotiation Checklist

Stages of Negotiation:

- Planning
- Actual Negotiations
- Completion

Planning

- Formulate your objective
- List alternatives if negotiations are unsuccessful.
- Identify any alternative approaches that can be offered during negotiations if agreement can't be reached on the primary objective
- Access the other side's alternatives if agreement isn't reached
- Establish maximum and minimum negotiation positions
- Develop your negotiation strategy
- List items that are non-negotiable
- Prioritize any concessions that can be made
- Determine timeline for negotiation
- Organize your team
- Select the team leader
- Establish the roles of the team
- Begin documentation of the negotiation
- Assess the strengths, weaknesses, and business reputation of the other party
- Determine whether outside experts are needed
- Have the documentation to support your position
- Develop the arguments that support your position
- Establish the first offer to be made
- Establish where the negotiations will be held
- Make travel arrangements if necessary

Actual Negotiations

- Go over logistics of the site
- Determine the negotiating authority of your counterpart
- Determine behind the scenes decision makers
- Assess your counterpart's negotiation style
- Determine tactics they are using and develop options to counter
- Control your emotions

- Communicate clearly
- Break when needed to regroup
- Close any gap left in negotiations
- Adjust your plan depending on the negotiation progression

Completion
- Explore trade-offs
- What are final concessions?
- Do higher ups need to be involved to complete the negotiations?
- Deal with your side to overcome any opposition to the negotiations
- Leave option available to reopen negotiations if they break down
- Prepare to move to another source if agreement can't be reached
- Agree on terms
- Write up the agreement
- Secure any required legal or other reviews

Source: Fuller, G. (1991). *The negotiator's handbook*. Englewood Cliffs, NJ: Prentice Hall.

CHAPTER 8

Contract Writing: Terms and Conditions

Introduction

*T*erms and conditions are the heart of any contract. They define and describe the rights and responsibilities of all of the parties. This chapter provides information on how to write terms and conditions that will guarantee strong contract performance.

The phrase "terms and conditions" is only one of the references that lawyers use to identify the substantive parts of a contract Other terms used are "clauses," "provisions," "paragraphs," and the word "terms" by itself. The use of these terms covers a whole range of items, such as specifications, scopes of work, delivery and repair response time lines, warranties, pricing for contract option or renewal periods, milestones for performance, termination of the contract, assignment of the contract to another supplier, indemnification, ownership of work products, and notification of debarment or suspension.

Procurement Official's Role in Drafting Terms and Conditions

*M*ore often than not, there are two types of public officials who develop the language of a public contract on behalf of a jurisdiction. The procurement representative, or the end-user with procurement's review, will prepare the specifications for goods by describing the item to be purchased as well as language addressing related issues, such as delivery, packaging, repair and maintenance; or, for service contracts, the Scope/Statement of Work (SOW), including service elements and delivery, desired contract outcomes, and the level of expertise required from the vendor and vendor staff. Typically, each agency has a standardized contract format that has been drafted to be directed at the law that affects the formation and operation of the contract, such as indemnification, certifications about independent, non-collusive pricing and gratuities, contract termination, and preservation of remedies.

While the actual responsibility for scripting contract language will vary depending on the size and resources of the jurisdiction and the level of training of the buyer, it is important for the procurement official to remember two things. First, the language that is used in describing the item being purchased; the specifications or scopes/statements of work serves not only to inform vendors what the agency desires to purchase; it also becomes a part of the contract that results from the solicitation and establishes whether the successful offeror is in compliance with the contract's requirements.

Additionally, the contract administrator should monitor whether other parts of the contract are working, i.e., those that the jurisdiction's attorney drafted. While it may be appropriate for an attorney to draft, or at least review, certain contract terms such as an indemnification clause, the procurement official needs to determine whether those terms are reasonable for the acquisition. If good suppliers are taking exception to a clause or deciding not to compete because they consider the clause too onerous, procurement should alert the attorney and discuss whether other suitable language could be used that protects the jurisdiction but would be more palatable to vendors.

Types of Contracts

There are many types of contracts that an entity can enter into with a vendor, depending on varying factors.

Purchasing Options. If the decision to purchase goods or services is ultimately made, the buyer must determine the type of purchase needed. An open market purchase is an acquisition made one single time rather than in volume or with a continuous purchase arrangement. Typically, it is used for low-value, small-volume items, one-time purchases, or purchases of items or services needed only on an occasional or infrequent basis. Occasionally, this purchase is referred to as "hand-to-mouth buying."

Blanket Contracts. A blanket contract is an agreement for a supplier to provide the purchaser's requirements for items or services on an "as-needed" basis. This type of contract is used when the exact items or services cannot be specifically defined. These contracts are for a specified period and usually include minimum/maximum order limits and a maximum overall expenditure amount.

Term Contracts. Term contracts establish a source of supply and pricing for specified items or services for a specific time frame. They are usually based on known or estimated quantities to be ordered, as needed.

Both blanket and term contracts may be referred to as "forward buying." Forward buying represents a win/win situation for both the jurisdiction and the selected supplier or contractor. The agency is able to obtain better terms in exchange for the longer-term commitment. The selected supplier or contractor can look forward to larger contracts. Procurement must remember that when such a commitment has been made, it should be honored. Any attempt to transfer responsibilities to the supplier weakens the agreement and closes the door to any future contracts of this nature.

Both blanket and term contracts may be referred to as "forward buying."

If purchasing takes place in sensitive or fluctuating markets, such as oil and oil products, the agency should look for approaches that minimize future risks. One technique entails the use of hedging transactions in the futures market. Governments use this technique to minimize risks on commodities that fluctuate in price and may depend on international politics as well as normal market conditions. Hedging is an option to buy a commodity in the future at a fixed price. If procurement officials want to purchase oil for delivery in six months, there are two ways to structure a contract—to either pay the price in effect at the time of delivery or to establish a fixed-price contract with escalation clauses. The selected supplier or contractor does not want to take a chance that future prices will be to his disadvantage and will not commit to a firm fixed price. On the other hand, the ability to forecast is limited, and the degree of uncertainty may mean unacceptable risks to the buyer. The risk can be reduced by the use of a futures contract.

Using the above example, the governmental unit can also purchase a futures contract at a fixed price for the amount of oil to be delivered at a specific time. If the price of oil rises and the selling price at the time of delivery is higher than the price in the futures contract, the value of the futures contract also rises, since it is a firm contract to buy the oil only at the lower price. Therefore, the agency will make a profit on this type of futures contract, the proceeds of which will offset the increase in oil prices. If the price of oil goes down, the futures contract is worthless. The agency will get the oil at a lower price but will have paid for the futures contract. Hedging may be looked upon as a form of insurance. It protects an entity against rising prices and enables accurate budgeting for projected costs.

Procurement should be aware that all contracts involve some degree of risk. Most agencies prefer to have the selected supplier or contractor assume most, if not all, of the risk. If, for instance, a city chooses to buy a large amount of material to avoid the risk of a subsequent price increase, it may be left with a large amount of inventory on hand that may not be used. If the city chooses to purchase on a hand-to-mouth basis, the buyer may end up paying higher prices at a later date. Therefore, choosing the proper contract is a balance between eliminating most of the agency's risks and uncontrollable market forces that determine what a supplier is willing to do.

Compensation arrangements can be classified into three broad categories: fixed-price contracts, cost-reimbursement contracts, and time-and-materials contracts. Under a fixed-price arrangement, the supplier is obligated to deliver the product called for in the contract at an agreed-upon price and to make delivery regardless of any unforeseen increase in costs. The amount of profit the supplier may earn will depend upon his actual costs. Naturally, this type of contract can only be used when specifications are well defined and the supplier is able to fully assess all of the potential risks in fulfillment of the contract. A supplier will normally anticipate and provide for contingencies when determining the price to be charged.

Under a cost type arrangement, the buyer's obligation is to reimburse the supplier for all allowable and allocable costs incurred and pay an agreed-upon fee or profit over and above the supplier's costs. Both types of contracts (fixed and cost plus) have variations.

Firm Fixed Price Contract

A firm fixed price contract (FFP) is the most common pricing practice in everyday purchasing transactions. In this agreement, the price agreed to by both the agency and supplier will not change during the period of the agreement. Generally, the establishment of a firm price should be the basic objective for procurement for most of the orders placed. In this type of contract, the selected supplier or contractor assumes all of the risk.

Firm Fixed Price with Economic Adjustments

A firm fixed price with economic price adjustment contract (FPEPA) contains escalation and de-escalation clauses that allow for modification of the prices in the contract for items that typically are subject to fluctuations. Cost adjustment clauses are generally used in long-term raw materials contracts. On occasion, this type of clause may appear in contracts for capital equipment that have an extended construction schedule. This type of contract can be used successfully when it is linked to an objective benchmark upon which to base the price variations.

Fixed Price Re-determination

A fixed price redetermination contract (FPR) is one that has a re-determination or renegotiation clause. These contracts provide for firm fixed prices for the initial period of the contract. A re-determination of the pricing either up or down would be made at a stated time during the contract performance. Typically, contracts for janitorial services are of this type: initial pricing applies to the first year of the contract, and a price re-determination is made for the second year. A pre-selected method to use as a basis for this process is required.

Price in Effect at Time of Shipment

Occasionally, a price is determined at the time the shipment contract is entered into; the price is established when the shipment is made. This type of contract is used if pricing for raw materials or labor is very unpredictable. As a general rule, agencies should avoid this type of contract, since the price is not known at the time of commitment. If this is not possible, procurement should attempt to tie the pricing to some published benchmark.

Cost Plus Fixed Fee

When the specifications or SOW cannot be well defined or the entity is willing to share some of the risk with the selected supplier or contractor, a cost plus contract is applicable. In this type of contract, the selected supplier or contractor is reimbursed for their costs and then paid an agreed-upon-fee, which is independent of the costs. The fee should always be a specified dollar amount. This is called a cost-plus-fixed-fee contract (CPFF). The disadvantage of this type of contract is that it does not offer any inducement to the selected supplier or contractor to reduce costs. The agency may overcome this problem by using a CPFF contract with a guaranteed maximum amount for the contract or "cap" that sets a budget ceiling. If the selected supplier or contractor exceeds the cap, no additional monies are paid. Governments should never enter into a cost-plus contract that aligns the fee to be paid as a percentage of the costs. Most jurisdictions prohibit this type of contract, because it tends to offer an incentive to the selected supplier or contractor to increase expenses.

Time and Materials

A time and materials contract (T&M) is used if the precise amount of work (labor) and the needed materials cannot be predicted, as is common with repairs. Under a T&M contract, the parties agree to a fixed hourly rate for labor that includes all overhead and profit. Parts are usually supplied at the contractor's cost, or procurement officials may allow a nominal handling charge, e.g., 5%.

Performance Based Contracts

Recent trends in purchasing have focused on the development of new perfor-mance-based or cost-incentive contracts. The purpose of these new constraints is to encourage the supplier to find new and more cost effective ways to make the product or furnish the service. The most frequent application of incentives is in the area of cost savings; however, incentives can be offered to improve the contractor's performance in other areas as well.

Cost incentive contracts can be used with fixed price and cost plus contracts. Typically, all construction contracts that are fixed price (lump sum) will contain a value engineering clause, which will pay the contractor a percentage of any savings incurred by finding an alternate way of carrying out the task. Other types of fixed price incentive contracts will require the agency and selected supplier or contractor to agree to target costs and a target profit, making them very similar to cost plus fixed fee contracts.

A target cost for an incentive contract is the cost that both the agency and the supplier determine to be the most applicable for the effort involved. Target costs should be based on costs resulting from normal business transactions. If contractors are able to reduce the costs, then they will benefit by receiving additional payment. A target profit is a profit amount that the buyer and selected supplier or contractor considers being fair and reasonable, considering the risks and the dollar amount of the contract.

Cost Plus Incentive Fee

In a cost plus incentive fee contract (CPIF), cost and fee targets are established for both the most optimistic and most pessimistic projections. These points are used to establish the sharing arrangements. If a supplier has incurred costs above the target, the target profit will be decreased by a given percentage. If the suppliers' costs are below target, their profit will be increased by a given percentage. In order to make this an effective contract, well-defined parameters must be established and an objective monitoring system used.

Cost Plus Award Fee

A new type of a contract that is gaining favor is called a cost plus award fee contract (CPAF). This contract provides that the agency will reward the supplier on a periodic basis for efforts in meeting the agency's stated needs. The key difference between the award fee and a fixed fee is that in a CPAF contract, the supplier's fee is based on the subjective evaluation of how well the supplier applies its efforts in meeting the jurisdiction's needs. This type of contract requires a great deal of administrative effort by the agency to monitor both cost and performance. Rather than simply negotiating one fixed fee, an agreement is reached for a minimum and a maximum fee based on the buyer's decision as to how much of the fee the selected supplier or contractor has earned. When properly used, an award fee-based contract can benefit both the buyer and the supplier. Superior performance receives superior rewards; poor performance receives lesser awards. The various contract structures are summarized in Table 33.

Table 33

Contract Summary

Types of Contracts	Description
Firm Fixed Price	No change permitted to contract price. Selected supplier or contractor assumes all risks.
Fixed Price with Economic Adjustment Clause	Fixed-price contract that allows for some adjustment. Adjustment must be based on agreed-upon index. Suitable for commodities whose prices fluctuate.
Fixed Price with Re-determination Clause	No changes permitted for agreed time period. Changes may be made at that time based upon index.
Fixed Price Incentive	Very similar to CPIF described below. Jurisdiction reimburses selected supplier or contractor for all allowable costs. No risks to selected supplier or contractor since all costs are reimbursable.
Cost Plus Fixed Fee	Selected supplier or contractor is paid fixed amount as fee independent of cost. A modification to this type of contract establishes a cap or not-to-exceed amount. Any costs over this amount become the selected supplier's or contractor's risk.
Cost Plus Incentive Fee	Selected supplier or contractor is reimbursed for all allowable costs. Target costs are agreed to. Selected supplier or contractor's fee is fixed amount. Selected supplier or contractor is paid incentive fee for lowering target costs.
Cost Plus Award Fee	Very similar to CPIF except that fee paid to selected supplier or contractor is determined subjectively by agency.
Time and Materials	Selected supplier or contractor is paid contract price for any labor. Material costs are reimbursed at selected supplier's or contractor's cost or slight markup for handling.

Private and Public Contracts Compared

The extent to which procurement's daily tasks requires the drafting of a wide range of contract terms and conditions depends somewhat on the procurement law and policies in place within the particular jurisdiction. For instance, if the law does not require certain purchases to be acquired competitively, the agency may engage in extensive negotiations with vendors for those purchases, including drafting and redrafting the terms of the contract. A purchasing department may have established a set of terms and conditions that are standard for all contracts, and the procurement official need only attach a copy of that section to solicitations issued for competitive procurements.

Whatever responsibilities purchasing has in drafting or reviewing contract terms and conditions, they will differ from the responsibilities and flexibility that parties have in the private sector. A brief discussion on the general differences between how contracts form in the public and private settings follows.

Formation of Private Contracts

In the commercial world, parties create contracts in one of three ways. First, one party may present the other with a prepared document for signature, and the second party has little bargaining power to change the terms of the agreement. Many consumer sales agreements fall within this category.

Secondly, a contract may be formed at the time each party sends the other its prepared document, setting forth differing terms from the first party's document. For example, one party may issue a purchase order for certain goods, and the other sends a confirmation that contains terms that vary from the purchase order. The goods are often shipped despite the differences in the documents, and those differences do not become important unless a problem arises.

Finally, a contract may be created through the process of negotiation, in which the parties bargain for the terms of the contract. Both parties sign the agreement that results from that negotiation. The contract may be a complex document with pages of tightly drafted clauses, or it may consist of a letter that one party drafts for the other to sign.

Formation of a Public Contract

Overview

For the most part, public contracts are created through a different process. As in the world of private commerce, a public procurement official, for some small dollar purchases, may issue a purchase order to a vendor based on items and prices in the vendor's general catalogue. The vendor may ship the goods requested with a confirmation or invoice that contains terms that vary from the purchase order. This scenario generally creates a contract, despite the fact that the parties did not reach an agreement on its precise language.

For larger dollar purchases, a contract arises as a result of a formal, arms-length process. The jurisdiction issues a solicitation that invites vendors to make an offer that complies with the specific terms of the solicitation. Where the jurisdiction seeks a contractor through the competitive sealed bids process, there is no real bargaining. Under the competitive sealed proposals method, the opportunity for discussions and negotiations exists but is limited.

Even in a qualifications-based selection process, if the procurement official negotiates price after selecting the most qualified professional service vendor, the subject matter of the negotiation is generally restricted to price or fee. Thus, in much of public contracting, the bargaining that is a normal part of private commerce is absent, due in large part to the mandate placed on public purchasers to ensure that the contractor-selection process is fair to all.

Once the procurement official selects the winning bid or proposal and notifies the offeror of its selection, a contract comes into existence in most cases. If contract award requires the vote of a town council or board of supervisors, the action taken at the vote becomes the event creating a contract. A solicitation that clearly defines the terms and item description in conjunction with the offer and the subsequent acceptance by the jurisdiction becomes the contract.

Separate Contract Document

In some jurisdictions, procurement officials prepare a separate contract document for signature once they have selected and notified the successful offeror. A separate contract document is unnecessary, as the contract arises under the principles of contract law once the jurisdiction indicates acceptance of the vendor's offer.

Occasionally, an agency will issue a solicitation without many terms, particularly when buying commodities, and award a contract through a simple blanket purchase order. Unless the solicitation addresses issues such as force majeure or contract remedies including termination and payment, the jurisdiction may not be adequately covered, or covered at all, depending on the language of the blanket purchase order.

The supplier may afford itself an advantage in the future through the terms it includes in its confirmation or invoice document. Some contractors seek to make the jurisdiction bound to the contractor's terms and conditions by asking unwitting users to sign separate agreements at the time of initial ordering from a contract.

The Best Approach

The best approach to protect an agency is to include in the solicitation all the terms that should be a part of the contract. Purchasing should have a set of standard contract terms, approved by the jurisdiction's attorney, addressing issues common to all of its contracts, and might consider drafting additional standard terms that are applicable, for instance, to contracts for the purchase of goods. The official may either include those standard terms explicitly in every solicitation or simply include language in the solicitation that incorporates them by reference, making copies available to vendors online, via fax-on-demand, or at the purchasing office.

Purchasing officers will engage in more negotiating, or bargaining, of the type that occurs in the commercial world, if the agency law does not require the agency to engage in a formal competitive process, such as competitive sealed bidding; if the purchase of certain services is qualifications-based without consideration of fees, as with architects and engineers for construction; or in situations where there exists only one source for the item, such as operating software for a large, mainframe computer. Whatever role procurement professionals have in creating the language of the contract, they must have the skills to recognize and draft sound contract provisions.

Overview of Contract Law

*D*rafting contract language for Request for Proposal (RFP) requires a basic knowledge of contract law, including types and sources of contract law, the legal force of the written document, law relating to contract creation and its application to drafting, general interpretation of the contract, and governing rules.

Types and Sources of Contract Law

Primary Source of Contract Law

With one important exception, the law of contracts emanates primarily from longstanding principles announced in common law. Common law consists of written decisions of judges. Legal principles announced in judicial decisions have the same legal effect as statutory law, where statutory law does not change them and courts adhere to common law principles just as they do to those announced in statutes.

The Uniform Commercial Code

The exception is commercial contract law. It emanates in large part from statutes, although case law interpreting those statutes is common law. The Uniform Commercial Code (UCC) is a set of statutes addressing a wide range of commercial topics, from bulk sales of goods to the negotiability of certain documents. It also covers the sales of goods and embodies many of the principles of the common law of contracts, while changing them in certain areas. Today, all 50 states have adopted some version of the UCC, but the State of Louisiana has not adopted those portions of it that address the sale of goods.

Sources of Public Contract Law

The sources of public contract law are more varied. Often, the genesis for public contract law is a statute or ordinance setting forth specific procedures that the jurisdiction must follow in purchasing the goods, services, and construction that it needs.

Like the general law of contracts, the law of public contracts has its own body of common law. Decisions of courts on legal challenges to contract awards and on claims filed under contracts form much of that common law, but there are other important sources for it as well. Certain jurisdictional administrative entities, particularly within the Federal jurisdiction, have the responsibility to decide bid protests and contract claims, and many of those administrative decisions are an important source of jurisdiction contract law principles.

...the genesis for public contract law is a statute or ordinance...

The U.S. General Accounting Office, an arm of Congress, has decided bid protests for the Federal jurisdiction since 1921. The legal principles of public purchasing announced in its written decisions over the years have been the basis for many of the essential concepts that drive the practice of public contracting at the Federal, state, and local levels. Many of those concepts have now found their way into the language of statutes and ordinances.

Likewise, the decisions of the Federal jurisdiction's boards of contract appeals, responsible for deciding claims filed under contracts, are key sources of direction on contract interpretation and administration. While these administrative sources of public contract law do not have the same legal effect as do decisions of courts and, thus, do not meet the narrow definition of "common law," they are, nonetheless, important and often provide guidance to state courts on issues relating to public contracts.

Application of Contract Law to Public Purchasing

As a general rule, the principles of general contract law apply to the government procurement process, except where the law of public contracts specifically displaces them. If statutes and rules that establish procedures for the award of public contracts are detailed, such as those that regulate the means by which the United States does so, there is a broad displacement of general contract law, and the requirements of public contract law predominate. The public contract laws of most state and local jurisdictions are not as specific as those of the Federal jurisdiction; and general contract law will play a greater role in the procurement processes of those entities.

Written or Oral Contracts

Contracts may be written or oral. Both common and statutory law, however, require certain promises or agreements to be supported in writing. For those types of promises and agreements, neither party to the contract may enforce an unperformed contract through legal means if there is a dispute.

Statute of Frauds

In 1677, the English Parliament passed a law called the "Act for the Prevention of Fraud and Perjuries" requiring certain promises and agreements to be evidenced in writing. That law, generally known as the Statute of Frauds, became the common law of this country through court decisions, and state legislatures have enacted their own versions of it. Additionally, the UCC contains its own requirements that certain agreements be supported by written documentation.

Agreements That Must Be Supported By Written Documentation

The Statute of Frauds generally mandates that the following types of promises or agreements be evidenced in writing: agreements for the sale of land or of interests in land; agreements in consideration of marriage; a promise by the executor or administrator of a deceased person's estate to pay from their own pocket a debt of the deceased; certain promises made by a person to answer for the debt of another; and contracts that are not to be performed within one year from the time they are made, including leases. For procurement, the key elements on that list are *the sale of land or an interest in land and contracts not to be performed within a year.*

Satisfying the Writing Requirement

The type of writing that will satisfy the Statute of Frauds varies. A memorandum, exchange of correspondence, or receipt, for instance, may suffice if that writing identifies with reasonable certainty the contracting parties, the subject matter of the contract, and the contract's essential terms. The writing needs to be signed in some fashion by the party against whom the contract is being enforced. Any mark or sign that is written, printed, stamped, or otherwise placed on the writing may serve as a signature. Electronic signatures probably satisfy the requirement under appropriate circumstances.

The UCC governs the requirements for writing contracts for the sale of goods. It directs that a contract for the sale of goods for the price of $500 or more be in some written form sufficient to indicate that a contract has been made and signed by the party, or his/her agent or broker, against whom enforcement is sought.

For the writing to satisfy the UCC's requirements, it must demonstrate the following. First, it must certify a contract for the sale of goods. Additionally, it must be "signed," which includes any authentication identifying the party against whom enforcement of the contract is sought.

Law Relating to Contract Creation and Its Application to Drafting

*T*here are some key issues relating to contract formation that purchasing should address in solicitations and contracts. To clarify these issues, the following discussion is a brief reminder of the legal principles of contract creation.

Definition of "Contract"

For the purposes of this chapter, the term "contract" refers to promises or agreements for which the law establishes enforceable duties and remedies.

Elements of a Contract

There are six essential elements that must exist for a contract to be formed.

- Offer and Acceptance;
- Definiteness;
- Consideration;

- Mutuality of Obligation;
- Capacity of the Parties; and
- Legality of Purpose.

Two of them—consideration and mutuality of obligation—are related. Because of the formal nature of the public contracting process, there seldom is a dispute about whether the jurisdiction and its vendor have complied with some of these elements. Nonetheless, issues arise from time to time.

Offer and Acceptance

The process by which persons reach an agreement is the offer and acceptance process. An offer generally involves a promise or commitment to do or not to do a specified thing in the future. That promise demonstrates a person's intent to assure that the thing promised will or will not be done.

Acceptance occurs when the person to whom the offer is made exchanges their own promise or performance for the promise made in the offer. In the common law, the acceptance may not vary at all from the terms of the offer. If it does, it may be a counteroffer and constitutes a rejection of the original offer.

The UCC moderates the harsh common law rule, providing that an acceptance is valid even though it states additional or different terms, unless acceptance is conditioned on agreement to those terms. Those varying terms are considered proposals for additions to the contract if they do not vary significantly.

In public purchasing in the United States, a solicitation, such as an RFP, is not an offer but, instead, requests vendors to submit offers. The proposals submitted in response are offers. Acceptance occurs when the public official authorized to award contracts signifies that the jurisdiction has selected the successful vendor. That official may be the procurement official or may be an elected official. This is different in Canada where obligations to the offerors may exist upon issuance of a solicitation and receipt of offers.

Drafting Tips. Following are some common offer and acceptance issues in public contracts. They demonstrate how the language of the solicitation and other documents may change the outcome of a dispute on matters such as whether acceptance occurred.

- Procurement should ensure that contract terms define the point at which acceptance occurs and state that letters identifying a proposal as, or inferring that the proposal is, the apparent awardee do not constitute acceptance. Should procurement need to send a letter to an apparent awardee, such as to request certain financial information for determining that offer's responsibility, the letter should state explicitly that it is not an acceptance of the proposal.

- Solicitations should include wording, generally in the instructions section, stating that in submitting the proposal, the offeror agrees to hold its proposal open for a stated period of time. Use of this type of language clarifies that the vendor's "offer" is irrevocable; that is, the offeror may not withdraw it and must hold it open for a specified period of time. If the solicitation does not contain that language, a jurisdiction may have no recourse against a low bidder who wishes to withdraw its bid after hearing the other bidders' prices. Some procurement laws or rules limit the instances in which a vendor may withdraw its proposal after submission and thereby provides the jurisdiction with a remedy. The better practice is to include language in the solicitation making the proposal irrevocable for a period of time.

Definiteness

Under common law, an offer must include the important, or material, terms of the proposed agreement so that, when a person accepts the offer, the resulting agreement is enforceable. Important terms include subject matter, price, payment terms, quantity, quality, duration, and the work to be done. If the parties purport to agree on a material term but do so in a vague manner in contrast to omitting the term altogether, there is no agreement because it is too indefinite.

Again, the UCC alters the common law rule to provide a more practical one. It states that a contract for sale will not fail due to indefiniteness if the parties intended to make a contract and there is a reasonably certain basis for curing its vagueness.

Because of the formal competitive process that most jurisdictions follow in purchasing items above a certain dollar limit, indefiniteness of the offer is not a problem. Under the law of public contracts, a bid must be responsive; it must show the vendor's commitment to comply with the solicitation's requirements, which includes supplying a set price. If, for example, a vendor submits a bid that says the price will be the one in effect at the time it supplies janitorial services, the bid is non-responsive; it is also too indefinite.

Under that same scenario, but involving the sale of goods, the UCC might treat the offer's indefiniteness as curable under commercial standards. Note that the bid would still be non-responsive under the solicitation's terms and, thus, unacceptable under public contract law.

Consideration

The term "consideration" generally means that the person making the offer intends that the person to whom it is made does or promises to do something they are not legally obligated to do and that the person accepting the offer actually does or promises to do something not legally required.

In the common law, a person agreeing to make any legal commitment, no matter how economically inadequate, generally provides sufficient "consideration" to support a promise. The UCC changes that principle by permitting a court to refuse to enforce a contract or part of a contract that it finds unconscionable at the time it was made. Courts have used that UCC provision to release consumers from harsh installment sales contracts, where the value of the items purchased is substantially lower than the monthly payments and high interest charges assessed.

A good example of a consideration issue in jurisdiction contracts arises under what are called term or indefinite quantity contracts. Public purchasers establish these contracts for items commonly used throughout the jurisdiction. Under this type of contract, a vendor agrees to supply particular goods or services at a set price for a specific period of time, but the quantity of the goods or services that the jurisdiction will need is unknown, only estimated. If a dispute arises because a vendor claims that the jurisdiction has ordered too great a quantity of the items under the contract, the estimated quantity in the contract as well as the size of past orders will define whether the disputed order is reasonable.

Drafting Tip. If a term contract does not require the jurisdiction to buy all of the specific goods or services that it needs from the contractor, but reserves the discretion to buy them elsewhere, the jurisdiction has not given any consideration; it has not legally obligated itself to the terms of the contract. Lack of consideration is solved by mandating that the jurisdiction purchase all of the specific goods or services it needs under the contract.

Mutuality of Obligation

This element is really a sub-element of consideration. It applies in situations where the offer requires the person accepting it to make a promise in return rather than by performing immediately. A simple statement of the element is "both parties must be bound or neither one is bound." It really means that both parties must supply consideration to the other. For example, if a contracting party reserves a means by which it may avoid performing completely, the contract may not be enforceable, since both parties are not legally obligated to perform.

Competent Parties

There are certain classes of persons whom the law deems incapable of entering into a contract. A person who lacks the authority to contract for someone else under the law of agency is an example. Others are infants and mentally infirm individuals. In common law, a person remained an infant until the age of 21. Today, statutes and court decisions generally place the age at 18. In the public purchasing setting, the capacity issue generally arises because a jurisdiction's employee or a vendor's representative is not authorized to contract.

Drafting Tip. The wording in the solicitation addressing vendor signatures on a proposal should state that the person signing for the offeror should be an authorized representative. Additionally, the solicitation should state that only an authorized procurement official can make a contract award. Contract terms should also provide that only an authorized procurement official is able to make a modification to the contract.

Legal Purpose

Courts generally will not enforce an agreement, or part of an agreement, that violates criminal law or public policy. The extent to which a court will assist one person to enforce an "illegal" contract against another will depend on the type of violation of law involved and the requirements of applicable statutes or ordinances.

Drafting Tip. Statutes and ordinances often require public contracts to contain certain terms. Examples of the subjects that those types of terms may address are rights to audit and inspect contractor records, retention of records, availability of funds, and conflict of interest. Purchasing should ensure that the solicitations, contracts, and purchase orders contain those required terms. More often than not, the statutes that require these clauses are not the procurement laws of the jurisdiction. Instead, the requirements will be in laws that address, for instance, ethics or budgetary matters.

General Interpretation of a Contract

Procurement officials should keep in mind that someday, someone will read what they have written and try to find something wrong with it. Common law provides rules of contract interpretation that courts apply when the parties to a written contract disagree about what the terms mean.

Rules of Interpretation

A court's first step in a contract dispute will be to determine the meaning of the contract's language to decide whether the parties adopted it as a complete and final reflection of their thinking. The rules of interpretation are used to aid in deciphering the intent of the parties.

If the court decides that the parties meant for the agreement to be final and complete, the parol evidence rule (see below) prevents one of the parties from bringing up the terms of any written or oral agreements that existed before the contract to explain it. The court will consider parol evidence, or evidence outside of the contract language itself, where the parties did not intend the contract to be final and complete and its language is ambiguous but the rules of interpretation do not resolve that ambiguity.

Parol Evidence Rule

If the procurement official has written concrete terms and conditions, the agency would want the parol evidence rule to apply to exclude explanations of the contract outside of the written terms themselves. To help ensure that it does so, purchasing should insert a merger clause in the contract stating that the contract is a complete and final expression of the parties' intentions, e.g., "This written document embodies the entire contract. It constitutes the final expression of the parties' agreement and is a complete and exclusive statement of the terms of that agreement."

The UCC offers its own version of the parol evidence rule as it applies to contracts for the sale of goods.

The UCC offers its own version of the parol evidence rule as it applies to contracts for the sale of goods. It states that terms of sale on which the parties' confirmation memos agree, or that appear in something written that the parties intended to be a final expression of their agreement, may not be contradicted by prior or contemporaneous oral agreements. However, unlike the common law, the UCC permits those terms to be explained or supplemented by evidence of how the parties dealt with each other in the past, industry custom, or how the parties deal with each other during the current contract. The merger clause would not prevent a party from explaining the terms of a contract for the sale of goods through prior dealings or trade custom, because the UCC permits these types of explanations even if the parties adopted the contract as the final and complete statement of their agreement.

Drafting Tip. If in the past the agency has permitted a "grace period" for delivery and does not wish to do so any longer, it could draft a specific clause to eliminate that "grace period."

Using the Rules for Interpreting a Contract in Drafting

A court uses the common law rules of interpretation to determine and implement the intention of the parties to the contract. As a starting place for drafting,
the purchasing agent should be somewhat familiar with those rules in order
to understand how a court will interpret a contract's language. Following is a
simplified version of the rules:

- Words will be given their plain and normal meaning in most instances.

- Every part of a contract is interpreted to carry out its general purpose,
  if possible.

- If, after applying those primary rules, the meaning is still not clear,
  the secondary rules apply.

- Obvious mistakes in writing, grammar, or punctuation will be corrected.

- A contract susceptible to two meanings will be given the meaning
  that will render it valid.

- A contract will, if possible, be interpreted to render it reasonable
  rather than unreasonable.

- Words will be construed most strongly against the person drafting them.

- In case of doubt, the interpretation given by the parties is the best
  evidence of their intention.

Clearly, the best approach is to avoid using language that may require relying
on these rules.

Drafting Tip. If a dispute arises, a court will view the language for its objective
meaning; the meaning that a reasonable person would give it and not necessarily the meaning that the drafter intended. Burnham (1987) in his book,
Drafting Contracts, suggests a simple way for drafters to objectively review
what they have written: engage in a "dialogue" with the contract language by
constantly asking three questions.

- What am I trying to say?
- Could the language be interpreted in more than one way?
- How could I say it better?

It is also a good idea to let someone else read the draft contract language and
critique it. Following are some additional tips Burnham recommends to avoid
interpretation problems.

Vagueness and Ambiguity

There is a difference between vague language and language that is ambiguous. Some drafters purposely use vague language to permit flexibility. Examples of vague language are "reasonable time," "in a workmanlike manner," and "prompt and best efforts." Burnham (1987) describes vagueness as a matter of degree or a shading of meaning. Before using this type of wording, always ask whether it serves a useful purpose or whether more specific language would be better.

Never intentionally use ambiguous language or language that permits totally different meanings. Burnham (1987) uses as an example the word "red." If an agreement says, "Party A orders ten red shirts from Party B," the term "red" is vague because there are many different shades of red. On the other hand, use of the word "red" is ambiguous in the phrase "Party A orders ten red ballpoint pens from Party B." In this case, it is unclear whether the pens ordered are red in colored or whether they contain red ink.

And/Or. Ambiguity often arises in agreements because of the inexact use of the terms "and/or." The term "and" connects things together and means both; the term "or" separates them and means either. For instance, the phrase "Joe shall ship apples and oranges" does not mean the same thing as "Joe shall ship apples or oranges."

Never use "and/or." While it is a shorthand way of saying X or Y or both, problems arise because of the numerous possible combinations the term's use can create. A simple example that Burnham (1987) offers to demonstrate the confusion the term may cause is language in a will that leaves a bequest to A and/or B. The executor of the will has no idea how to dispose of that bequest.

Another pitfall to avoid is using "and" to connect things that overlap, e.g., consider the sentence: The corporation shall pay a bonus to directors and shareholders. Does the language mean that a bonus goes to persons who are both directors and shareholders or to each person who is a shareholder and each person who is a director?

Modifiers. A problem area in drafting often occurs in the use of modifiers. If the selected supplier or contractor is obligated under the agreement to ship frozen vegetables or fruit, do they violate the contract by sending fresh fruit? The issue is whether the term "frozen" applies to both vegetables and fruit, or just to vegetables. The drafter may cure the problem by including the word "frozen" before the word "fruit," or stating that the selected supplier or contractor shall ship frozen (1) vegetables or (2) fruit.

Definitions. A good way of avoiding ambiguity is to define key terms that appear in the agreement. For instance, if an agency is purchasing beans and rice for a prison cafeteria, it should define what those terms include.

Tabulations. Tabulations may help avoid ambiguity. Tabulate the language in order to make it more clear. For example, the copier shall:

1. collate,

2. staple, and

3. perform two-sided copying.

The procurement official may wish to leave this contract language in tabular form to ensure that offerors clearly understand it.

General and Particular. Sometimes a general word is used to describe a group or series of items. An example is the usage of the term "parts" in a maintenance agreement for the upkeep and repair of certain equipment. It is risky if the procurement official tries to specify what the term "parts" includes. If various parts are enumerated or listed without specifying that they are "examples only," the offeror, or a court, may interpret the language to exclude everything not listed. The better approach is to precede the listing of the items that the general word represents with, for example, "including but not limited to."

Drafting the Contract

Overview

Before writing the draft with the principles and tools discussed in this section, there are some additional critical steps that should be reviewed.

Developing a Drafting Strategy

Before drafting any contract language, the purchasing official should understand the objective of the purchase and the contract and develop a strategy based on that objective. It is critical that the buyer's agent have a good understanding of both the marketplace and the requirements of the internal customer before preparing language that will govern how the purchase and delivery of an essential service or product will operate.

Copying language used in the past or from forms is not helpful if the language does not achieve the objective. Remember that specifications and scopes or statements of work are part of the contract and the process of writing them is subject to the same good writing habits and professional drafting skills used in drafting other terms and conditions.

Drafting Language to Fit the Type of Contract Used

Another decision that will affect some of the language is the selection of the type of contract to use. For instance, different contract types necessitate various types of cost or pricing provisions as well as contractor documentation requirements. A contract for a simple commodity that establishes a firm fixed price may not need to state anything further than that the price is fixed for the period of the contract and perhaps describe situations in which there may be a price increase or decrease.

A firm fixed price contract for a consulting study may state that the contractor is not entitled to anything but the fixed price for its services unless the jurisdiction directs changed or additional work that increases the cost. Additionally, the contract may provide that the contractor must, nonetheless, submit monthly time sheets as evidence of work performed, particularly if the contract allows progress payments or requires the contractor to meet specific milestones to obtain progress payments.

Procurement should ensure that the terms included in the solicitation advise competing offerors of the type of contract to be awarded and address all the other issues that relate to that type of contract. Offerors need to know the jurisdiction's performance and documentation requirements for payment, because those requirements may be, depending on the type of contract used, key components of the costs that the offerors need to factor into their prices.

Use of Legal Counsel

Before drafting contract language, consider whether any of the issues that need to be addressed in the contract's terms require the assistance of an attorney. The language of a contract may change the outcome that the common law or the UCC may otherwise dictate on a matter. If it is decided that in keeping with the objectives of the purchase the contract should address a legal issue in a particular way, procurement should consult with the jurisdiction's attorney to make sure that the drafted language achieves the necessary legal objective sought.

Writing Style for Drafting: Good Writing Rules to Remember

There are some good, simple principles that can be used to draft clear, concise contract terms and conditions. Before drafting any contract language, the procurement official should remember these principles, the rules of interpretation, and the tips for avoiding ambiguity. Burnham (1987) suggests a good series of questions that drafters should ask themselves when reviewing a contract:

- Is the language clear and coherent?
- Does it use words with common everyday meanings?
- Is it divided and captioned by sections?
- Does it use a typeface of readable size?

These good writing rules are not hard to understand or follow and will improve the clarity of what is written into a contract.

Use the Present Tense

Even though a contract generally addresses events that will take place in the future, the contract should describe them in the present tense. For instance, instead of stating "if the contractor shall violate any terms of this agreement," the contract should state "if the contractor violates any terms of this agreement."

Use the Active Voice

Contracts require each party to do something. If, in creating a requirement, the language fails to identify who is responsible, the contract is confusing. Here is a sentence that suffers from that affliction: "The equipment shall be kept in good repair." That is what is known as the passive voice, and its use leaves unclear who is obligated to perform. The better way to write the sentence is in the active voice: "The contractor shall keep the equipment in operating condition at all times."

Provide a Remedy

While the agency may have written a contract based on good drafting techniques, there still may be something missing. Ask whether the contract term should answer the question, "What happens if the contractor does not do what the term requires?" If the provision is key, be sure to include in the terms a statement of some further obligation or a sanction for breach.

Use Cross References

If a contract condition refers to another term or subparagraph of the same found within the section, good drafting dictates that the reference include the specific number or letter of that other term or subparagraph. Using the phrase "as set forth below," for instance, does not identify the reference sufficiently.

Use Plain Language

Contract terms ought to be in plain language. There is no simple definition of plain language; but, at a minimum, it means not using legalistic terms, such as heretofore, whereas, and promises and covenants. The procurement official should use common terms in the most direct way. For instance, instead of writing "this agreement, made this 5th day of February, 1997, by and between Joe and Harry. . .," use a simpler version "Joe and Harry, on February 5, 1997, agree. . . . " Burnham (1987) suggests some steps to help the drafter use plain language:

- Know the law;
- Identify the problem;
- Outline a solution;
- Reorganize;
- Read for precision;
- Read for style; and
- Make it look good.

Do Not Vary the Language

In an effort to make a document sound less tiresome or repetitive, drafters sometimes make the mistake of using a variety of words to mean the same thing. That is not a good practice. The language should not be changed unless the drafter wishes to change meanings. Do not use "reasonable efforts" in one place and "best efforts" in another, if the intent is to keep the meaning the same.

Organization of a Basic Contract

Good organization of a contract's terms is as essential to its meaning as are the words used in the contract itself. This section provides a general understanding of the organization of a basic contract.

Most basic contracts result from the parties to them bargaining equally and, through a give-and-take process, executing a document that reflects their bargain. There may be situations in which purchasing must negotiate directly with a vendor to create a contract for purchases exempt from the procurement law, sole source procurements, or inter-jurisdictional agreements.

Description of the Document

Contracts have subject matters. If the title of a contract merely says "Agreement" at the top of the page, it does nothing to describe for the reader the type of agreement involved. The better practice is to identify the type of agreement in the title, such as Contract for Professional Services, or Agreement for the Lease of Software.

Caption

The caption in a contract identifies the parties to the contract and the legal action they are taking. This section of the contract need not be identified literally as the caption, but it should contain the appropriate language. For example:

> AGREEMENT FOR THE PURCHASE OF GOODS AND
> SERVICES PARTIES
>
> The City of Timbuktu (City) and Contractor X (Contractor) enter into this agreement on October 11, 1997, for the purchase of certain software upgrades and services (Agreement). The City and Contractor (Parties) agree as follows:

The date of agreement is generally placed in the caption or at the end of the contract. The date of the contract may not be its effective date. A contract term may provide a different date for the agreement to become effective, that is, for performance to begin.

Transitional Language

The contract should contain language showing that the parties have agreed. The procurement official should use the term "agree" to meet that requirement; the phrase "enter into an agreement" is insufficient to do so. The example used above meets this test. If the agreement contains a recitals section, the language should be placed after the recitals.

Recitals

Sometimes, drafters include a recitals section in a contract to provide the background information, often for the purpose of clarifying the parties' intentions. Traditionally, recitals begin with whereas clauses. The term "whereas" should be avoided when possible because it does not meet the plain language principle of contract drafting.

Recitals should be short and consist of a bare statement of key facts. They should not contain representations, or substantive contract terms and conditions or indicate agreements. Those sections should appear in the body of the agreement. For example:

BACKGROUND

- The City maintains its automated financial system on an XYZ mainframe computer that operates exclusively on BBB operating software. That software requires upgrading and maintenance from time to time.

- The Contractor manufactures BBB software.

- The City and Contractor want to enter into an agreement for the purchase of BBB software upgrades and maintenance.

The parties agree as follows:

Definitions

Follow the caption section, or the recitals section, if used, with definitions of key terms in the contract, and consistently use the words or terms as they are defined.

Operative Language

The portion of the contract that contains the operative language is the meat of the agreement. The procurement official may title the section "Agreement" or not title it at all. If the contract includes definitions, the title should appear before them.

The operative component of the contract should consist of the terms that answer the what, where, when, and how questions about the purchase. The structure may be divided into subsections with separate headings, and those subsections might separately address matters such as specifications or SOWs and performance of the contract—delivery, warranty, maintenance, and payment, for commodities contracts. For a consulting contract, this section would include documentation of work hours; milestones for any progress payments; format for a final report; and standard and special terms and conditions, such as those addressing indemnification, conflicts of interest, termination of the contract, and liquidated damages.

The types of statements in the body of the contract generally fall within three distinct categories, which are briefly discussed below.

Obligations

Statements of obligation concern things that the vendor has promised to do in the future and are signified by the use of the word "shall." They will appear in the contract's specifications or scope/statement of work and in the description of the type or course of performance required.

Representations and Warranties

Representations and warranties should reside in the contract in the same place as the obligations. Contract language should include any representations about the supplier and the supplier's product that the public agency has relied on in entering into the contract. Unlike obligations, the agency must demonstrate in this section that the representations are in the present and are a basis for the jurisdiction contracting with that offeror. For instance, if the contract is for consulting work, the contract language should read along the lines of "the contractor represents that it has ten years' experience in consulting, and the specific expertise to conduct a study in the nesting habits of the endangered blue and pink owl." By placing all essential representations in the contract, the agency avoids having parol evidence problems if a dispute arises.

The same is true of warranties. Warranties may either be representations of current facts or may relate to a promise of something in the future. The language in the owl consultant example could also be a warranty as well as a representation. If the agency wishes to ensure that the clause is also a warranty, it should insert the words "and warranties" after the word "represents."

Many warranties involve the performance over time future performance of commodities for items such as computers, ergonomic chairs, copiers, fax machines, and carpet. The manufacturer and dealer may offer their own warranties, but the procurement official may wish to include their own language in the contract. For example:

In addition to all other warranties, Contractor warrants that its ergonomic chairs will be free of any defects in mechanics or materials for one year after purchase.

It is important to ask whether the contract term should include a remedy for the situations in which the promise is not kept or the fact is not as represented. If so, the term should spell out the consequences.

Declarations

Declarations address the legal principles that govern the parties' agreement. In most cases, those declarations will be the standard terms and conditions and any special clauses developed for the particular contract, such as liquidated damages. To ensure that the contract contains all of the necessary declarations, the procurement official should ask whether the terms and conditions answer the possible situations that could arise under the contract.

Closing

The closing of a contract should show that the parties consent to the agreement. It is the place where signatures demonstrating consent are placed. The parties who sign the agreement should be the same ones whose names appear in the caption. Since neither a corporation nor a jurisdiction can actually sign an agreement, the closing should designate their signatures as follows:

THE CITY OF TIMBUKTU   ABC CORPORATION

By _____   By _____

The closing should include the date that the parties signed it, represented by simply stating at the end: Signed November 11, 2003. If the parties are likely to sign the contract at different times, there should be a place for the date under each signature line.

Drafting Terms and Conditions

For most purchases, a complete contract is not drafted, but the solicitation and the documents are used as the format for the contract. The drafting principles and tips that this chapter has already discussed apply equally to this important exercise. The solicitation is the starting point for a good contract.

The organization of the solicitation is just as important as it is for a basic contract. Each of the parts of the solicitation should be distinct to make the document clear and easy to use. Instructions to offerors, for instance, should not include language defining the circumstances under which the agency may terminate the contract. Instead, those instructions should be restricted to advising offerors about the how, when, where, and what of preparing and submitting their bids or proposals. Likewise, specifications defining the commodity to be supplied should not be mixed with other performance requirements that the contract may establish, such as documentation to be submitted with payment requests.

One key to creating a good contract is the identification, development, and use of some general solicitation provisions instructions to offerors and terms and conditions that can be consistently used in every procurement for that jurisdiction. An attorney should be a participant in the drafting process and should approve the final version of the contract.

Standard Terms and Conditions

Coverage

Terms and conditions that are basic for every contract should be established as a standard boilerplate. By asking the question, "what if," the procurement official, along with the jurisdiction's attorney, should identify those legal issues that they want to be consistent in all contracts. Those legal issues should become terms and conditions that are standard in every contract that the jurisdiction awards.

Laws often require that certain terms appear in every contract of the jurisdiction, and those clearly are candidates for the standard terms and conditions. Following are some other possible topics that could be included as standards:

- Definitions of terms;
- The law applicable to the contract (generally the law of the contracting state or, for other public entities, the law of the state where they are located);
- Authority of the procurement official;
- Contract interpretation (excluding parol evidence)—called a merger clause—and provided that instances in which the public entity ignores a contractor's noncompliance with the contract does not waive that entity's right to enforce the contracts requirements—called a no waiver clause);
- Public records laws (describing that the contract is a public record);
- Severability (stating that, if a court deems part of the contract as invalid, the remainder of the contract is still valid);
- Relationship of the parties (providing that the contractor and its employees are independent contractors and not employees of the jurisdiction);
- Assignment and delegation (prohibiting the contractor from assigning its contract rights or delegating its contract duties without the written approval of the authorized procurement official);
- General indemnification (stating that the contractor will hire an attorney to represent the public entity and pay any damages or other costs that the entity incurs due to the negligence of the contractor under the contract);
- Indemnification for patent and copyright infringement (requiring the contractor to indemnify the public entity for any violations of patent and copyrights laws that arise out of performance of the contract);

- Subcontracts (requiring the authorized procurement official's approval);

- Compliance with applicable laws (stating that the contractor must comply with all laws applicable to the performance of the contract);

- *Force majeure* (identifying those instances in which the jurisdiction will excuse the contractor's noncompliance with the contract, such as acts of God and strikes);

- Amendment of the contract (providing that the sole manner for changing the requirements of the contract is through a written amendment to the contract that the authorized procurement official signs);

- Nondiscrimination (prohibiting the contractor from discriminating on racial, sex, religious, or disability grounds, and identifying specific laws and executive orders that are pertinent);

- Advertising and promotion of the contract (requiring approval of the authorized procurement official before using the contract for promotional purposes);

- Ethics, including conflicts of interest, gratuities, and kickbacks;

- Availability of funds in the next fiscal year;

- Right of the jurisdiction to audit and inspect the contractor's books and records;

- Retention of records (requiring the contractor to maintain records relating to the contract for a set period of time);

- Termination for default (authorizing the jurisdiction to terminate the contract for nonperformance or defective performance);

- Termination for the convenience of the jurisdiction (authorizing the jurisdiction to terminate the contract with proper notice and providing recovery of certain contractor costs and profits); and

- Nonexclusive remedies (reserving to the jurisdiction all remedies for violation of the contract that the law allows).

There are some additional terms and conditions that can be included as standards in every solicitation for the purchase of commodities. Those terms address issues that arise under the UCC, such as:

- Risk of loss (defining which party must bear the cost of the commodities if they are lost or destroyed during delivery or before the public entity accepts them);

- Inspection and testing (allowing the public entity to test the commodities and thoroughly inspect them without being deemed under the UCC to have accepted them); and
- Nonconforming product (permitting the public entity greater leeway than the UCC allows to reject an untimely delivery or delivery of defective commodities under an installment contract calling for multiple deliveries).

Incorporation by Reference

It is clear from the list in the section above that the standard terms and conditions can be lengthy. One good way to reduce the size of the solicitation is to incorporate those terms and conditions by reference. The way to do that is to place a term in the solicitation stating:

> This solicitation incorporates by reference the Standard Terms and Conditions, Form _____, and those terms and conditions are a part of the solicitation as if it specifically set them forth. Copies of them are available. . . .

Copies may be available in the purchasing office, online, or via fax-on-demand.

Special Terms and Conditions

It is often useful to include in a solicitation a category of terms and conditions designated as special because they, like the specifications or scopes/statements of work, are unique to that particular purchase or type of purchases, or require adjustment for particular purchases. Procurement professionals should be careful not to react to a one-time problem they have encountered with a bidder, offeror, or supplier by drafting a special term to include in every solicitation for printing. The term "drafted" in those situations is often too narrow and may simply confuse the meaning of the contract without achieving any commensurate benefit.

An example of a special term is one addressing liquidated damages. Include a liquidated damages clause in a contract only where it will be difficult for the public entity to determine what its actual damages are if the contractor breaches the contract. Liquidated damages are a substitute for actual damages clauses should appear in a contract and must be a reasonable approximation of the actual damages amount. If the dollar amount of the liquidated damages is too high, a court will view it as a penalty and refuse to enforce it.

Conclusion

*T*he writing of a contract is a team effort consisting of the procurement official, end-user and the government agency's legal staff. The process is similar to that of writing specifications or scopes/statements of work requirements and must be clearly and concisely written. The contract must be written in plain language and in the present tense. After the procurement official has prepared the final draft, the attorney should review it. The contract is a concise summary statement of all of the terms, conditions and the other contents of the solicitation document, the successful vendor's offer, and the jurisdiction's acceptance. These documents, together with any drawings, addenda, bonds, insurance certificates and any correspondence between the jurisdiction and the successful vendor, form a package properly designated as the Contract Documents. The contract must specify the order of priority of these documents.

References

Burnham, S. J. (1987). *Drafting contracts*. Charlottesville, VA: The Michie Company/ LEXIS Law Publishing.

National Association of Purchasing Management (1993). *Contract terms and conditions (T's and C's)*. Available from www.napm.org.

National Contract Management Association (1990). *Using contract warranties*. McLean, VA: National Contract Management Association.

National Institute of Governmental Purchasing, Inc. (NIGP) (2001). *Advanced public procurement* (2nd ed.). Herndon, VA: NIGP.

Reid, T., & Bowen, B. (1990). *Selecting contract types*. McLean, VA: National Contract Management Association.

CHAPTER 9

Completing the RFP Process

Introduction

*A*t this point in the Request for Proposal (RFP) cycle, most of the work has been completed: funding was obtained; specifications were written; the RFP document was created, advertised and issued; a pre-proposal conference was held and addenda issued; proposals were received and evaluated; and offeror presentations were held. In some jurisdictions, a second set of proposals was evaluated as the best and final offers. The contract details were negotiated and finalized and, in many cases, agencies may have contributed significant effort up to this point over a period of as much twelve months or even longer. All that remains is the relatively simple process of confirming the successful offeror, dealing with the unsuccessful offerors, and closing the project file.

For all government jurisdictions, when they have selected the successful offeror, the offeror and proposal judged best able to satisfy the jurisdiction's requirements must be awarded. Following selection, specific tasks must be completed, dependent on each jurisdiction's policies and procedures. Confirming the successful offeror may involve nothing more than having the evaluation committee's choice confirmed by management. In some jurisdictions, it involves a quality assurance step—a review of the RFP process.

Once the award recommendation is made, the results of the process are made public. Documents and information are often made available under Freedom of Information laws or as a matter of policy. The public is permitted to inspect the process and the results. Offerors having submitted proposals are often entitled to a debriefing.

The RFP file has to be completed. Completing the RFP file involves not only additional paperwork but also reviewing or auditing the just-completed selection process. Although care and due process have been given throughout the RFP process, protests often occur. These protests must be handled effectively and efficiently. Finally, after a contract is awarded, the Project Manager or Contract Administrator issues a notice to proceed that sets the contract administration phase in motion (National Institute of Governmental Purchasing, Inc. [NIGP], 2001, p. 255). The job of the Contracting Manager is to ensure that the terms of the contract are met and that the interests of the buying jurisdiction are protected.

Confirming the Successful Offeror

*F*or most government jurisdictions, once they have selected the successful offeror (the offeror and proposal judged best able to satisfy the government jurisdictions' requirements) and negotiated an acceptable contract, an award is made. The specific set of tasks that remains varies from jurisdiction to jurisdiction.

Reviewing the Results Before the Award

The review process by either a management team or review group that was not a part of the evaluation team is an excellent way to discover any potential problems prior to award. Smaller jurisdictions benefit from using this process, because they lack sufficiently trained staff to handle both the evaluation and final review. An easy solution is to call upon a peer group located within the area to take a look at the final product and the evaluation path it took. This could be a group from within or outside the jurisdiction, depending upon availability of expertise. The cooperative nature of procurement officials and their desire to enhance overall procurement professionalism is enough motivation for peer participation. The nature of RFPs requires long lead times and much planning and critical evaluation. Sometimes, small items tend to be overlooked as everyone concentrates on the big picture. Reviewing the results of an RFP takes both time and expertise. A lengthy document with multiple items to be satisfied takes a trained eye, the eye of an individual or individuals who know what to look for in an RFP.

Procurement officers willing to review a peer's long hours of work and effort can quickly focus on issues that could lead to controversy, and even protest. A quick fix can improve the RFP and ensure that any challenge can be set aside.

Larger more sophisticated jurisdictions will have a highly skilled in-house review team to compliment work done by the Evaluation Team. Whatever group reviews the final product ensures quality of the decision and should reduce the likelihood of any successful protest launched by an unsuccessful offeror. The format chosen by the jurisdiction will aid the review process, as one can step through each section of the document and review its content. The same scrutiny given the document when it is developed is again used to review each offeror's response. Those in procurement who deal with the entire RFP become knowledgeable of the document construction, content, requirements, and ultimate award. The regulations of most agencies require that a notice of intent to award be publicly posted for a certain period of time in order to notify interested parties of the intended award, especially those offerors submitting a response the opportunity to be debriefed by the jurisdiction prior to actual award. The notice of intent to award allows those who may have a legitimate objection to the pending award an avenue to air their grievances. After the award, the unsuccessful offeror must pursue its case in court where a decision of validity can be made.

The Evaluation Committee Report

In the simplest approach, management is informed of the results and confirms the choice of offeror and the contract. Documentation consists of a brief memorandum from the procurement officer to management. In many jurisdictions, this memorandum is called the Evaluation Committee Report.

In many agencies, the decision is formalized and made a part of the public record. The procurement official documents the results of the RFP process and contract negotiations in a written presentation to the governing board manager. This report typically identifies the successful offeror, its score, the proposed cost, and the most important features of its proposal. The memo seeks approval of the selection and authority to enter into a contract with the successful offeror.

Reviewing the RFP Process

Recent best practices reflect a review of the entire RFP process and the contract prior to the award. While this adds both time and cost to the procurement process, it does assure quality. In some jurisdictions, the procurement process is run by the end-user. Most often, however, there is a central group responsible, often by statute, for the proper exercise of this function. This review recognizes some of the problems associated with decentralized procurement and its lack of time and training of end-users to ensure that the specified process is followed.

In Australia, for example, the Victoria Government Purchasing Board has developed a "Probity Policy" to ensure that the government contracting process is carried out in an open and fair manner. This policy has been translated into a program in which a department will develop a procurement plan for all major procurements. An independent group then audits the process, and all auditor reports are made public.

The State of New Mexico performs a quality assurance review prior to an award. The review provides a last chance to correct errors that might jeopardize the award, avoids embarrassing public errors, and possible litigation (Table 34).

Table 34

Quality Assurance Review

- The purpose of the review is to insure that the procurement process was completed properly and thoroughly prior to an award. If an error or omission occurred there is an opportunity to correct the error or omission without jeopardizing the procurement. Whereas some typographical errors in evaluation committee reports and other public documents are simply embarrassing, procedural errors and omissions discovered after the award are generally the subject of formal protests and lawsuits. Approximately one-half of the materials submitted for award have to be revised or corrected.

- The State Purchasing Agent has established a standard set of award requirements.

- The procurement must have been conducted in accordance with the procurement regulations and procurement procedures, practices and methodology contained in this guide.

- The proposals must have been evaluated based upon the specifications and evaluation factors set forth in the RFP.

- The agency management must have reviewed the Evaluation Committee Report and recommend the award in a signed Management Recommendation Letter.

- The Evaluation Committee Report must be thoroughly and professionally prepared as well as signed by every member of the Evaluation Committee. The report must contain verifiable documentation regarding the differences between the proposals.

- The role of the Purchasing Division staff is to review and insure that the procurement process was conducted properly.

Source: State of New Mexico (2002). *Request for proposals procurement guide* (p. 116). Available from www.state.nm.us/clients/rfpguide.

Award Recommendation and Approval

The authority and approval for the award of a contract will depend on the spending limits and signing authority granted through a jurisdiction's policy framework. Regardless of the hierarchy established for award approval and agreement execution, once a recommendation for award or "Notice of Award" is issued, accepted and approved by the appropriate authorities, it may be executed by anyone who has been delegated that authority and responsibility. In some jurisdictions, contracts greater than a certain value must be reviewed, authorized, and attested to by the agency's legal department or legal counsel.

Evaluation Team Recommendation

Normally, each entity has a formal written policy, procedure and practice manual which sets out the terms, protocols and methodology for taking a solicitation award recommendation through its various stages up to and including approval, execution, and award. At this stage, the Evaluation Committee that typically has representation from the jurisdiction's Purchasing Service Department will have consensus and a unified recommendation for award.

If the recommendation is not the consensus, the Committee is often consulted to assist in resolution as to the factors that are causing non-unanimity. Often, the root causes of not being able to reach a unanimous recommendation are:

- Not applying the evaluation criteria consistently and equitably to all response submissions;
- Ranking of response submissions on a preferential basis with emphasis on relationships and subjective criteria/factors;
- Bias of evaluation committee/team members;
- Ranking based on "gut-feeling"; or
- Any other number of factors that are not objective in nature or that have been introduced into the evaluation process subsequent to closing.

The Committee may choose to review their process one more time to reconfirm their decision.

End-User Sign-Off

Whether the acquisition involves products and/or services, prior to an award the end-user should be provided with the opportunity to acknowledge and accept the recommendation for award. In situations where the products or services are as specified by brand, make or model, user sign-off is not essential, since the conditions of law of agency will have been met; however, where there are any variations from what was specified, sign-off should be attained. When considering awards resulting from an RFT, the internal client's review, acceptance, and approval should always be secured prior to award.

Finance Office/Funding

During the evaluation, recommendation for award and contract approval processes, due to the high value of the acquisition, should there be a variation from the original estimate compared to the response submission cost of the selected offeror, or as may be required by policy, finance or funding, final approval should be sought. Finance approval is basically a reconfirmation of budget prior to executing the final contract, since initial approval was obtained prior to issuance of the RFP. Approval should be conducted after technical evaluation but prior to recommendation to management for approval. Some jurisdictions require acquisition over a specified value to be forwarded to and approved by another level of finance when allocation of funds, particularly for infrastructure, capital or long term commitment type contracts, is needed.

Executive Approval

Most acquisitions over a specified value that fall within high risk or may be sensitive from an environmental, political, or economic development perspective often will require Executive (management) level approval. Once the Evaluation Committee has conducted its review and due consideration, the recommendation for award is forwarded to the Executive Officer who then takes the recommendation for award to the governing Board. As each jurisdiction establishes its own approval process, a prudent procurement officer is sure to verify approval procedures.

Governing Body/Board Approvals

The laws, ordinances and policies of many jurisdictions require that the governing body make the final decision for award. In some cases, the governing body or higher-level jurisdiction approval is required in advance of acquisition and commitment of funds. Often, large capital and infrastructure projects require prior advanced approval by the senior level governing body, such as a federal, state or provincial jurisdiction.

Award to Successful Offeror

In some jurisdictions, a Notice of Award is published or distributed to all of the offerors. This Notice provides a formal mechanism for any of the offerors to protest the award prior to a contract being signed. In Alaska, the

Procurement Code provides that each offeror be informed of the intent at least 10 days before the formal award of a contract. Procedures for notification vary by jurisdiction.

If such a notice is not required, the procurement department should furnish a contract or other notice of the award to the successful offeror. If the award document includes information that is different from the negotiated proposal, as amended by the offeror's written correspondence, both the offeror and the agency's representative must sign a contractual agreement. When an award is made to an offeror for less than all of the items that may be awarded and additional items are being withheld for subsequent award, each notice must state that the government may make subsequent awards on those additional items within the proposal acceptance period (Federal Acquisition Regulation [FAR] 15.505).

Releasing the Results

RFP closure consists of three tasks: announcing the award, debriefing unsuccessful offerors, and releasing information as required by law.

Announcing the Award

Unsuccessful Offerors

When the American Bar Association (ABA) *Model Procurement Code* was first published, jurisdictions found themselves awarding contracts using the RFP approach, anticipating that protests would not emerge. However, protests were not prevented. Jurisdictions faced the problem of dealing, usually in court, with any angry proposer who had just lost a contract and a new proposer trying to get the re-award of a recently cancelled contract. The Notice of Award requirement was implemented to provide the offerors public notice of an impending award, thus allowing time for a protest to be dealt with for resolution.

Most agencies have a procedure for announcing contract awards to unsuccessful offerors as well as the general public. Unsuccessful offerors—those whose proposals were not selected—are sometimes sent a Pre-Award Announcement or Notice of Award. The award is then made as scheduled, unless a protest is received. More often, these unsuccessful offerors are sent a courtesy announcement, identifying the successful offeror. In some jurisdictions, this Announcement also contains a summary of the evaluation, or Evaluation Committee Report.

In the Federal Government, within three days after the date of contract award, the contracting officer must provide written notification to each offeror whose proposal was in the competitive range but was not selected for award (10 U.S.C. 2305[b][5] and 41 U.S.C. 253b[c]). The notice includes:

- the number of offerors solicited;
- the number of proposals received;
- the name and address of each offeror receiving an award;
- the items, quantities, and any stated unit prices of each award. If the number of items or other factors makes listing any stated unit prices impracticable at that time, only the total contract price need be furnished in the notice. However, the items, quantities, and any stated unit prices of each award should be made available to the public, upon request.
- in general terms, the reason(s) the offeror's proposal was not accepted. In no event should an offeror's cost breakdown, profit, overhead rates, trade secrets, manufacturing processes and techniques, or other confidential business information be disclosed to any other offeror (FAR 15.503).

Moreover, upon request, the contracting officer must provide the post-award notice to unsuccessful offerors that received a pre-award notice of exclusion from the competitive range.

Public At Large

There are a number of different ways to announce an award. Most entities employ more than one method.

- Posting a notice in a newspaper, or an official journal of record;
- Posting a notice in a pre-selected spot in a public building (such as the purchasing department)
- Posting a notice in a pre-selected spot in a public building;
- Posting a notice on the agency's official Web site;
- Issuing a press release; and/or
- Holding a news conference.

Debriefing Unsuccessful Offerors

A debriefing is an attempt by the agency to provide unsuccessful offerors with insight as to why their offer was not selected. It is recognition that the preparation of proposals is time intensive and expensive. Each offeror has invested considerable time, effort, and money into preparing and submitting its proposal. Fairness dictates that the agency explain why a proposal was not successful. Debriefings should help the offeror compete more effectively the next time and encourage the offeror to pursue other government business.

Most jurisdictions provide debriefings when requested by offerors that submitted a proposal. The ABA does not make a debriefing mandatory but, rather, leaves it to law and local policy makers.

Debriefings may be given orally, in writing, or by any other method acceptable to the purchasing officer. A post-award debriefing may include: (a) the [agency's] evaluation of significant weaknesses or deficiencies in the proposal, if applicable; (b) the overall evaluated cost or price (including unit prices) and technical rating, if applicable, of the successful offeror and the debriefed offeror; (c) the overall ranking of all proposals, when any such ranking was developed during the source selection; (d) a summary of the rationale for award; and (e) reasonable responses to relevant questions about whether source selection procedures contained in the RFP and applicable law were followed. Post-award debriefings should not include point-by-point comparisons of the debriefed proposal with those of other offerors. Any debriefing should not reveal any information prohibited from disclosure by law or exempt from release under the applicable public laws, including trade secrets, or privileged or confidential commercial or manufacturing information. A summary of any debriefing should be included in the contract file (ABA, 2000, p. 29).

Law or policy generally establishes the requirement for a debriefing.

Law or policy generally establishes the requirement for a debriefing. FAR 15.1004 outlines the requirements for debriefing of offerors for the Federal Government. In other jurisdictions such as Massachusetts, a debriefing is given, not as a right of the offeror or as a requirement imposed on the jurisdiction but, rather, as a courtesy and allows the requesting offeror the opportunity to ask questions regarding the evaluation of its response. Debriefings are designed to identify any weak areas of a response and suggest improvements for future procurements (Commonwealth of Massachusetts, 2000, p. 46). In some jurisdictions, an offeror must attend a debriefing before being permitted to protest an award.

Often, the opportunity to obtain a debriefing is announced in the RFP itself. In a recent RFP from California, the Rules Governing Competition included the following:

A debriefing will be held after contract award at the request of any offeror for the purpose of receiving specific information concerning the evaluation. The discussion will be based primarily on the technical and cost evaluations of the offeror's final proposal. A debriefing is not the forum to challenge the RFP specifications or requirements (State of California, 2000, p. II.15).

Releasing Information as Required by Law

Most jurisdictions have laws providing public access to procurement information. These laws generally regard procurement information as public, except when its release will harm the commercial interests of one of the offerors. In some jurisdictions, only the successful proposal is a "public record." In other jurisdictions, all proposals must be made public after the award.

Releasing the Results as Required by Law

As the public becomes more knowledgeable of the RFP process and potential suppliers aggressively seek more business, jurisdictions are consistently asked for information involving procurements, especially RFPs. The apparent subjective nature of voting to award a contract raises questions in the minds of those who do not completely understand the RFP process and its procedures to ensure open competition.

The one area of weakness in the RFP process could come about in documenting how each evaluation team member voted or ranked each offeror to choose the successful offeror with the highest score. Remember, this is a somewhat subjective award based upon established criteria; therefore, the documentation of each member's notes and voting become a part of the public record. In addition, Evaluation Team members' e-mails concerning anything stated about an offeror is fair game for those who seek to overturn an award. In one jurisdiction, the evaluation team members had impeccable notes and ranking for the contract file, but a protesting offeror sued and won the right to have access to each Evaluation Team member's e-mails for the past six months. The protesting offeror was able to prove discrimination by certain team members via their e-mails. Although too late, a valuable lesson was learned--anything written or documented by an evaluation team member is possible matter of public record.

In Texas, the entire RFP contract file becomes a matter of public record and is open for review by the public and offerors upon final disposition of the purchase order (State of Texas, 2002). Montana and Florida have gone even further than Texas. In both states, all Evaluation Committee meetings are considered public meetings, with meeting notices and agendas posted 72 hours in advance. Offerors are even allowed to make recordings of the Evaluation Committee meetings. Names of all Committee members must be released, if asked. Even site visits to offerors are considered public meetings (if a quorum of the Evaluation Committee is in attendance). Anyone, including competing firms, can attend the offeror presentations, sit in on briefings, and observe the deliberations of the evaluation committee in action. (For further information on public records and the Freedom of Information Act, see *The Legal Aspects of Public Purchasing* (NIGP, 2004).

In many government jurisdictions, obtaining procurement information during the evaluation process is difficult. The existing systems do not make it easy for public review. A lot of manual intervention is required; existing laws often impose lengthy procedures; sufficient resources are not available to make this a high priority; and sometimes agency staff presents a barrier to information access.

Information That Should Not Be Released

Unless required by law or regulations, certain types of information should not be released. As procurement regulations vary by agency, it is important to consult the policy and procedures manuals and/or legal staff prior to releasing sensitive information.

Completing the RFP File

*D*uring the course of the procurement, much information will be obtained or generated. This information is collectively referred to as the RFP file or the project file and grows as the procurement proceeds through its various phases.

The RFP file consists of a variety of documents: the original project plan, the draft RFP, market research, proposals, draft contracts, and notes from meetings with offerors. Most jurisdictions lack an overall plan for collecting and organizing these project documents.

The purpose of file documentation is to provide an orderly record of the actions taken and decisions made throughout the contract process, beginning with the definition of requirements through the solicitation, evaluation, negotiation and award stages and continuing through performance or termination and contract close-out.

The RFP file serves many valuable purposes:

- It is the official factual record of events and decisions which can be used to defend against complaints or litigation.
- It provides the information required under freedom of information laws.
- It provides the information required by the Contract Administrator.
- It provides the information required for a pre- or post-award audit.

Information to be collected is prescribed by statute or policy for most agencies. In Alaska, the contents of the project file are prescribed by statute:

The commissioner shall keep a contract file open for public inspection and the contracting agency for each contract awarded under competitive sealed proposals. The file kept by the commissioner must contain a summary of the information in the file of the contracting agency. The file kept by the contracting agency must contain:

- a copy of the contract;
- the register of proposals prepared . . . and a copy of each proposal submitted; and
- the written determination to award the contract (State of Alaska, 2002, Section 36.30.510).

The information included in the RFP file varies by jurisdiction; however, it most often includes the following:

- Award Documents (winning proposal, contract, changes, best and final offer);
- Contract Administration Material (changes, problems);
- Evaluation Documents (Evaluation Committee Report, correspondence, evaluation forms, protest documentation);
- RFP (original, addenda);
- Planning Documents (market research, source selection plan); and
- Proposals (all proposals received, correspondence).

New Mexico has a good list (State of New Mexico, 2002).

Some material may be excluded from the file or shielded from disclosure to the public, depending on state or local statutes and ordinances. Documents that may be protected include personal notes of members of the evaluation committee, draft copies of documents, and data judged or declared as confidential or a trade secret. Procurement is advised to consult the legal staff for clarification of what is considered public record.

In most jurisdictions, all procurement information, except the information made public, is considered confidential, and its improper disclosure may be a criminal offense. Buyers sometimes forget the importance of keeping this information confidential. Often, there is insufficient education concerning the various laws and ethics issues that relate to procurement activities. California's approach to this issue serves as a model for other jurisdictions.

> Buyers are cautioned to protect documentation from improper disclosure, as required by law, regulation or established policies or procedures. Such documentation that may require protection is that which is identified as confidential, is identified as proprietary or contains trade secrets, is subject to a legal privilege or is otherwise exempt from disclosure. Protection from disclosure includes protection from all persons who are not authorized to review it, including State employees who do not have a need to know the contents of the document. Prior to releasing documentation to any person, the buyer must consult with legal counsel to determine the State's obligation to protect information from disclosure. Procurement Division employees who receive a request for documents under the California Public Records Act, coordinate with System Integrity and the Department of General Services Office of Legal Services in determining how to respond to the request. In no event shall a document that is identified as subject to a legal privilege be shared with anyone outside of the department(s) concerned or with any State employee who does not have a need to know of it. Documents subject to legal privilege may be excluded from the transaction file and securely stored separately until destroyed (State of California, 2002, Section 3.6.1).

Dealing with Complaints and Protests

*O*fferors can protest any procurement activity that they believe has not been conducted properly. To make matters even worse, some unscrupulous offerors have been known to initiate unfounded protests simply to delay the award of a contract, to penalize a competitor that won, or to maintain their position as the incumbent while the protest is being examined. There are hundreds of reasons why offerors can feel aggrieved (Michael Asner Consulting, 1999).

While each type of source selection has its own issues, problems and potential for creating adverse press. As discussed in this book, the RFP is the most complex form of procurement. Potential offerors can spend hundreds of thousands of dollars preparing a response to an RFP. The selection process employs evaluation criteria that are based on judgments about the offeror and its proposed solution. Unfortunately, there are always more unsuccessful offerors than successful offerors, and some of the unsuccessful offerors will feel aggrieved. They may believe that the requirements were too vague, that the time to complete the proposal was too short, that the selection process was arbitrary or, even worse, that the successful offeror was selected before the RFP was issued. They may believe that the incumbent was favored by insider information. They may also believe that some of the team members were biased and discounted their proposal. Some offerors develop suspicions about the environment within the agency and whether it truly promotes fair and open competition. Many protests are based on improper actions of the jurisdiction, whether real or perceived, such as deviation from the published process, new criteria being introduced in the evaluation process, or discriminatory application of criteria.

Most complaints and protests can be prevented. For those that cannot be prevented, many can be justified. Careful planning and much work can help a jurisdiction reduce the number of protests it receives. The term "reduce" is used, since there is no way to guarantee that an offeror will not file a protest; or that the protest will be set aside. Unfortunately, an agency will tend to take a very defensive approach thereby attempting to prove itself right rather than the protestor proving the jurisdiction wrong. For instance, do not defend the evaluation team's position, but show the other side why the team's position or action was in the best interest of the jurisdiction and taxpayer. A good negotiator shows the other side why it's position benefits the other party, not why their position is best.

Legislation has helped jurisdictions deal with protests by stipulating that frivolous protests will cost the protestor the amount associated with such an action. Once word gets out that frivolous protests can cost additional funds, only those with serious, legitimate concerns will bring them forth. Most agencies now require a protestor to file a bond with the agency, most often in the amount of 10% of the contract value.

This is not a simple task, nor is it a quick fix. To accomplish these goals requires leadership, much effort, diligence and desire expended over a number of years. The work must be directed both at the procurement process and its legal framework. There are numerous cases that can easily lead to protests.

- Persons external to the process attempting to influence offeror selection;
- Circumventing competitive RFP requirements;
- Splitting purchases in order to remain within small-purchase limits;
- Using emergency procedures in the absence of an emergency;
- Using sole source when competition is available;
- Denying one or more offerors the opportunity to offer or propose;
- Using unnecessarily restrictive specifications;
- Pre-qualifying some offerors on a discriminatory basis;
- Removing companies from the offerors list without just cause;
- Requiring unnecessarily high bonding;
- Making information available to some but not all offerors; or
- Giving unfavorable offerors inaccurate or misleading information. (Watt, 1995, p. 71).

Grinding to a Halt

There are serious implications in protests to a jurisdiction, its political over-seers, and the vendor community. In many jurisdictions, procurement activity ceases until the protest is resolved. If a contract has not been awarded, the process is suspended. If the contract has been signed, its execution is suspended. A finding in favor of the complainant can cause the contract to be canceled, and the procurement process begins anew.

Protests can introduce delays in a project of not only months but also years. These delays can derail major jurisdictional initiatives and raise questions that can cut into the public trust. The process itself can be subjected to public scrutiny and found lacking, especially where conflicting laws and regulations govern procurement. The competence and objectivity of the purchasing officer may even be questioned.

For an aggrieved offeror, protest procedures can be expensive, time-consuming, and cause the loss of good will with the jurisdiction. For a successful offeror, the initiation of a protest by one of its competitors may place the award at risk.

Adversary or Partner?

Offeror complaints can be dealt with in many different ways; however, an ounce of prevention is a lot less expensive and more professional than having to deal with a constant stream of complaints.

Occasionally, a procurement official or agency representative may commit an error or do something that compromises the process. The question is not whether these violations occur, but what is to be done when they have occurred. Most states, and some provinces, have laws that establish administrative procedures to address offeror grievances. The procedures are intended to be relatively simple, straightforward, fast, and inexpensive. Having failed to win its protest, an offeror can still resort to the courts.

...the protest process represents an attempt to reconcile competing goals of the stakeholders.

With procurement reform, many states are examining the offeror's right to protest. Some states, such as Massachusetts, have eliminated this administrative procedure and left the offerors with no formal recourse other than the court system.

Public entities exhibit a wide variety of approaches in dealing with offeror protests in these sometimes difficult and stressful circumstances. Approaches range from a visibly hostile, adversarial approach to one based on cooperation, open communication, and a desire to resolve the issue.

Larger local governments (state governments and agencies) recognize the right of offerors to protest and take steps to ensure that their concerns are dealt with in a fair and open manner. Some jurisdictions, usually smaller local governments, fail to provide offerors with any process for resolving concerns other than the political process.

Some senior government officials and politicians do not want any formalized approaches. They prefer retaining the power to deal with offeror complaints as they see fit. Often, their actions are seemingly arbitrary and possibly contrary to public policy. However, these actions can deter all but the most resolute of offerors from getting enough good information to understand the issue, file a protest, resolve the complaint, or warrant going public.

Putting Out the Fire

Like all politically imposed administrative processes, source selection and the associated protest process represent an attempt to reconcile competing goals of the stakeholders. The procurement official wants to obtain goods and services quickly and in a fair and open manner. The offerors (except the incumbent) want to compete on equal footing with each other. In some jurisdictions, the process favors the offerors; in others, the procurement official, the jurisdiction itself, or its project manager are favored. In several states with many different laws affecting procurement, each with its own definitions and sometimes over-lapping terms, the protest process (as well as the procurement process) favors no one and frustrates all of the stakeholders.

What are the requirements for a strategy to deal with offeror protests? Can the procurement official prevent offeror complaints? How should protests be handled? What should the procurement staff be trained to do? In considering these questions, we identified four major requirements.

Start with a Solid Foundation: Promote Fair and Open Competition

The first requirement is to ensure that offeror protests evaporate once the facts are known, i.e., the entire RFP process must be publicly defensible. The competition must be fair and open and, therefore, easily defended. The fundamental approach must be based on accepted public policy, which has been translated into appropriate jurisdictional policies and procedures. All jurisdictional staff must follow the procurement procedures. If the process and the jurisdiction's specific actions can survive close public scrutiny, then the Evaluation's Committee decisions will be upheld. The policy also must provide for fair and open competition.

Go the Extra Mile: Promote Excellence

The minimum requirements related to offeror protests are to ensure that the process is fair and easily defended and to provide a dispute resolution mecha-nism. But can this be done? Can the jurisdiction, through its actions and policy and by building in quality, actively discourage offerors from protesting its deci-sions or taking the jurisdiction to court?

Some jurisdictions have taken a proactive approach to ensure that there are few protests. These jurisdictions provide the vendor community with training and education about their policies and processes. They offer workshops on the RFP process, publish their policies, solicit input, and develop handbooks on How to Submit a Proposal. Others hire an RFP or legal expert to ensure that high-visibility RFPs are properly executed. Some jurisdictions provide unsuccessful offerors with extensive debriefings. Still others release their RFPs in draft form to obtain offeror acceptance prior to the competition itself.

A policy should encourage constant review of the jurisdiction's practices and continuous improvement. The jurisdiction should adopt practices designed to convince offerors of the fairness of the process and, thereby, deter them from a public protest.

When Best Efforts Fail, Handle Protests More Effectively

Even when a protest has no basis in fact, it can still cause a lot of damage by delaying the contract. The offerors can aggressively challenge all aspects of a decision—the requirements, the process, the competence of the staff, the analysis performed, the criteria, and the weights. It is always better that this be done through an internal process rather than in public. The third requirement of any policy is to promote the quiet resolution of disputes before they become public issues. Is there a way in which protests can be handled without making them public events? Can the questions by the politicians and the articles in the newspapers be avoided? Can the jurisdiction keep the protests out of court?

The jurisdictional policy should provide for an effective dispute resolution mechanism. In recent years, the U.S. Federal Government and some states have initiated procurement reform, which has included streamlined dispute resolution strategies and the introduction of other techniques such as third-party mediation. While these events are also occurring in Canada, their priority seems to be much lower here. (Note: The American Bar Association [2000] describes legal and contractual remedies. It offers the commentary that it is essential that offerders, offerors, and contractors have confidence in the procedures for soliciting and awarding contracts. This can best be assured by allowing an aggrieved person to protest the solicitation, award, or related decision.)

The Best Defense: Know the Law

All documents, policies, procedures, contracts and forms must accurately reflect all of the applicable laws and, more importantly, recent court cases. This may require additional training of staff or a legal audit of existing procurement practices, policies, and contracts.

Complex RFPs, especially those involving outsourcing or information technology, may require a lawyer as a member of the criteria development or evaluation team. The planning of the process and design of the RFP document can significantly affect the potential for protests. Legal advice may be needed to structure the Best and Final Offers process or to structure the process for negotiating contract terms and conditions.

Offerors are sophisticated and very aggressive when millions of dollars are involved. The typical offeror responding to an RFP for information technology services knows that the jurisdiction is required to conduct a fair and open competition. They know that the jurisdiction has in-house background papers, feasibility studies, cost estimates, etc. The vendor also knows that the evaluation process must be objective and defined prior to receiving the proposals.

Sellers are also aware of the access to information laws in the jurisdiction and their right to challenge the award. Finally, if the jurisdiction dismisses the protest, the matter need not be dropped. The offeror can still take the matter into court and have a judge review the facts and assess the merits of the protest.

Notice to Proceed

Once an award has been made, usually the procurement official issues a Notice to Proceed that sets the contract administration in motion (NIGP, 2001, p. 255). The contractor must perform the contract. This is more than simply providing the goods or services on time. The contractor must fulfill all of its other contractual obligations. It has to comply with labor laws, prepare required reports, seek changes as unanticipated events occur, manage and monitor subcontractors, prepare invoices, and a lot more. A complex contract lasting several years will require significant amounts of contract management time.

The job of the Contract Administrator is to ensure that the terms of the contract are met and that the interests of the agency are protected. The Contract Administrator may be required to handle several responsibilities with a large-dollar, high-volume, or multi-term contract. For instance, bonding requirements must be kept in force in the event it becomes necessary to proceed to collect for non-performance or any uncorrected default. (For further information on "Contract Administration, the Next Step in the Contract Process," see *Contract Administration* [NIGP, 2004].)

Conclusion

*T*he RFP process provides for best value procurement and offers the procurement official the opportunity to effectively work within a team and make a significant contribution to the jurisdiction.

References

American Bar Association (2000). *The 2000 model procurement code for state and local governments.* Chicago: American Bar Association.

Commonwealth of Massachusetts (2000, July). *Procurement policies and procedures handbook.* Available from http://www.state.ma.us/osd/phand/phand.pdf.

Michael Asner Consulting (1999). *Offeror complaints and protests: A guide for public officials and vendors* (2nd ed.). Available from www.proposalsthatwin.com.

National Institute of Governmental Purchasing, Inc. (NIGP) (2001). *Advanced public procurement* (2nd ed.). Herndon, VA: NIGP.

National Institute of Governmental Purchasing, Inc. (NIGP) (2004). *Contract administration.* Herndon, VA: NIGP.

National Institute of Governmental Purchasing, Inc. (NIGP) (2004). *The legal aspects of public purchasing.* Herndon, VA: NIGP.

State of Alaska (2002). *Procurement code.* Available from http://touchngo.com/ lglcntr/akstats/statutes//Title35/chapter30.htm.

State of California. (2002). *California acquisition manual.* Available from www. pd.dgs.ca.goov/acqui/camweb.asp.

State of California Department of Consumer Affairs, Bureau of Automotive Repair (2000). *RFP BAR-1110-104.* Available from http://www.pd.dgs.ca.goov/acqui/ camweb.asp.

State of New Mexico (2002). *Request for proposals procurement guide (prepare for public inspection).* Available from http://www.state.nm.us/clients/rfpguide.pdf.

State of Texas (2002). *Procurement manual.* Available from www.gsc.state.tx.us/ stpurch/rfp -16.

Watt, P. C. (1995). *An elected official's guide to procurement.* Chicago, IL: Government Finance.